THE UNCANNY AVENGERS

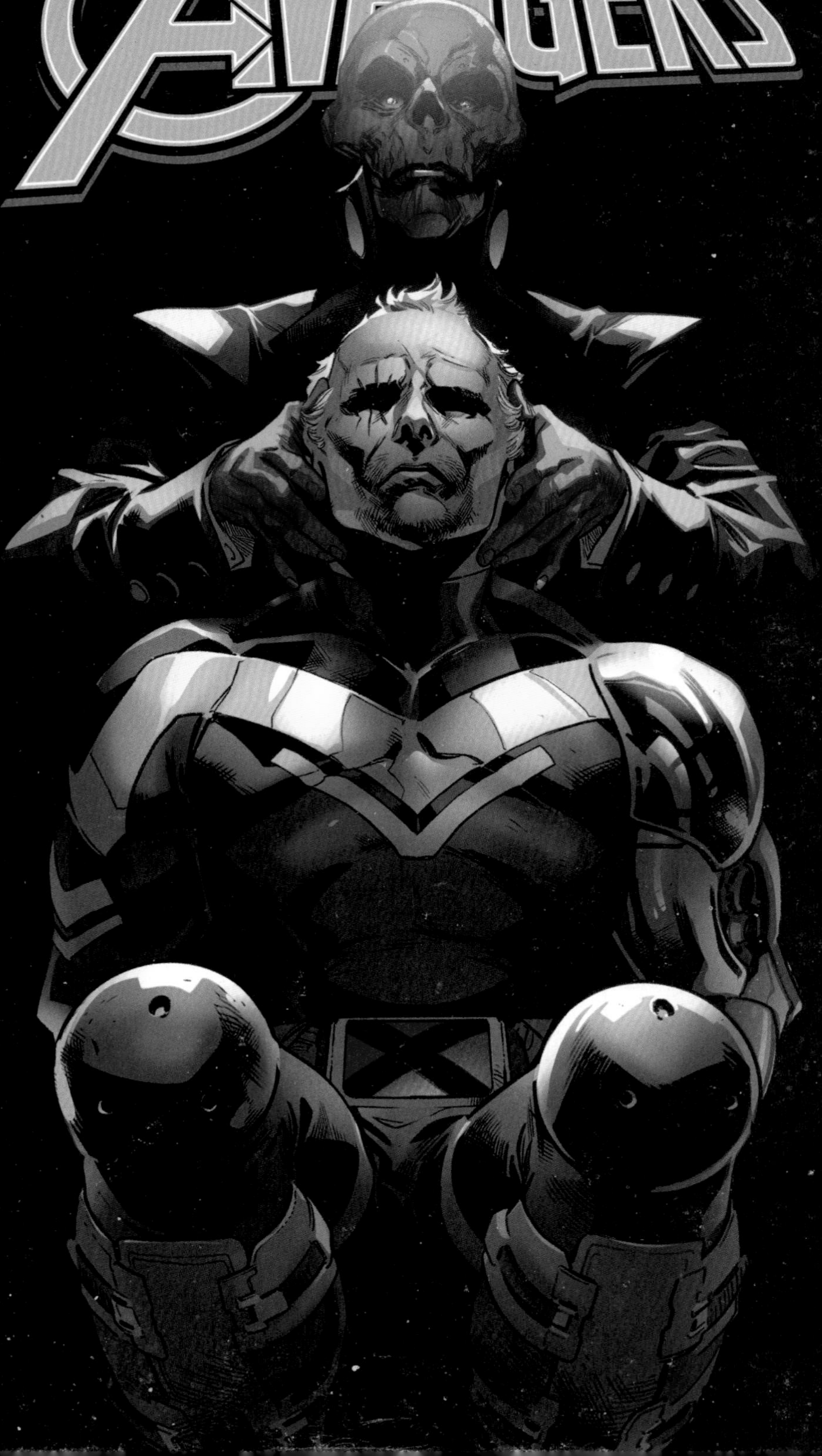

PREVIOUSLY

AFTER A BETRAYAL BY THE TEAM'S MUTANTS, CAPTAIN AMERICA BROKE UP THE UNITY SQUAD, BUT THEIR MISSION IS FAR FROM OVER. THE RED SKULL IS STILL IN POSSESSION OF CHARLES XAVIER'S TELEPATHIC BRAIN, AND THE TEAM WON'T REST UNTIL THE SKULL IS FOUND AND NEUTRALIZED. BUT THE HUNTERS ARE ABOUT TO BECOME THE HUNTED. ON A RECENT VISIT TO AVENGERS MANSION, QUICKSILVER'S MIND WAS INVADED BY THE SKULL, WHO IS FINALLY READY TO SPRING A DEADLY TRAP...

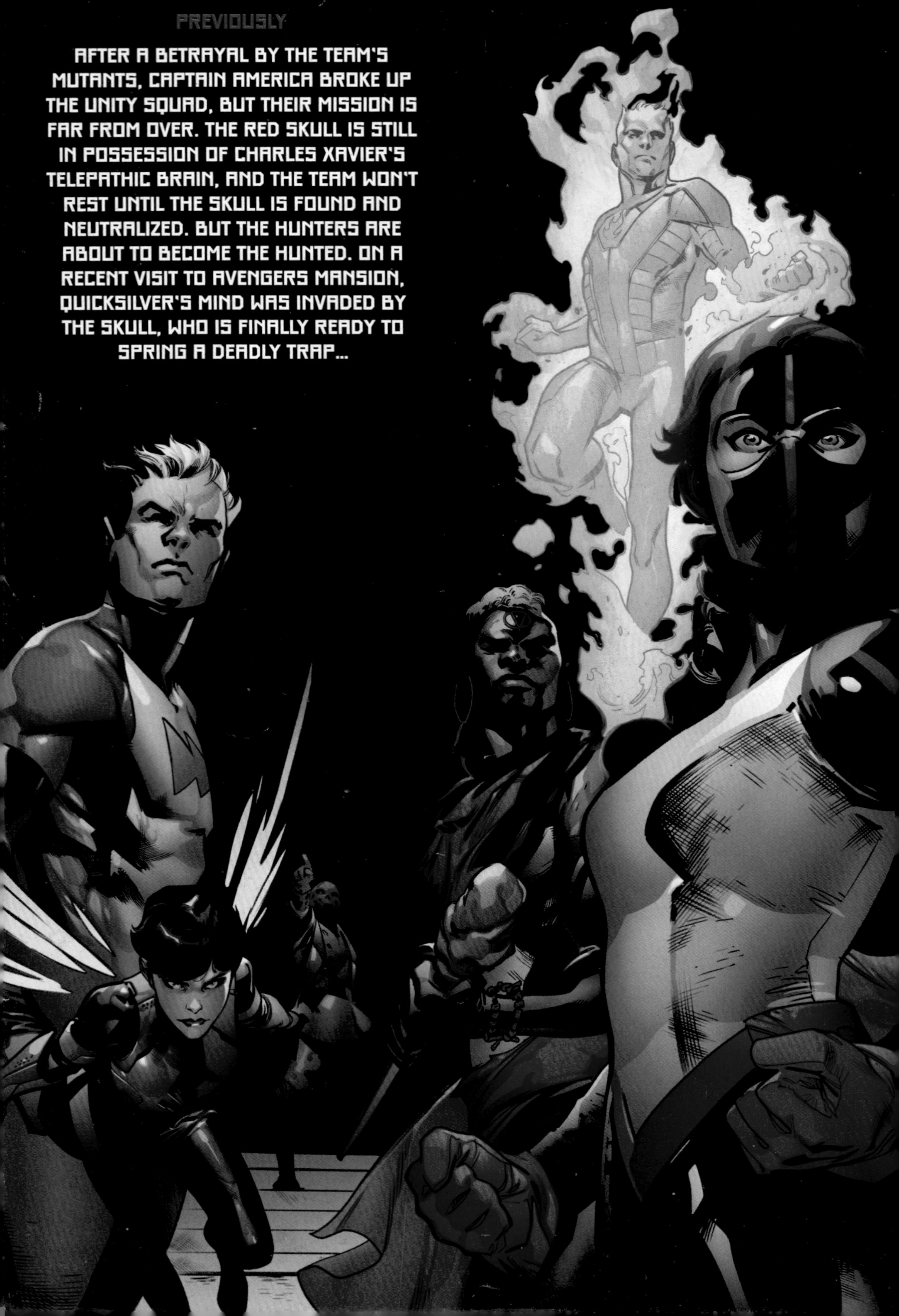

THE UNCANNY AVENGERS
RED SKULL

GERRY DUGGAN
WRITER

KEVIN LIBRANDA (#18, #21) & PEPE LARRAZ (#19-20, #22-23)
WITH RODRIGO ZAYAS (#19)
ARTISTS

DAVID CURIEL (#18, #22-23) &
DONO SÁNCHEZ-ALMARA WITH PROTOBUNKER (#19-21)
COLOR ARTISTS

STEVE MCNIVEN & DAVID CURIEL (#18);
STEVE MCNIVEN, JAY LEISTEN & DAVID CURIEL (#19);
ADAM KUBERT & DEAN WHITE (#20); ADAM KUBERT & PAUL MOUNTS (#21);
DAVID MARQUEZ & MARTE GRACIA (#22); AND
RYAN STEGMAN & JESUS ABURTOV (#23)
COVER ART

VC's CLAYTON COWLES
LETTERER

ALANNA SMITH
ASSISTANT EDITOR

TOM BREVOORT WITH
DANIEL KETCHUM
EDITORS

AVENGERS CREATED BY **STAN LEE** & **JACK KIRBY**

COLLECTION EDITOR: JENNIFER GRÜNWALD
ASSISTANT EDITOR: CAITLIN O'CONNELL
ASSOCIATE MANAGING EDITOR: KATERI WOODY
EDITOR, SPECIAL PROJECTS: MARK D. BEAZLEY
VP PRODUCTION & SPECIAL PROJECTS: JEFF YOUNGQUIST
SVP PRINT, SALES & MARKETING: DAVID GABRIEL
BOOK DESIGNER: JAY BOWEN & ADAM DEL RE

EDITOR IN CHIEF: AXEL ALONSO
CHIEF CREATIVE OFFICER: JOE QUESADA
PRESIDENT: DAN BUCKLEY
EXECUTIVE PRODUCER: ALAN FINE

UNCANNY AVENGERS: UNITY VOL. 4 — RED SKULL. Contains material originally published in magazine form as UNCANNY AVENGERS #18-23. First printing 2017. ISBN# 978-1-302-90644-3. Published by MARVEL WORLDWIDE, INC., a subsidiary of MARVEL ENTERTAINMENT, LLC. OFFICE OF PUBLICATION: 135 West 50th Street, New York, NY 10020. Copyright © 2017 MARVEL No similarity between any of the names, characters, persons, and/or institutions in this magazine with those of any living or dead person or institution is intended, and any such similarity which may exist is purely coincidental. **Printed in Canada.** DAN BUCKLEY, President, Marvel Entertainment; JOE QUESADA, Chief Creative Officer; TOM BREVOORT, SVP of Publishing; DAVID BOGART, SVP of Business Affairs & Operations, Publishing & Partnership; C.B. CEBULSKI; VP of Brand Management & Development, Asia; DAVID GABRIEL, SVP of Sales & Marketing, Publishing; JEFF YOUNGQUIST, VP of Production & Special Projects; DAN CARR, Executive Director of Publishing Technology; ALEX MORALES, Director of Publishing Operations; SUSAN CRESPI, Production Manager; STAN LEE, Chairman Emeritus. For information regarding advertising in Marvel Comics or on Marvel.com, please contact Vit DeBellis, Integrated Sales Manager, at vdebellis@marvel.com. For Marvel subscription inquiries, please call 888-511-5480. **Manufactured between 6/2/2017 and 7/4/2017 by SOLISCO PRINTERS, SCOTT, QC, CANADA.**

10 9 8 7 6 5 4 3 2 1

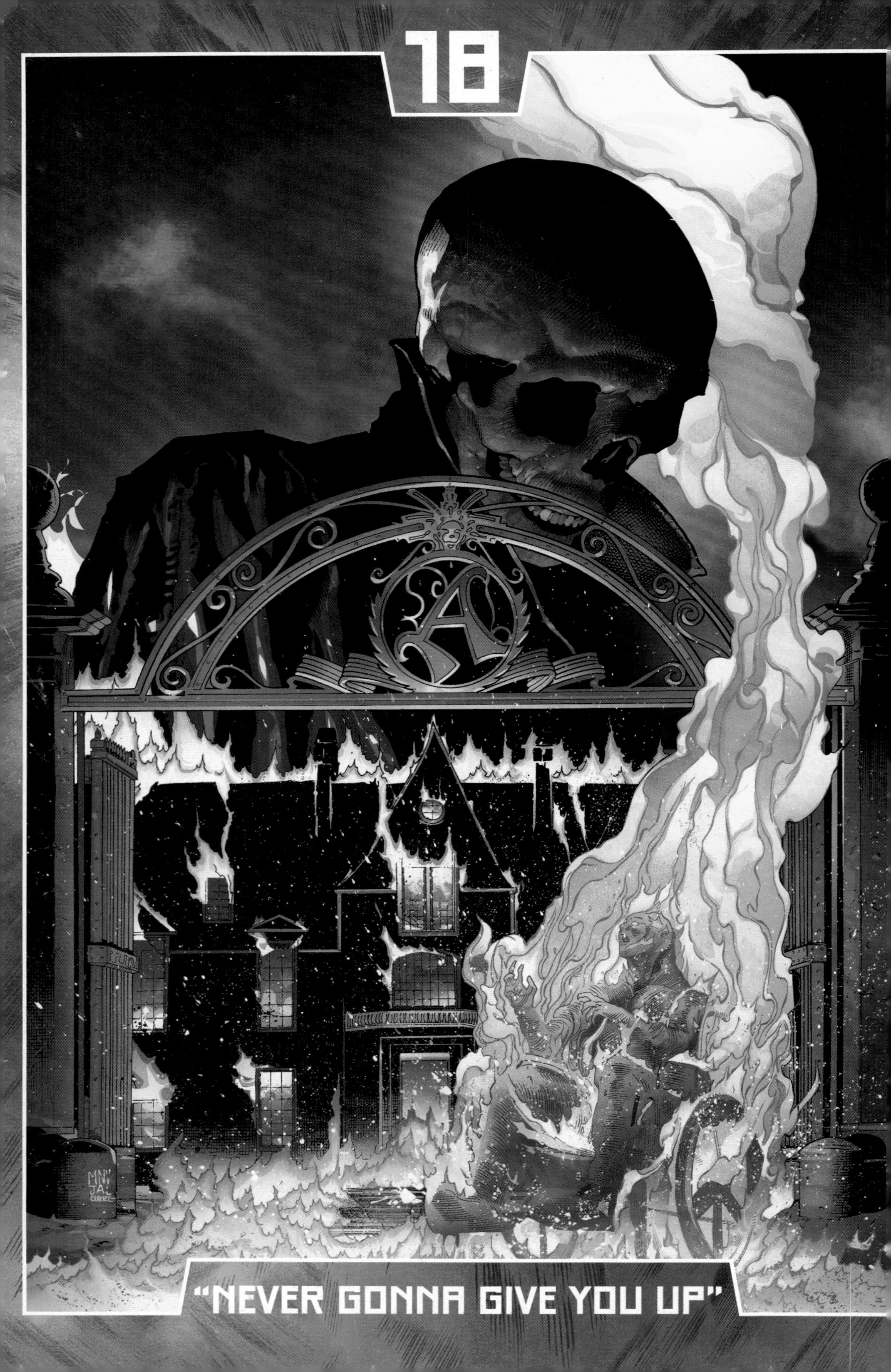
18
"NEVER GONNA GIVE YOU UP"

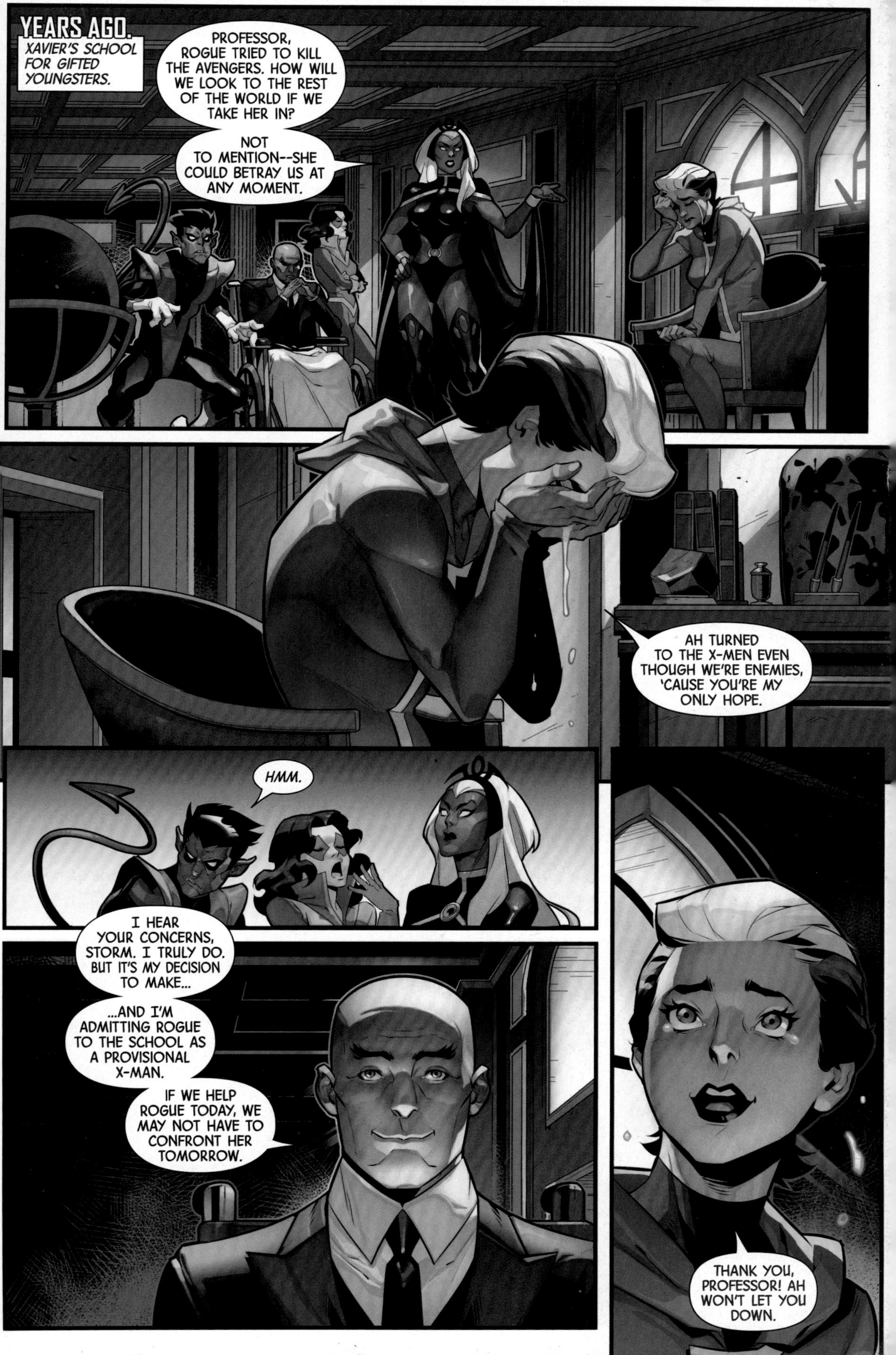
YEARS AGO.
XAVIER'S SCHOOL FOR GIFTED YOUNGSTERS.
PROFESSOR, ROGUE TRIED TO KILL THE AVENGERS. HOW WILL WE LOOK TO THE REST OF THE WORLD IF WE TAKE HER IN?
NOT TO MENTION--SHE COULD BETRAY US AT ANY MOMENT.
AH TURNED TO THE X-MEN EVEN THOUGH WE'RE ENEMIES, 'CAUSE YOU'RE MY ONLY HOPE.
HMM.
I HEAR YOUR CONCERNS, STORM. I TRULY DO. BUT IT'S MY DECISION TO MAKE...
...AND I'M ADMITTING ROGUE TO THE SCHOOL AS A PROVISIONAL X-MAN.
IF WE HELP ROGUE TODAY, WE MAY NOT HAVE TO CONFRONT HER TOMORROW.
THANK YOU, PROFESSOR! AH WON'T LET YOU DOWN.

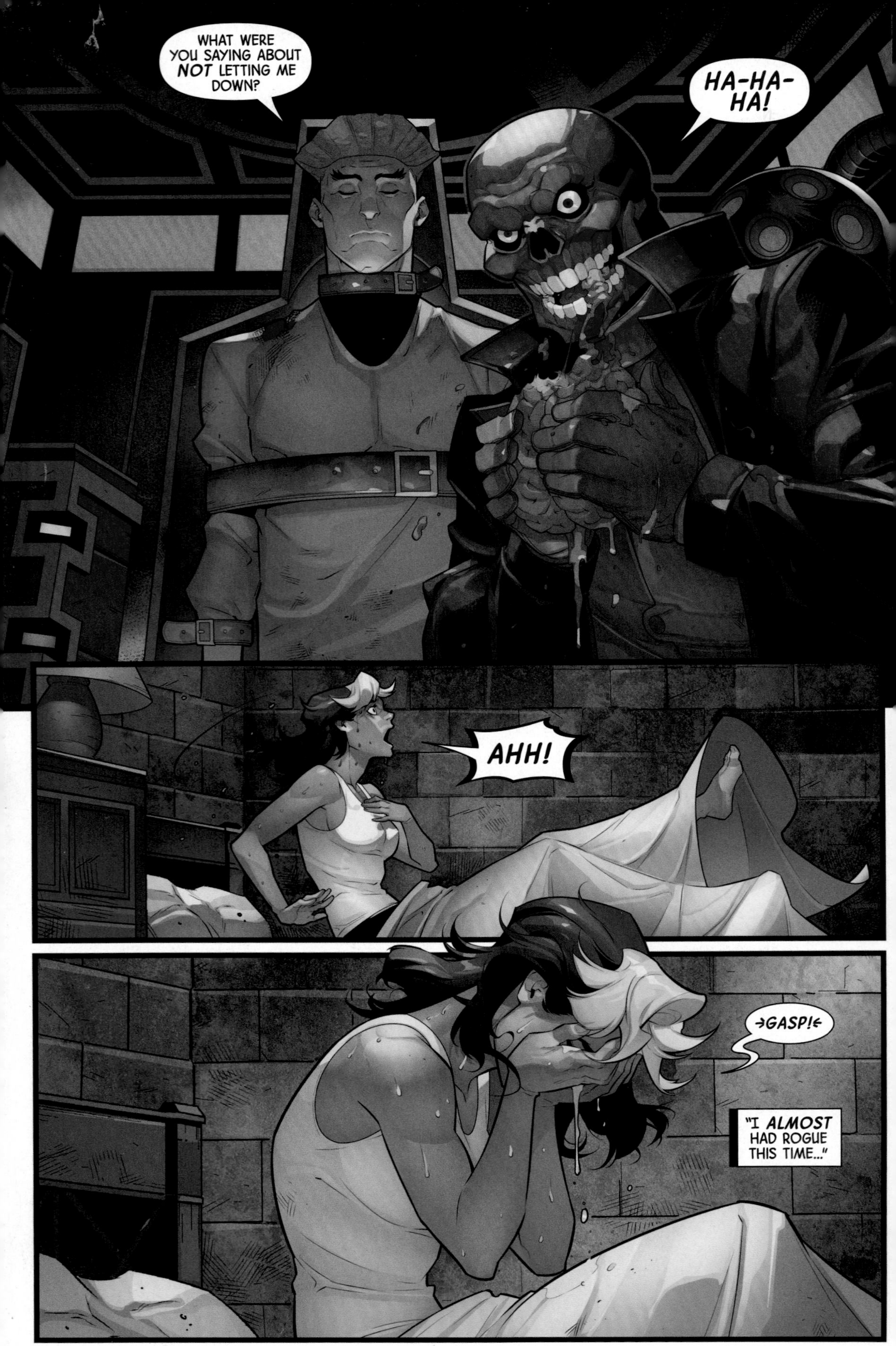
WHAT WERE YOU SAYING ABOUT NOT LETTING ME DOWN?
HA-HA-HA!
AHH!
GASP!
"I ALMOST HAD ROGUE THIS TIME..."

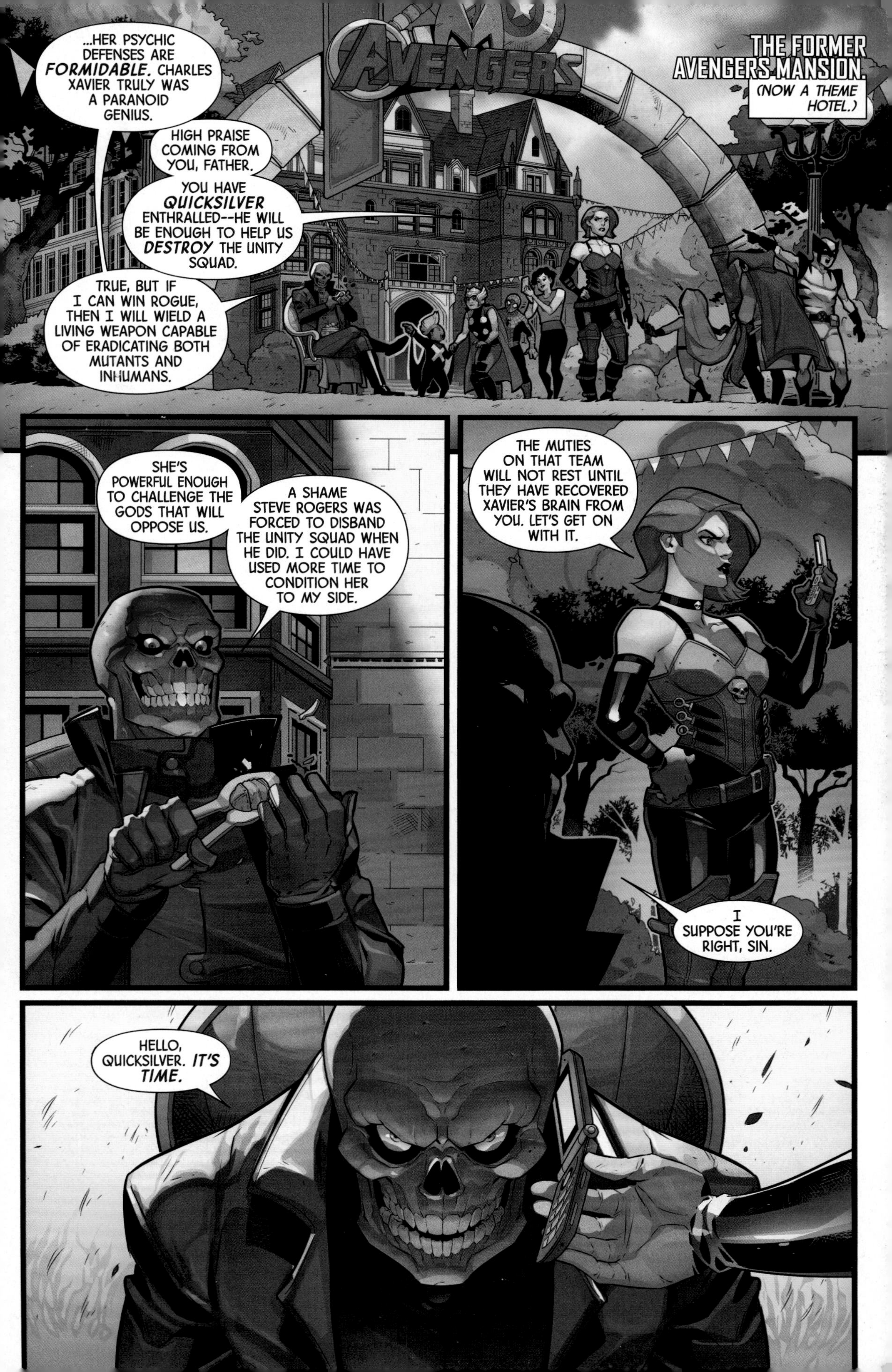
AVENGERS
THE FORMER AVENGERS MANSION.
(NOW A THEME HOTEL.)
...HER PSYCHIC DEFENSES ARE FORMIDABLE. CHARLES XAVIER TRULY WAS A PARANOID GENIUS.
HIGH PRAISE COMING FROM YOU, FATHER.
YOU HAVE QUICKSILVER ENTHRALLED--HE WILL BE ENOUGH TO HELP US DESTROY THE UNITY SQUAD.
TRUE, BUT IF I CAN WIN ROGUE, THEN I WILL WIELD A LIVING WEAPON CAPABLE OF ERADICATING BOTH MUTANTS AND INHUMANS.
SHE'S POWERFUL ENOUGH TO CHALLENGE THE GODS THAT WILL OPPOSE US.
A SHAME STEVE ROGERS WAS FORCED TO DISBAND THE UNITY SQUAD WHEN HE DID. I COULD HAVE USED MORE TIME TO CONDITION HER TO MY SIDE.
THE MUTIES ON THAT TEAM WILL NOT REST UNTIL THEY HAVE RECOVERED XAVIER'S BRAIN FROM YOU. LET'S GET ON WITH IT.
I SUPPOSE YOU'RE RIGHT, SIN.
HELLO, QUICKSILVER. IT'S TIME.

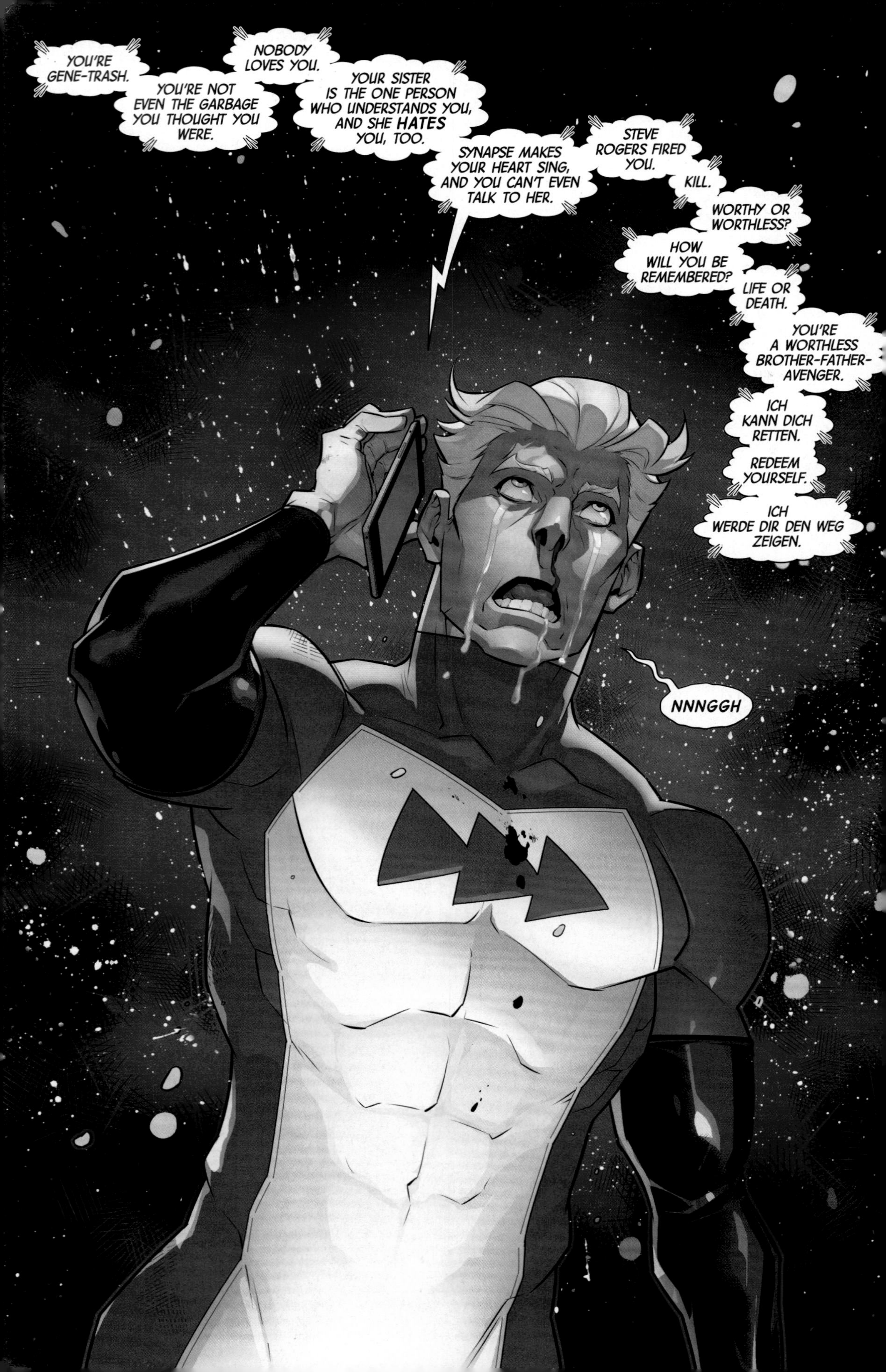
YOU'RE GENE-TRASH.
NOBODY LOVES YOU.
YOU'RE NOT EVEN THE GARBAGE YOU THOUGHT YOU WERE.
YOUR SISTER IS THE ONE PERSON WHO UNDERSTANDS YOU, AND SHE **HATES** YOU, TOO.
SYNAPSE MAKES YOUR HEART SING, AND YOU CAN'T EVEN TALK TO HER.
STEVE ROGERS FIRED YOU.
KILL.
WORTHY OR WORTHLESS?
HOW WILL YOU BE REMEMBERED?
LIFE OR DEATH.
YOU'RE A WORTHLESS BROTHER-FATHER-AVENGER.
ICH KANN DICH RETTEN.
REDEEM YOURSELF.
ICH WERDE DIR DEN WEG ZEIGEN.
NNNGGH

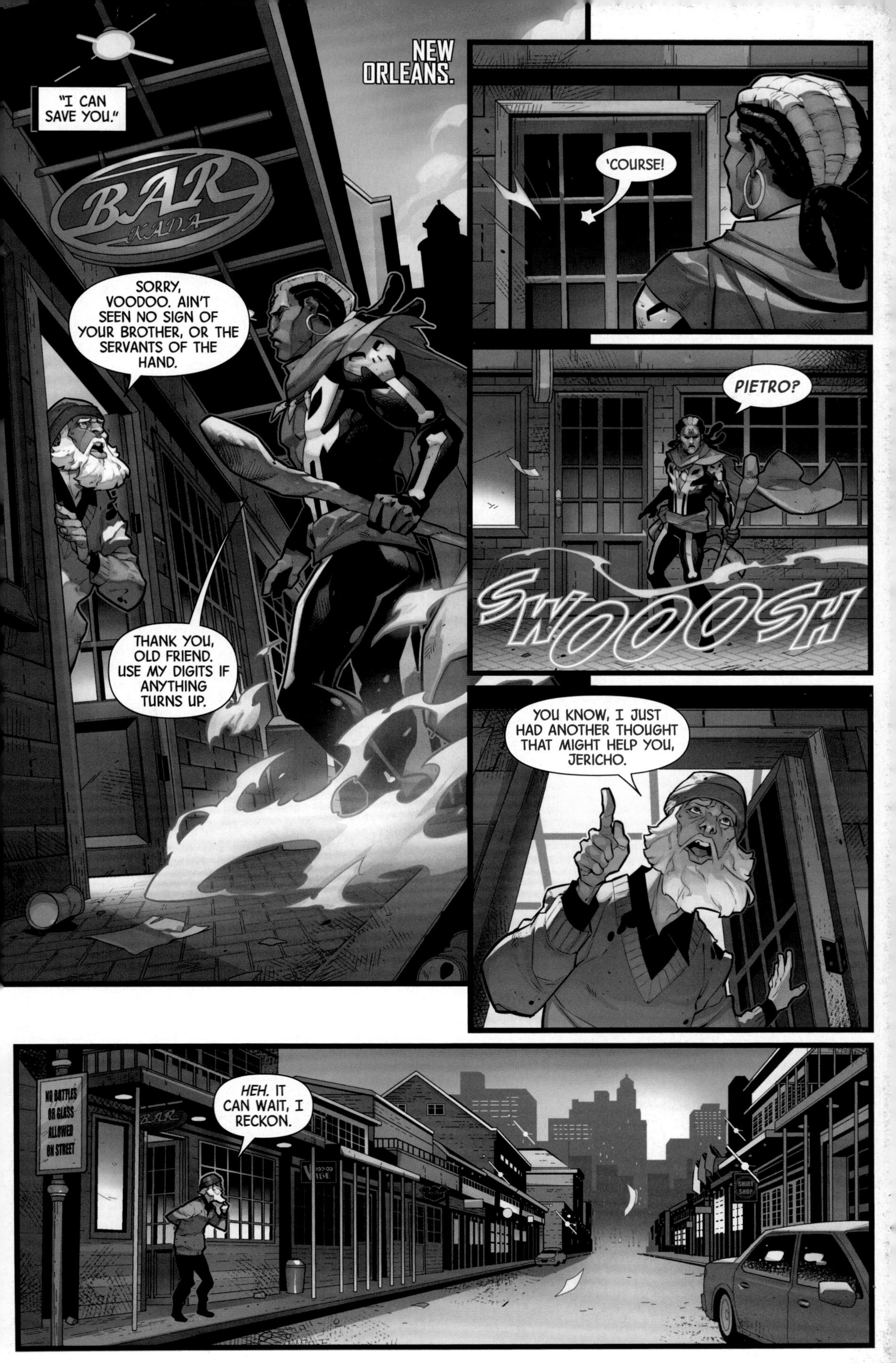
NEW ORLEANS.
"I CAN SAVE YOU."
BAR
KADA
SORRY, VOODOO. AIN'T SEEN NO SIGN OF YOUR BROTHER, OR THE SERVANTS OF THE HAND.
THANK YOU, OLD FRIEND. USE MY DIGITS IF ANYTHING TURNS UP.
'COURSE!
PIETRO?
SWOOOSH
YOU KNOW, I JUST HAD ANOTHER THOUGHT THAT MIGHT HELP YOU, JERICHO.
NO BOTTLES OR GLASS ALLOWED ON STREET
BAR
HEH. IT CAN WAIT, I RECKON.
SHIRT SHOP

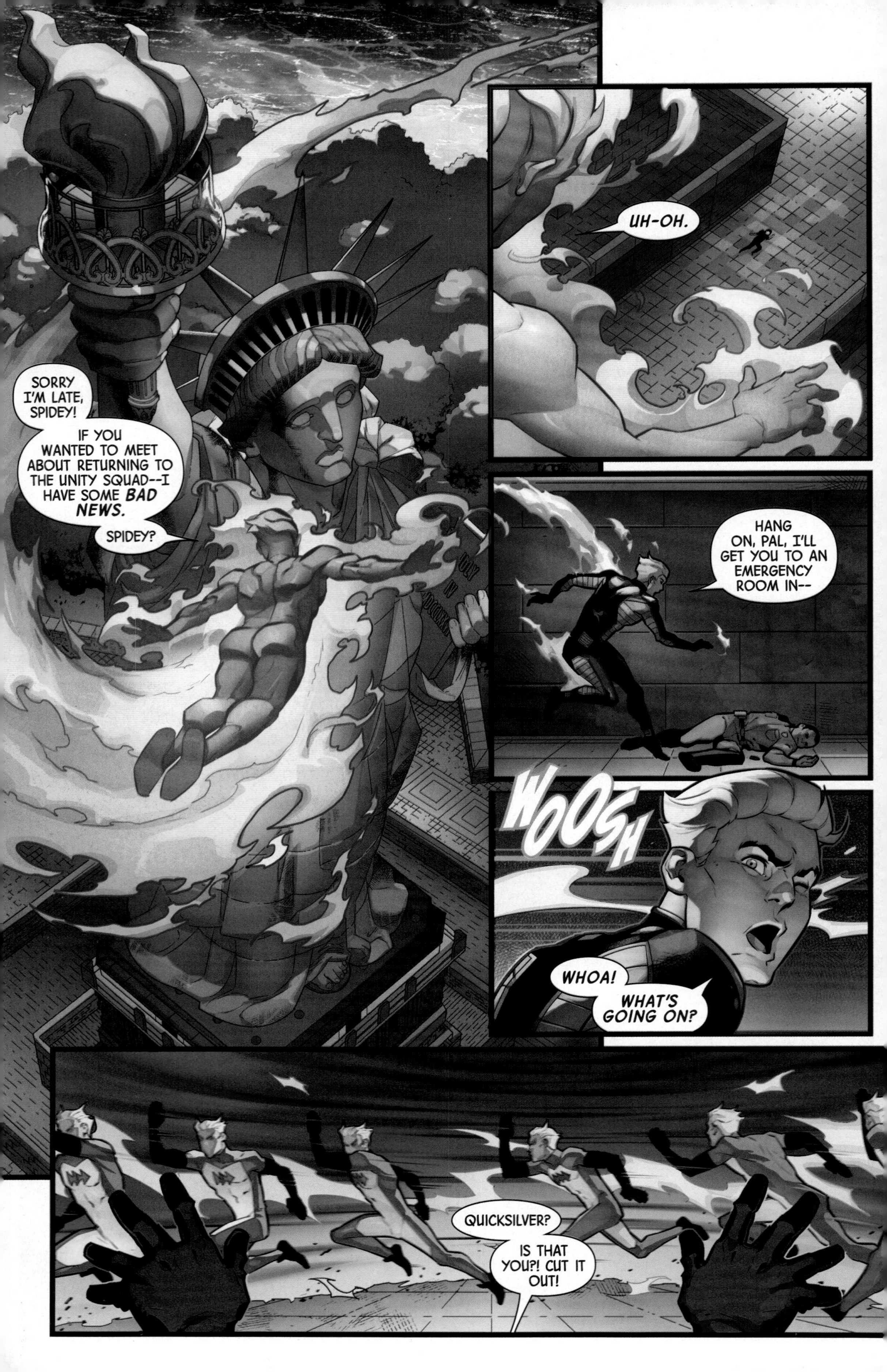
SORRY I'M LATE, SPIDEY!
IF YOU WANTED TO MEET ABOUT RETURNING TO THE UNITY SQUAD--I HAVE SOME BAD NEWS.
SPIDEY?
UH-OH.
HANG ON, PAL, I'LL GET YOU TO AN EMERGENCY ROOM IN--
WOOSH
WHOA!
WHAT'S GOING ON?
QUICKSILVER?
IS THAT YOU?! CUT IT OUT!

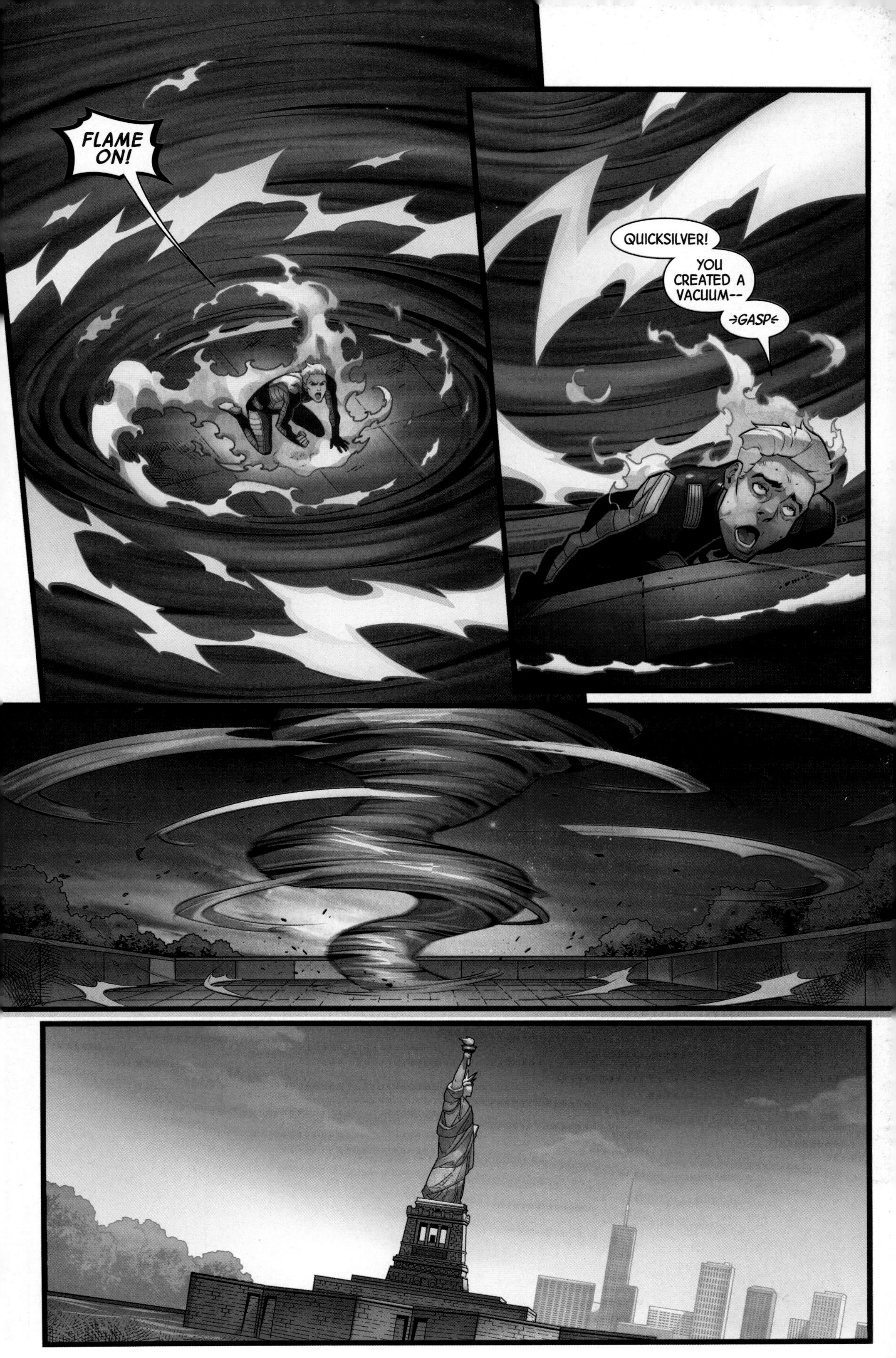
FLAME ON!
QUICKSILVER!
YOU CREATED A VACUUM--
GASP

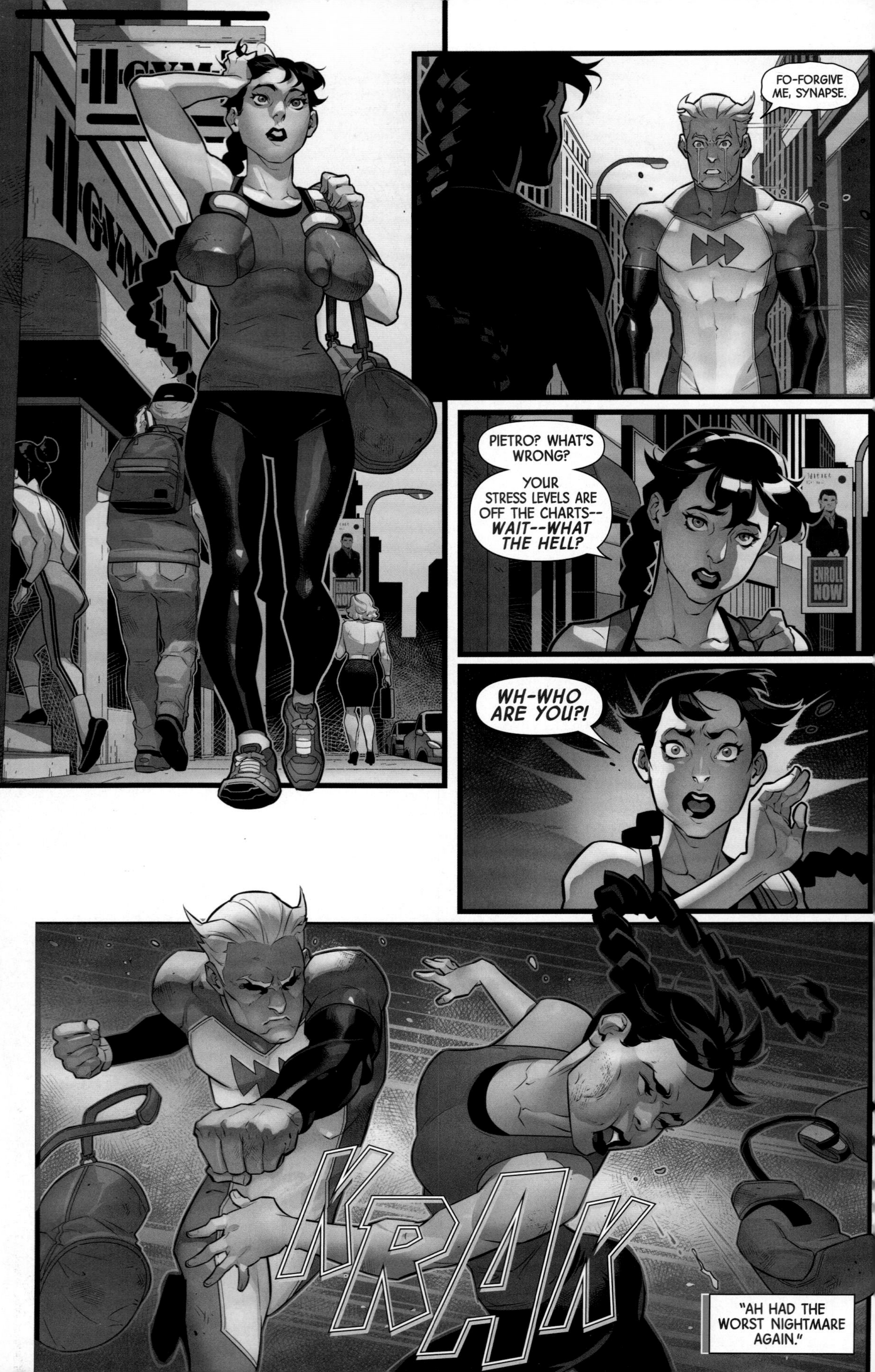
GYM
GYM
FO-FORGIVE ME, SYNAPSE.
PIETRO? WHAT'S WRONG?
YOUR STRESS LEVELS ARE OFF THE CHARTS-- WAIT--WHAT THE HELL?
ENROLL NOW
WH-WHO ARE YOU?!
KRAK
"AH HAD THE WORST NIGHTMARE AGAIN."

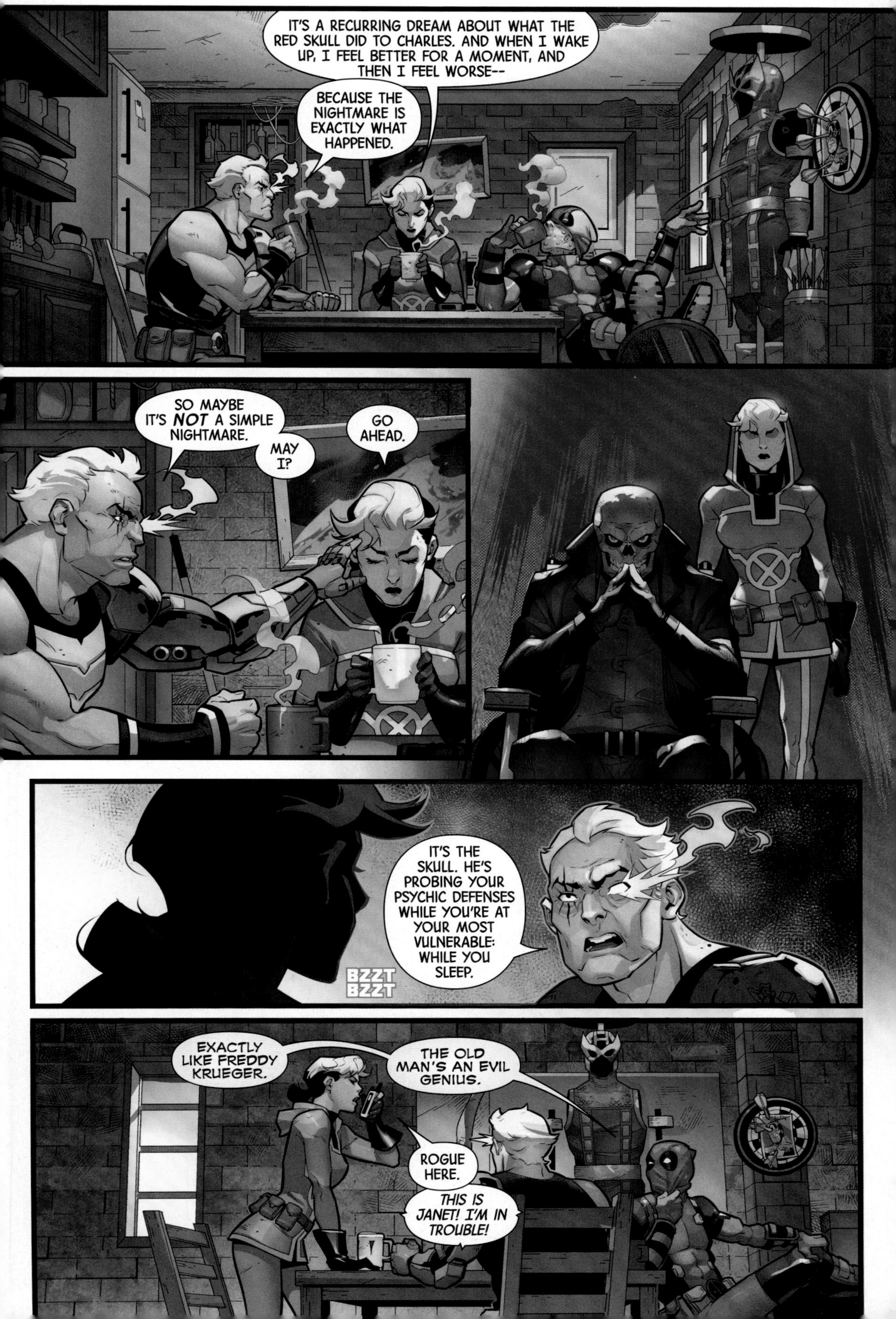
IT'S A RECURRING DREAM ABOUT WHAT THE RED SKULL DID TO CHARLES. AND WHEN I WAKE UP, I FEEL BETTER FOR A MOMENT, AND THEN I FEEL WORSE--
BECAUSE THE NIGHTMARE IS EXACTLY WHAT HAPPENED.
SO MAYBE IT'S NOT A SIMPLE NIGHTMARE.
MAY I?
GO AHEAD.
IT'S THE SKULL. HE'S PROBING YOUR PSYCHIC DEFENSES WHILE YOU'RE AT YOUR MOST VULNERABLE: WHILE YOU SLEEP.
BZZT BZZT
EXACTLY LIKE FREDDY KRUEGER.
THE OLD MAN'S AN EVIL GENIUS.
ROGUE HERE.
THIS IS JANET! I'M IN TROUBLE!

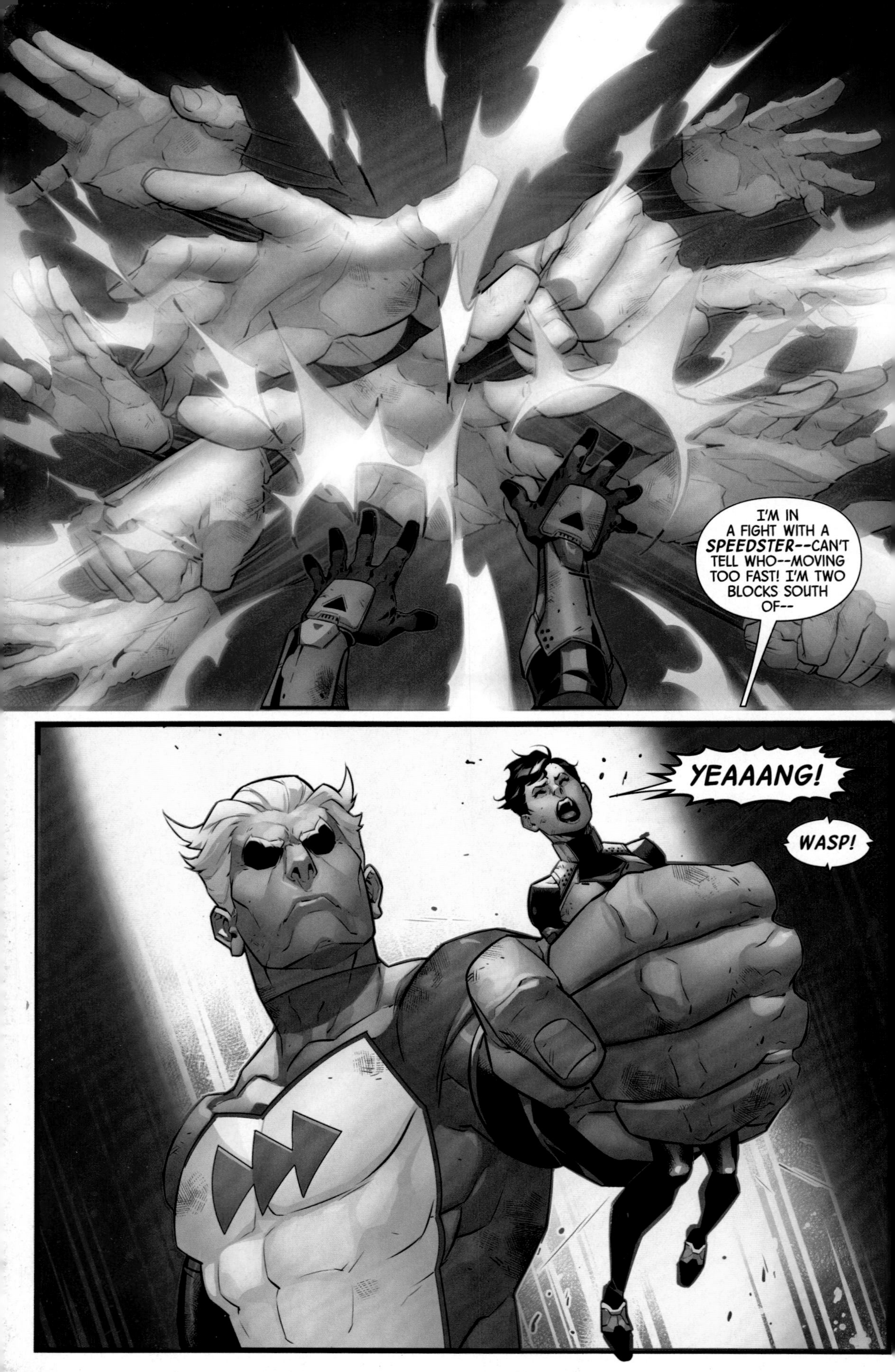
I'M IN A FIGHT WITH A SPEEDSTER--CAN'T TELL WHO--MOVING TOO FAST! I'M TWO BLOCKS SOUTH OF--
YEAAANG!
WASP!

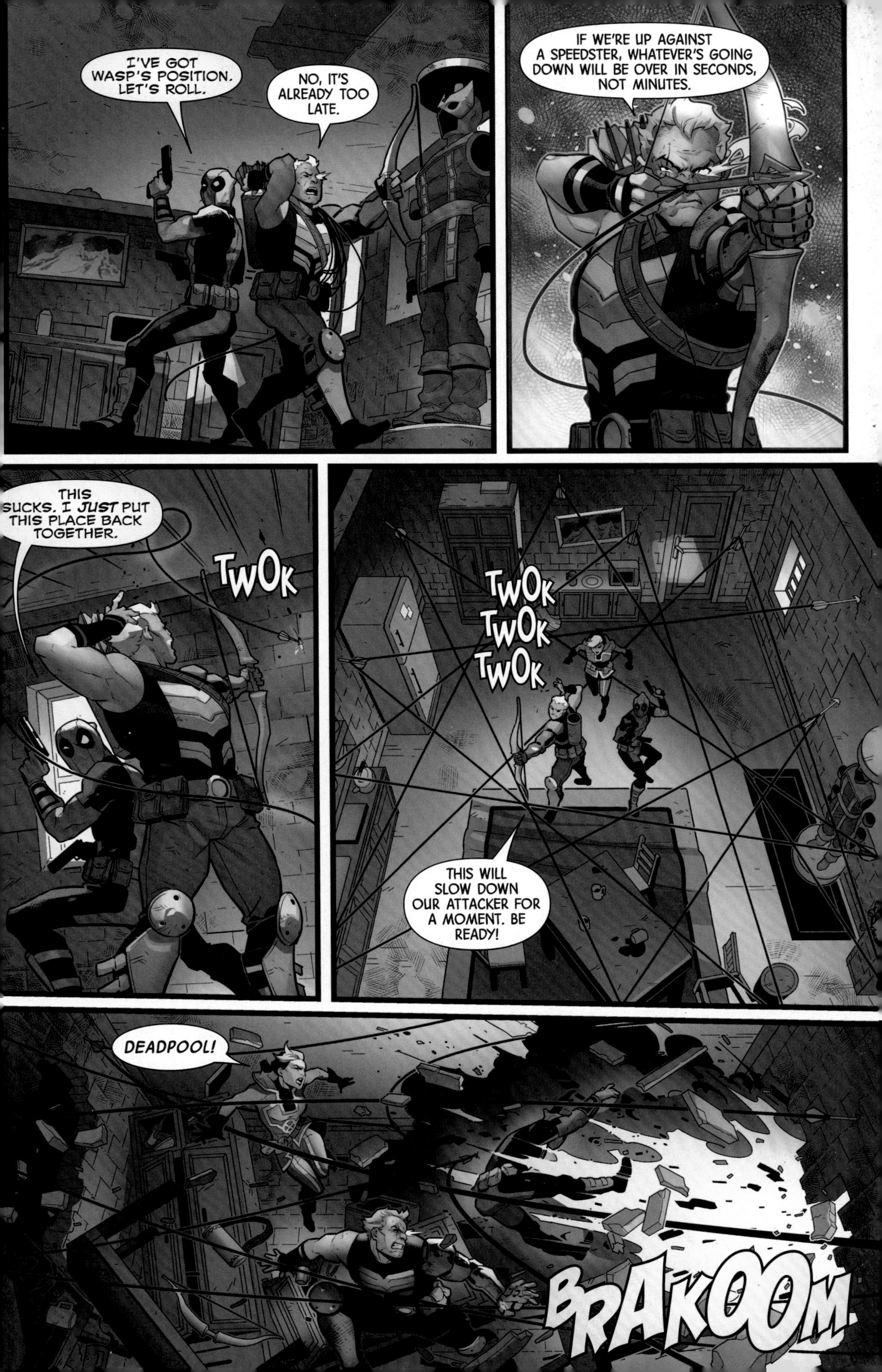
I'VE GOT WASP'S POSITION. LET'S ROLL.
NO, IT'S ALREADY TOO LATE.
IF WE'RE UP AGAINST A SPEEDSTER, WHATEVER'S GOING DOWN WILL BE OVER IN SECONDS, NOT MINUTES.
THIS SUCKS. I *JUST* PUT THIS PLACE BACK TOGETHER.
TWOK
TWOK
TWOK
TWOK
THIS WILL SLOW DOWN OUR ATTACKER FOR A MOMENT. BE READY!
DEADPOOL!
BRAKOOM

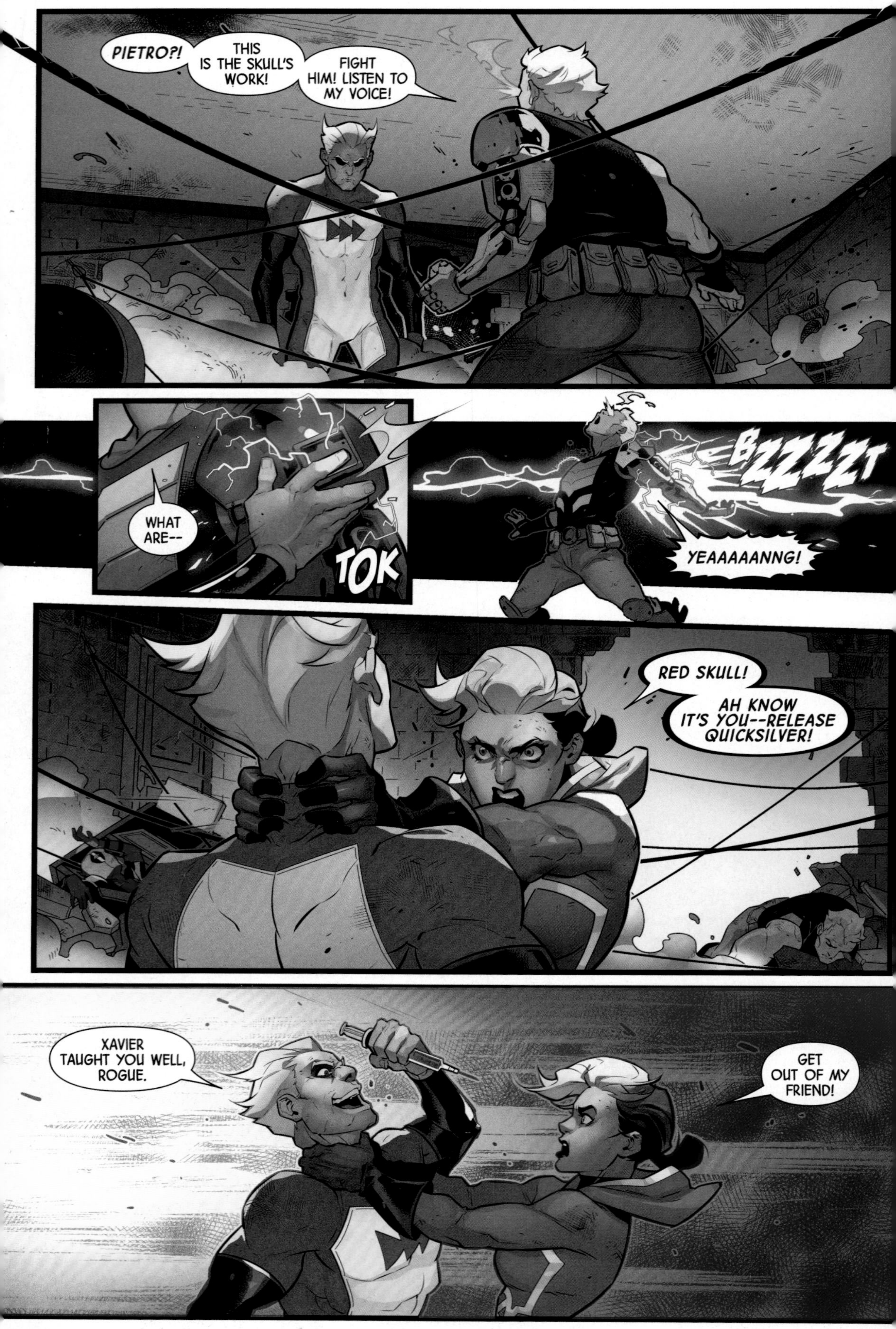
PIETRO?!
THIS IS THE SKULL'S WORK!
FIGHT HIM! LISTEN TO MY VOICE!
WHAT ARE--
TOK
BZZZZT
YEAAAAANNG!
RED SKULL!
AH KNOW IT'S YOU--RELEASE QUICKSILVER!
XAVIER TAUGHT YOU WELL, ROGUE.
GET OUT OF MY FRIEND!

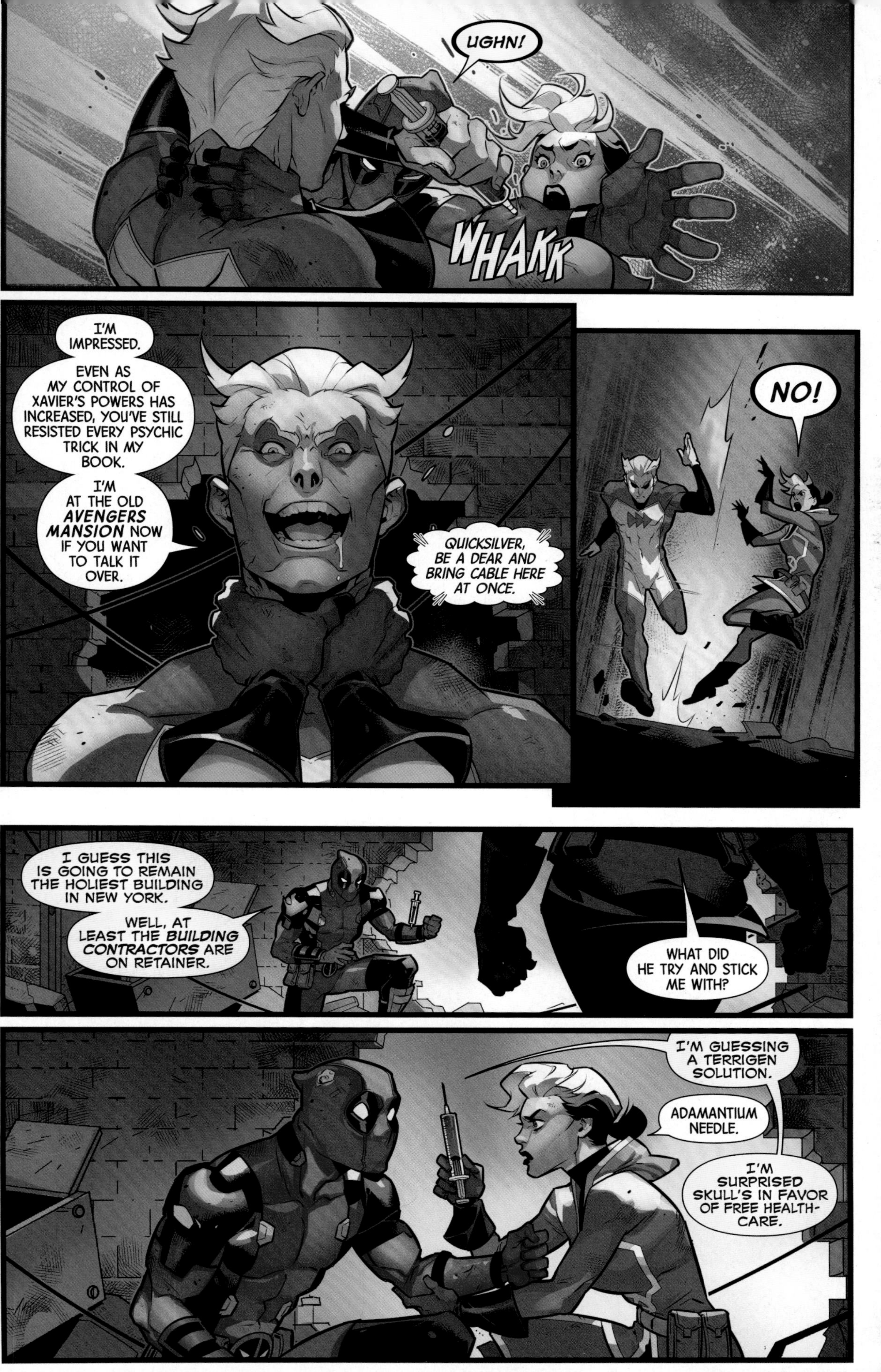
UGHN!
WHAKK
I'M IMPRESSED.
EVEN AS MY CONTROL OF XAVIER'S POWERS HAS INCREASED, YOU'VE STILL RESISTED EVERY PSYCHIC TRICK IN MY BOOK.
I'M AT THE OLD AVENGERS MANSION NOW IF YOU WANT TO TALK IT OVER.
QUICKSILVER, BE A DEAR AND BRING CABLE HERE AT ONCE.
NO!
I GUESS THIS IS GOING TO REMAIN THE HOLIEST BUILDING IN NEW YORK.
WELL, AT LEAST THE BUILDING CONTRACTORS ARE ON RETAINER.
WHAT DID HE TRY AND STICK ME WITH?
I'M GUESSING A TERRIGEN SOLUTION.
ADAMANTIUM NEEDLE.
I'M SURPRISED SKULL'S IN FAVOR OF FREE HEALTH-CARE.

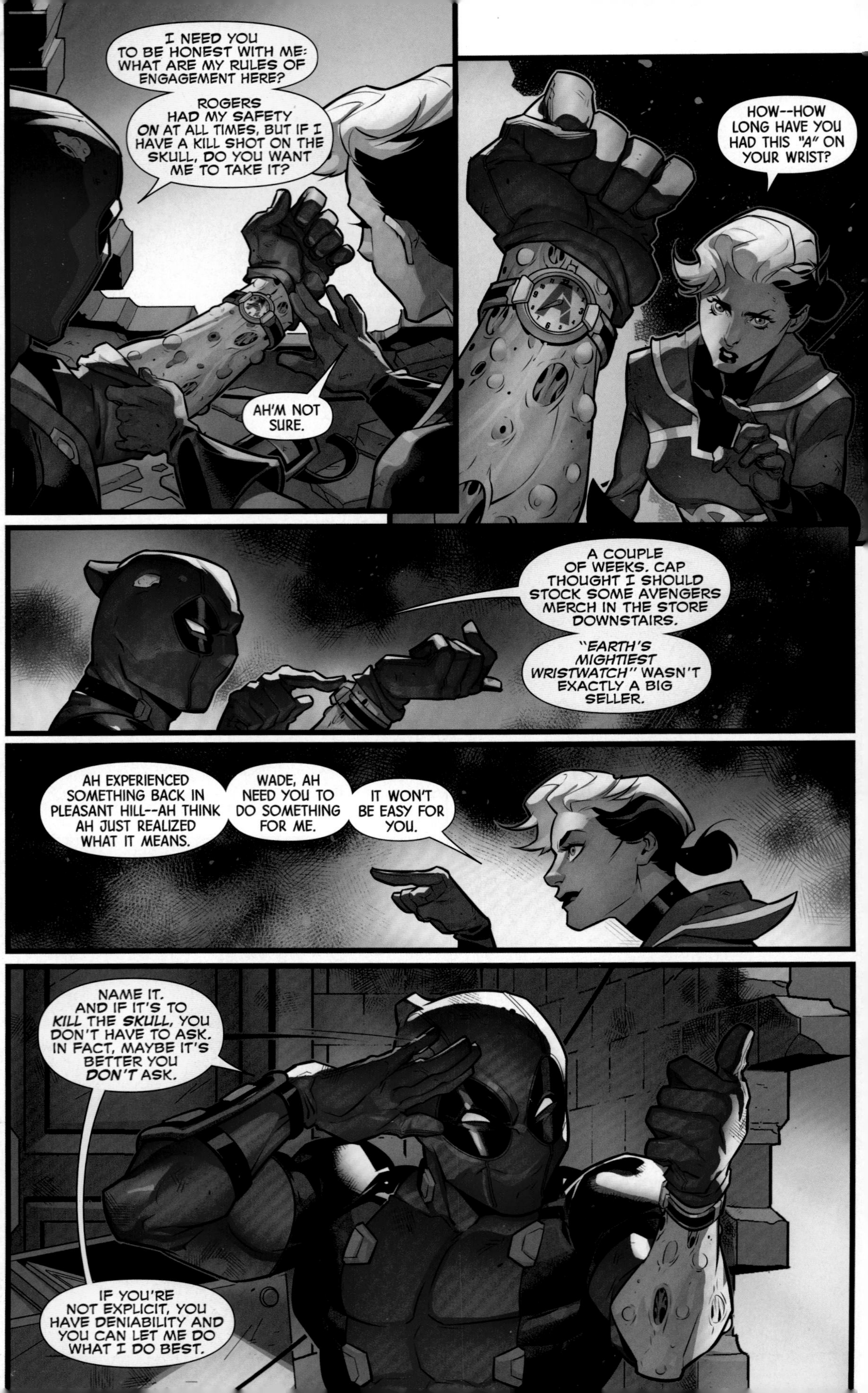
I NEED YOU TO BE HONEST WITH ME: WHAT ARE MY RULES OF ENGAGEMENT HERE?
ROGERS HAD MY SAFETY *ON* AT ALL TIMES, BUT IF I HAVE A KILL SHOT ON THE SKULL, DO YOU WANT ME TO TAKE IT?
AH'M NOT SURE.
HOW--HOW LONG HAVE YOU HAD THIS *"A"* ON YOUR WRIST?
A COUPLE OF WEEKS. CAP THOUGHT I SHOULD STOCK SOME AVENGERS MERCH IN THE STORE DOWNSTAIRS.
"EARTH'S MIGHTIEST WRISTWATCH" WASN'T EXACTLY A BIG SELLER.
AH EXPERIENCED SOMETHING BACK IN PLEASANT HILL--AH THINK AH JUST REALIZED WHAT IT MEANS.
WADE, AH NEED YOU TO DO SOMETHING FOR ME.
IT WON'T BE EASY FOR YOU.
NAME IT. AND IF IT'S TO *KILL* THE *SKULL*, YOU DON'T HAVE TO ASK. IN FACT, MAYBE IT'S BETTER YOU *DON'T* ASK.
IF YOU'RE NOT EXPLICIT, YOU HAVE DENIABILITY AND YOU CAN LET ME DO WHAT I DO BEST.

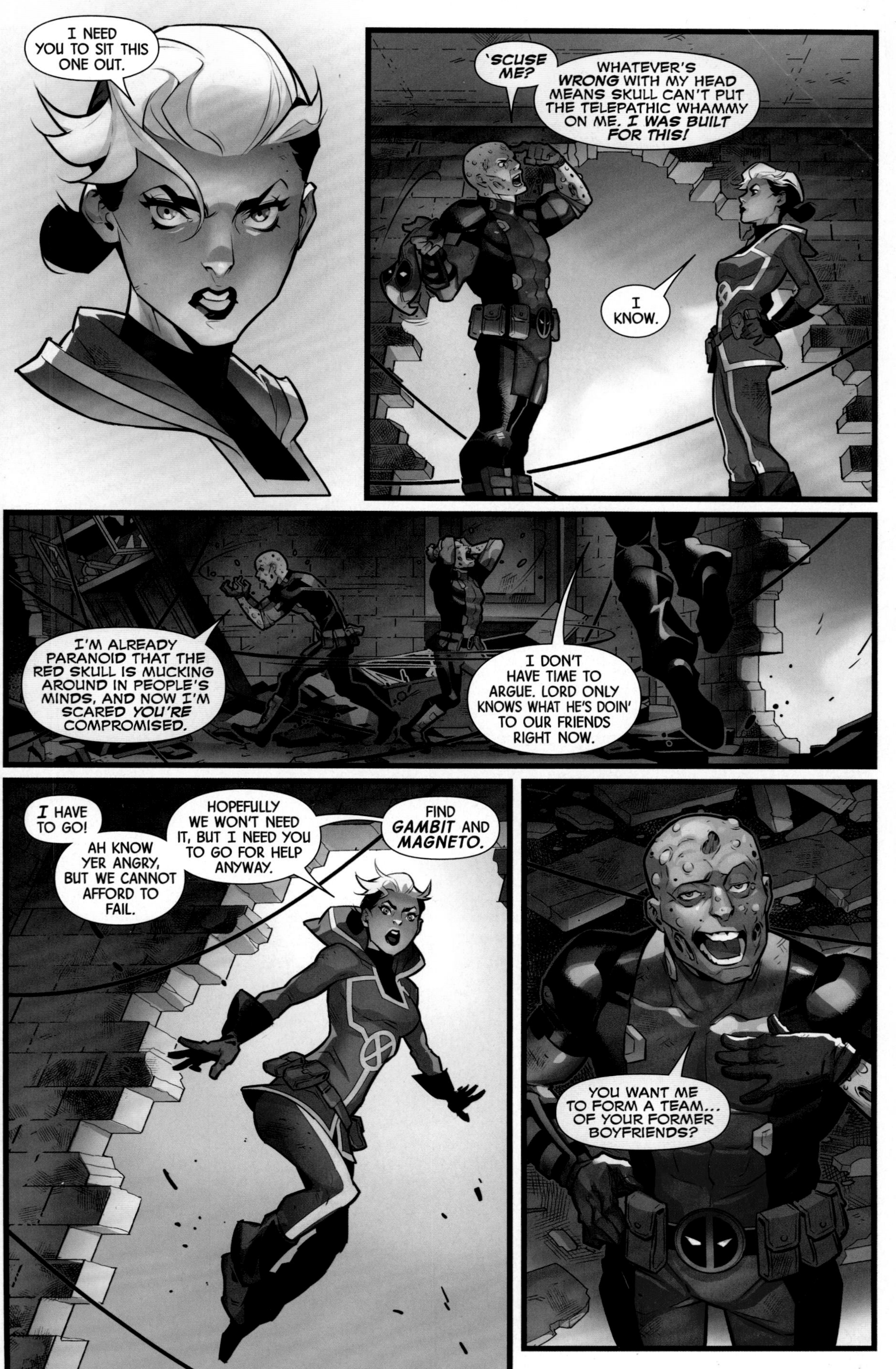

I NEED YOU TO SIT THIS ONE OUT.
'SCUSE ME?
WHATEVER'S *WRONG* WITH MY HEAD MEANS SKULL CAN'T PUT THE TELEPATHIC WHAMMY ON ME. *I WAS BUILT FOR THIS!*
I KNOW.
I'M ALREADY **PARANOID** THAT THE **RED SKULL** IS MUCKING AROUND IN PEOPLE'S MINDS, AND NOW I'M SCARED *YOU'RE* COMPROMISED.
I DON'T HAVE TIME TO ARGUE. LORD ONLY KNOWS WHAT HE'S DOIN' TO OUR FRIENDS RIGHT NOW.
I HAVE TO GO!
AH KNOW YER ANGRY, BUT WE CANNOT AFFORD TO FAIL.
HOPEFULLY WE WON'T NEED IT, BUT I NEED YOU TO GO FOR HELP ANYWAY.
FIND ***GAMBIT*** AND ***MAGNETO.***
YOU WANT ME TO FORM A TEAM... OF YOUR FORMER BOYFRIENDS?

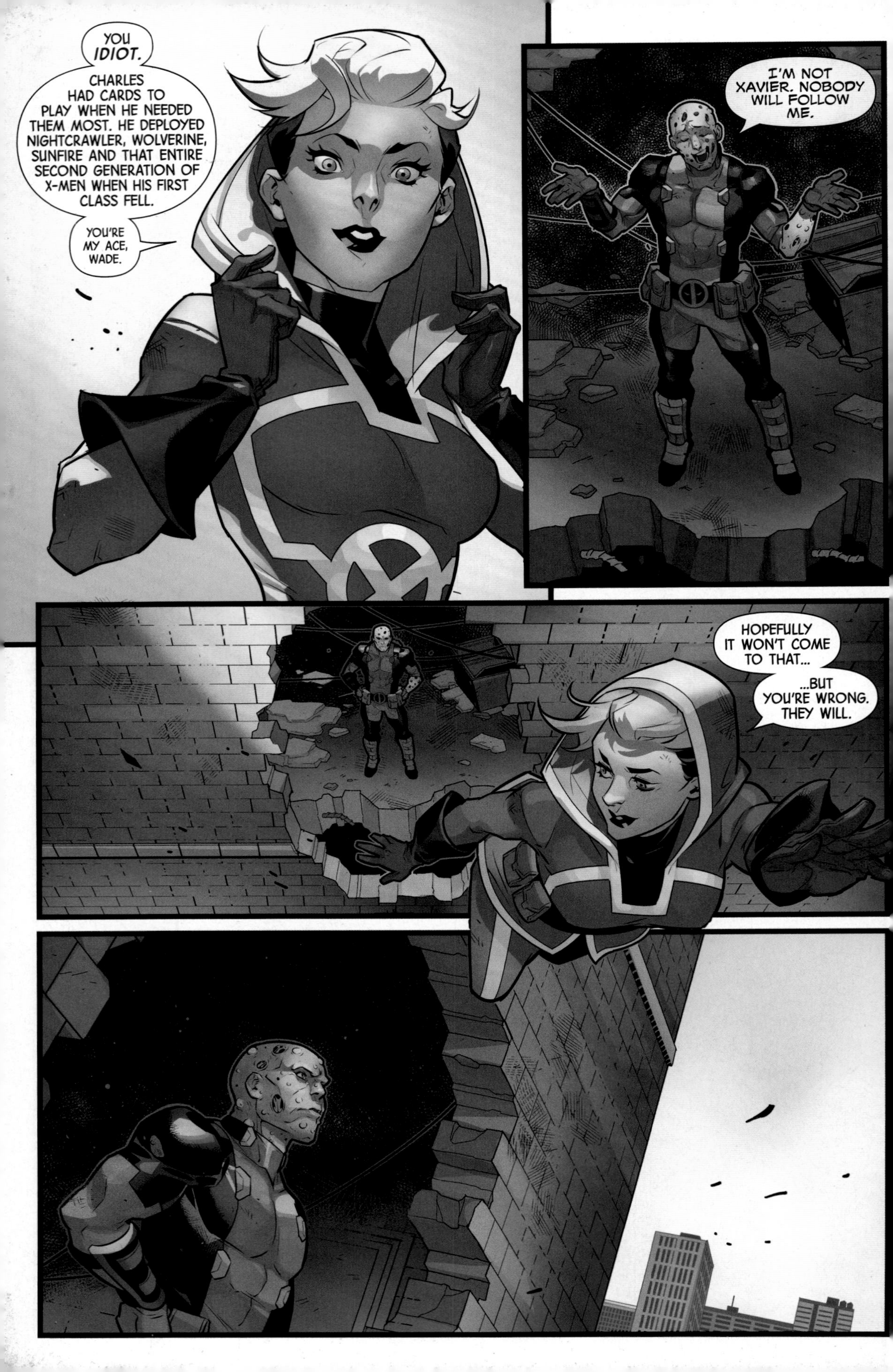
YOU *IDIOT.*
CHARLES HAD CARDS TO PLAY WHEN HE NEEDED THEM MOST. HE DEPLOYED NIGHTCRAWLER, WOLVERINE, SUNFIRE AND THAT ENTIRE SECOND GENERATION OF X-MEN WHEN HIS FIRST CLASS FELL.
YOU'RE MY ACE, WADE.
I'M NOT XAVIER. NOBODY WILL FOLLOW ME.
HOPEFULLY IT WON'T COME TO THAT...
...BUT YOU'RE WRONG. THEY WILL.

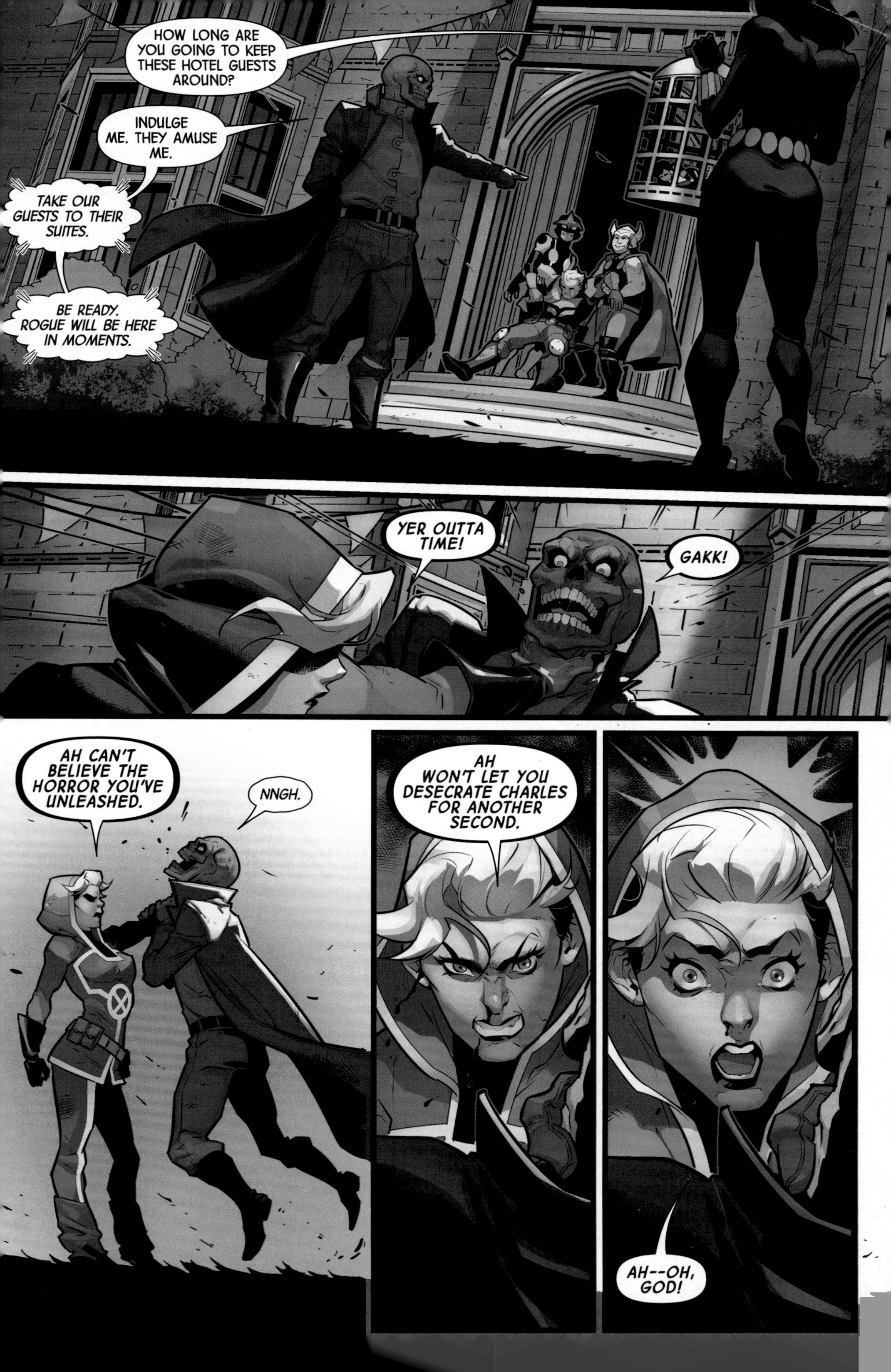
HOW LONG ARE YOU GOING TO KEEP THESE HOTEL GUESTS AROUND?
INDULGE ME. THEY AMUSE ME.
TAKE OUR GUESTS TO THEIR SUITES.
BE READY. ROGUE WILL BE HERE IN MOMENTS.
YER OUTTA TIME!
GAKK!
AH CAN'T BELIEVE THE HORROR YOU'VE UNLEASHED.
NNGH.
AH WON'T LET YOU DESECRATE CHARLES FOR ANOTHER SECOND.
AH--OH, GOD!

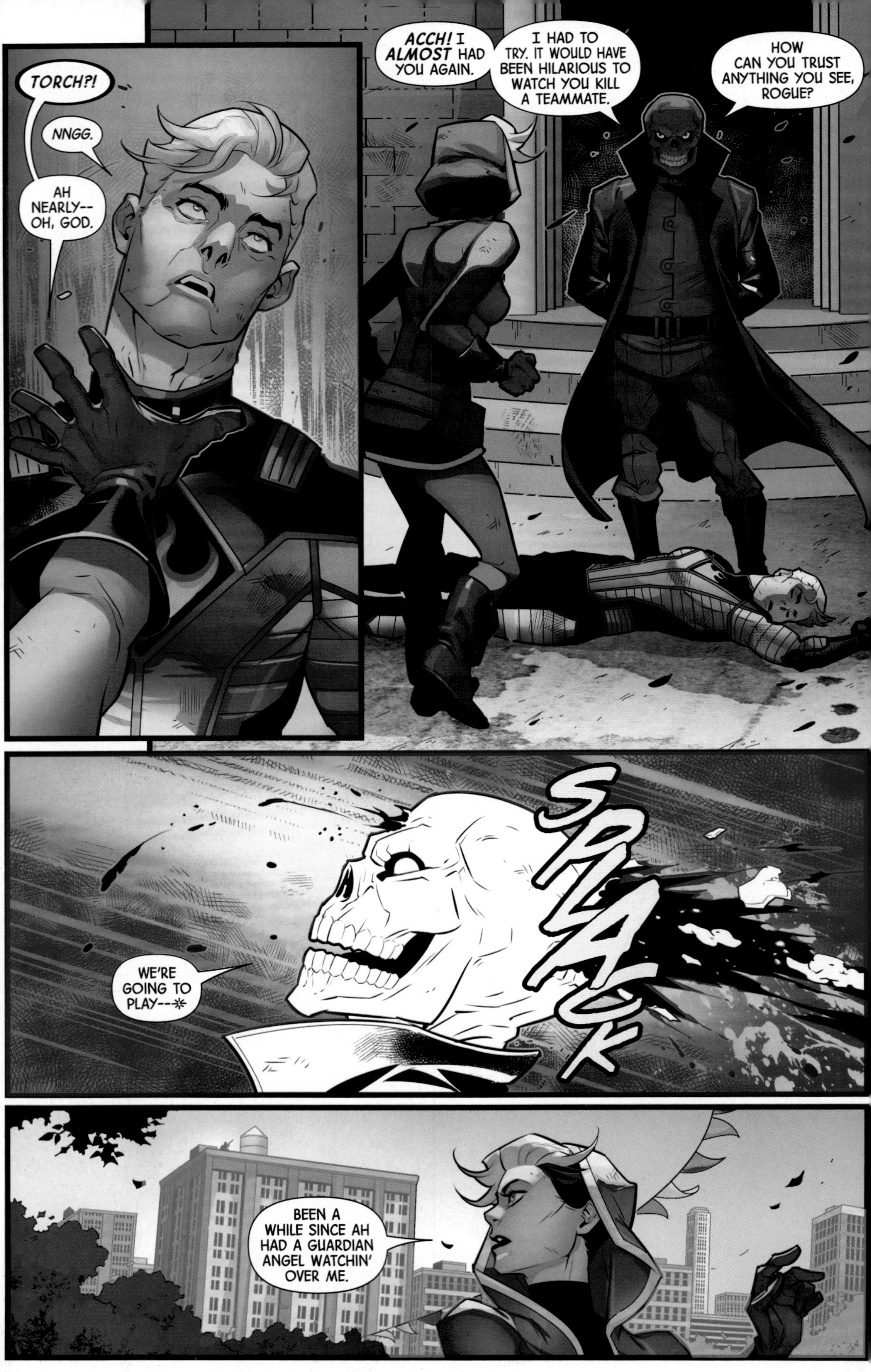
TORCH?!
NNGG.
AH NEARLY-- OH, GOD.
ACCH! I ALMOST HAD YOU AGAIN.
I HAD TO TRY. IT WOULD HAVE BEEN HILARIOUS TO WATCH YOU KILL A TEAMMATE.
HOW CAN YOU TRUST ANYTHING YOU SEE, ROGUE?
SPLAK
WE'RE GOING TO PLAY--
BEEN A WHILE SINCE AH HAD A GUARDIAN ANGEL WATCHIN' OVER ME.

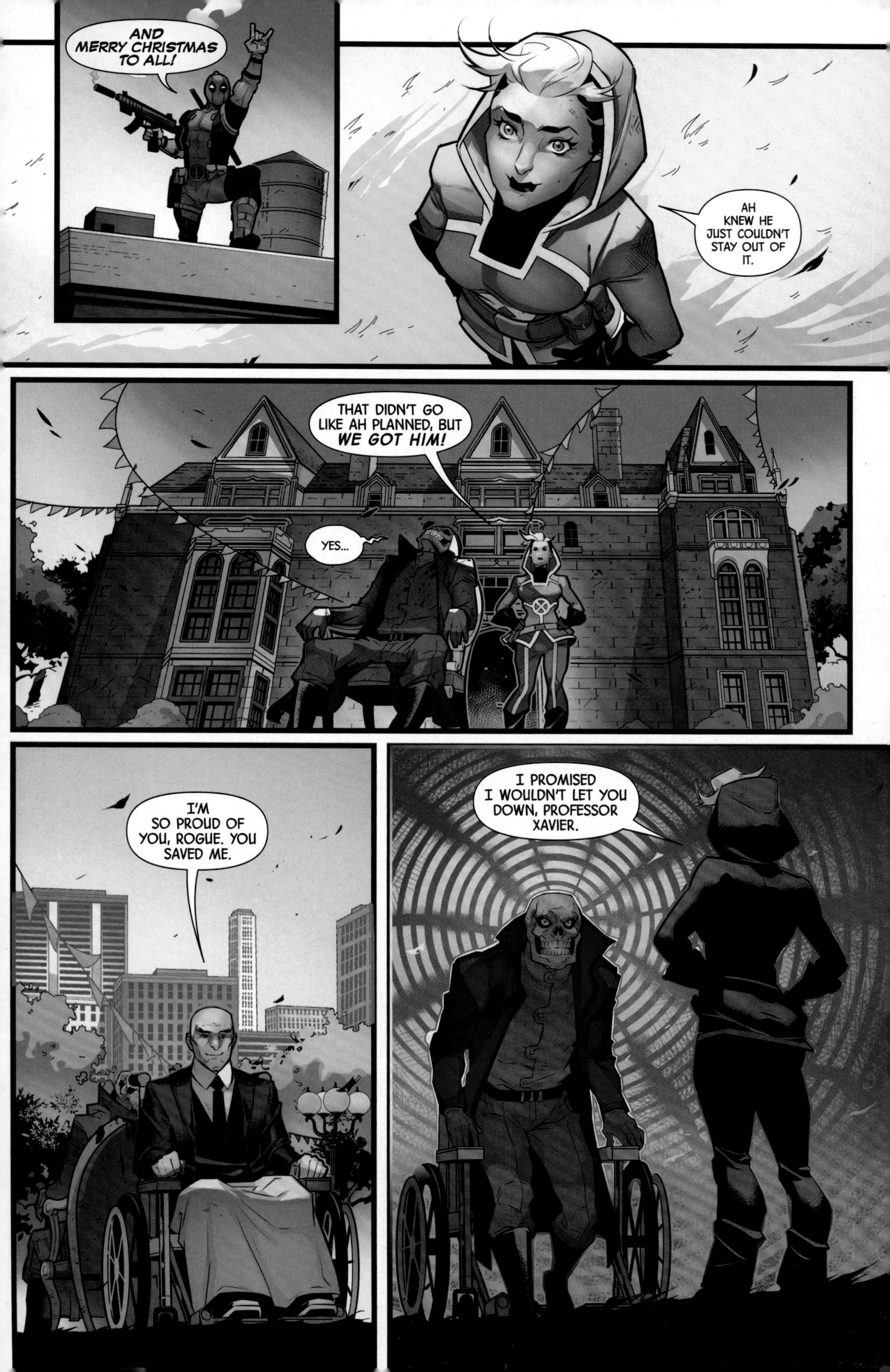
AND MERRY CHRISTMAS TO ALL!
AH KNEW HE JUST COULDN'T STAY OUT OF IT.
THAT DIDN'T GO LIKE AH PLANNED, BUT WE GOT HIM!
YES...
I'M SO PROUD OF YOU, ROGUE. YOU SAVED ME.
I PROMISED I WOULDN'T LET YOU DOWN, PROFESSOR XAVIER.

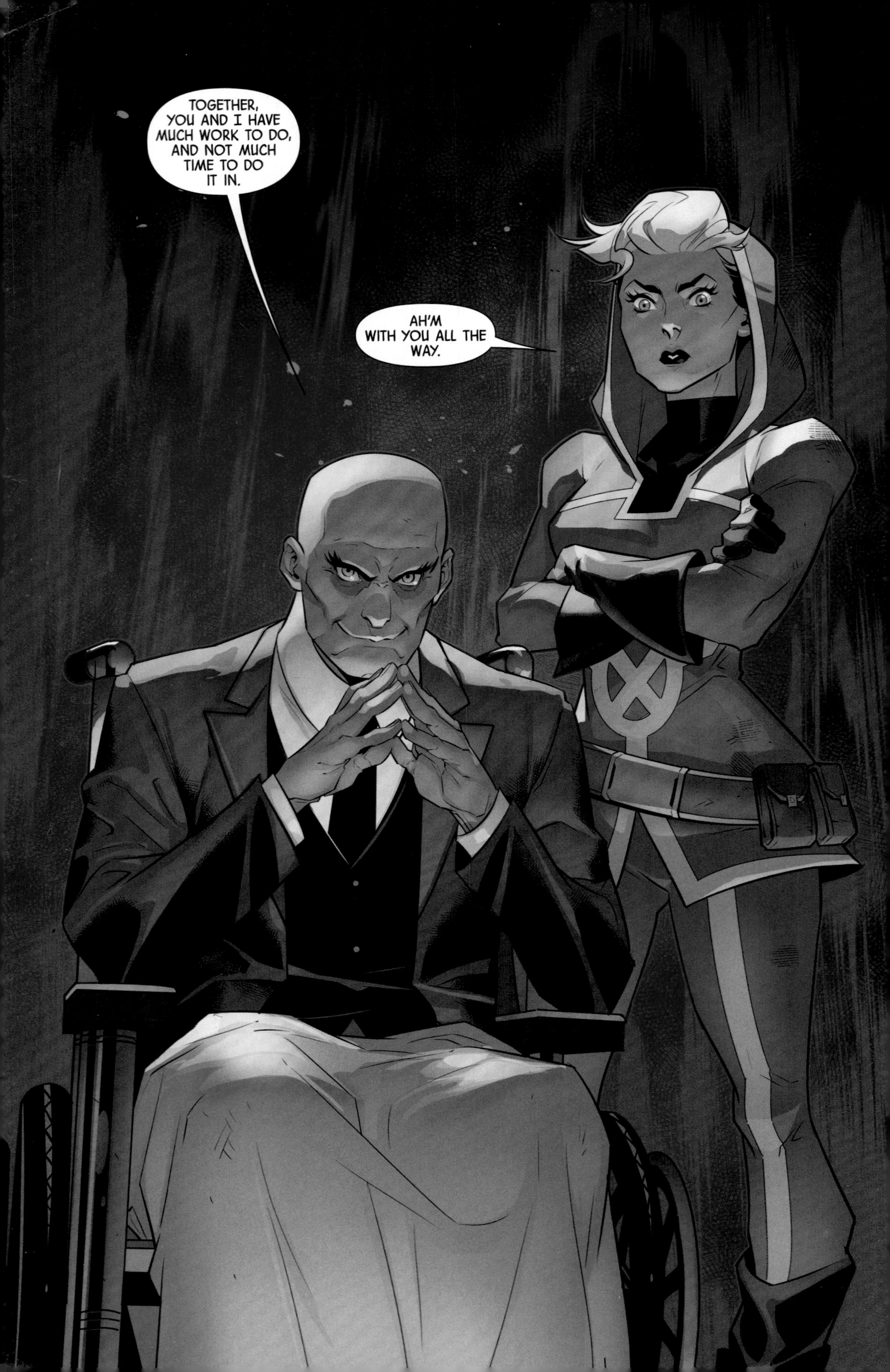
TOGETHER, YOU AND I HAVE MUCH WORK TO DO, AND NOT MUCH TIME TO DO IT IN.
AH'M WITH YOU ALL THE WAY.

19

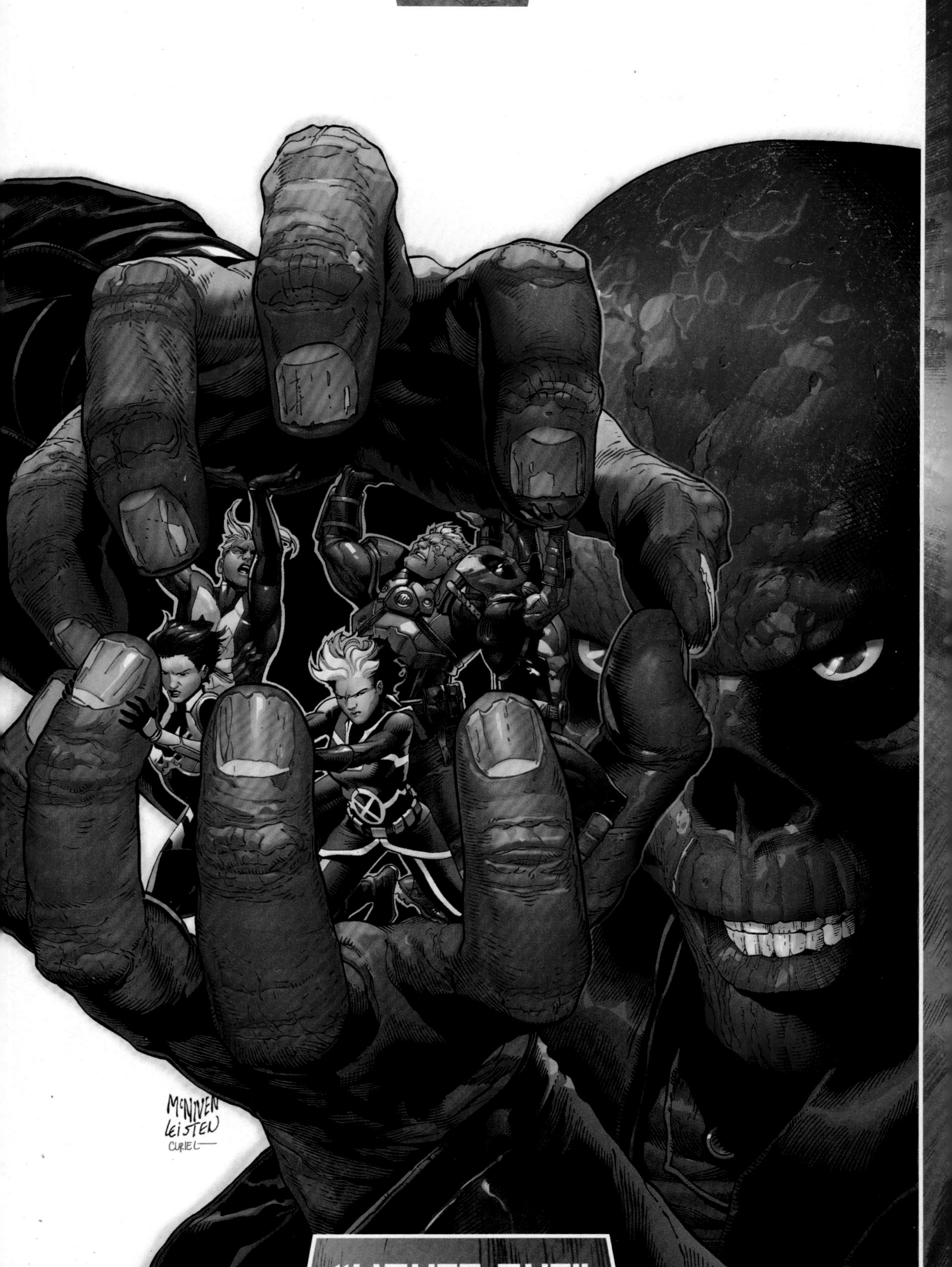
McNIVEN
LEISTEN
CURIEL

"LIGHTS OUT"

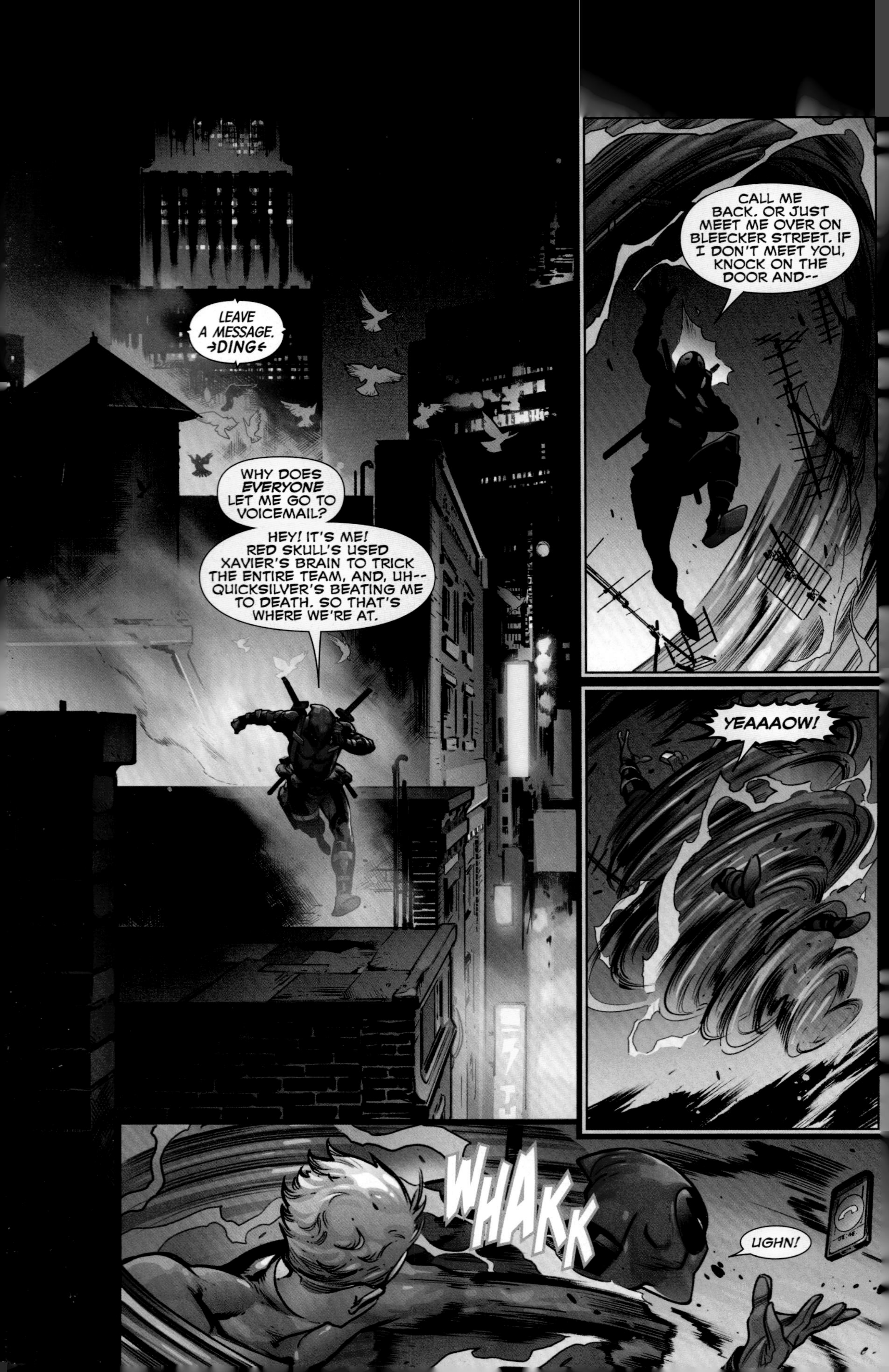
LEAVE A MESSAGE. →DING←
WHY DOES EVERYONE LET ME GO TO VOICEMAIL?
HEY! IT'S ME! RED SKULL'S USED XAVIER'S BRAIN TO TRICK THE ENTIRE TEAM, AND, UH-- QUICKSILVER'S BEATING ME TO DEATH. SO THAT'S WHERE WE'RE AT.
CALL ME BACK. OR JUST MEET ME OVER ON BLEECKER STREET. IF I DON'T MEET YOU, KNOCK ON THE DOOR AND--
YEAAAOW!
WHAKK
UGHN!

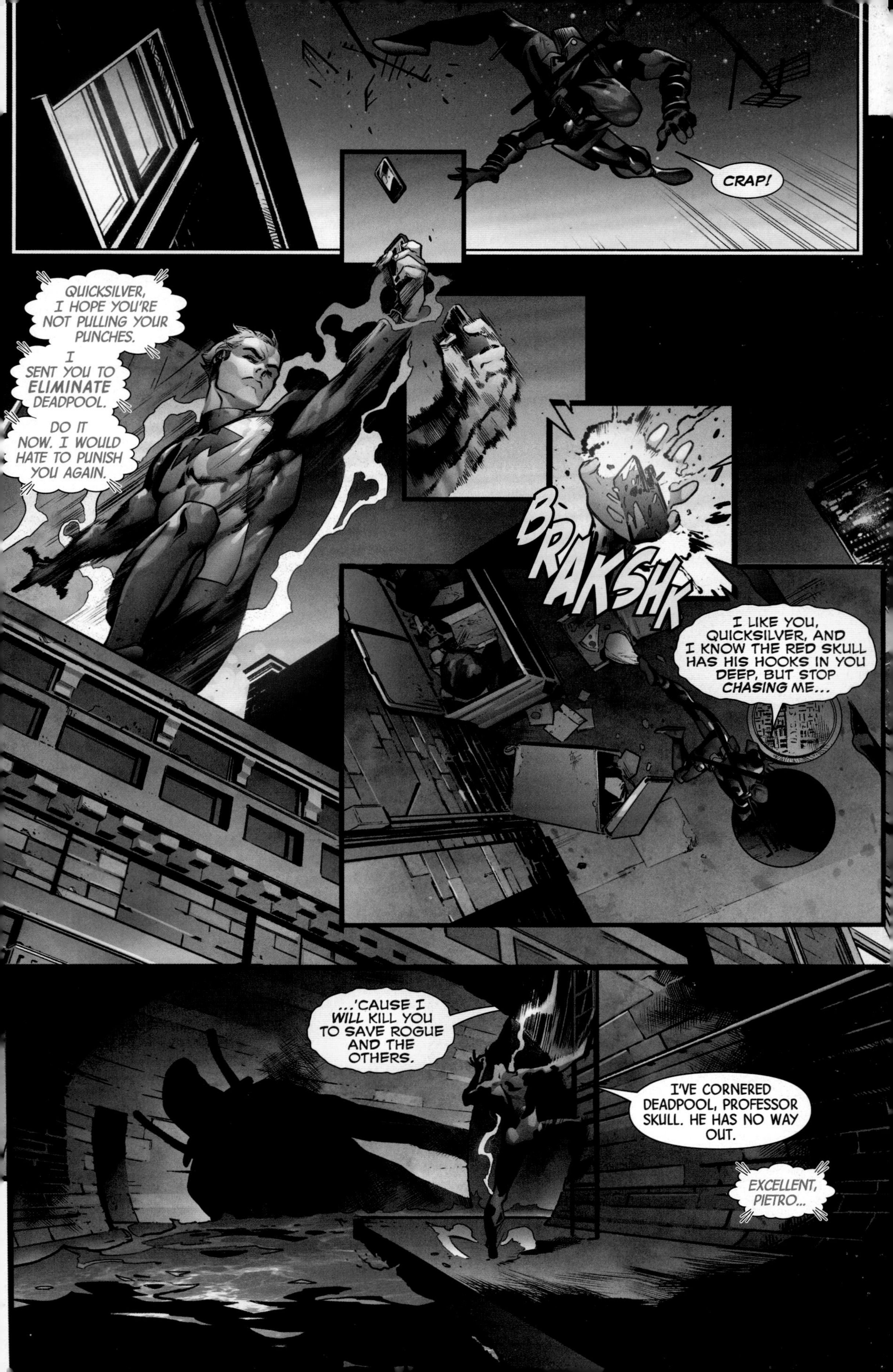
CRAP!
QUICKSILVER, I HOPE YOU'RE NOT PULLING YOUR PUNCHES.
I SENT YOU TO ELIMINATE DEADPOOL.
DO IT NOW. I WOULD HATE TO PUNISH YOU AGAIN.
BRAKSHK
I LIKE YOU, QUICKSILVER, AND I KNOW THE RED SKULL HAS HIS HOOKS IN YOU DEEP, BUT STOP CHASING ME...
...'CAUSE I WILL KILL YOU TO SAVE ROGUE AND THE OTHERS.
I'VE CORNERED DEADPOOL, PROFESSOR SKULL. HE HAS NO WAY OUT.
EXCELLENT, PIETRO...

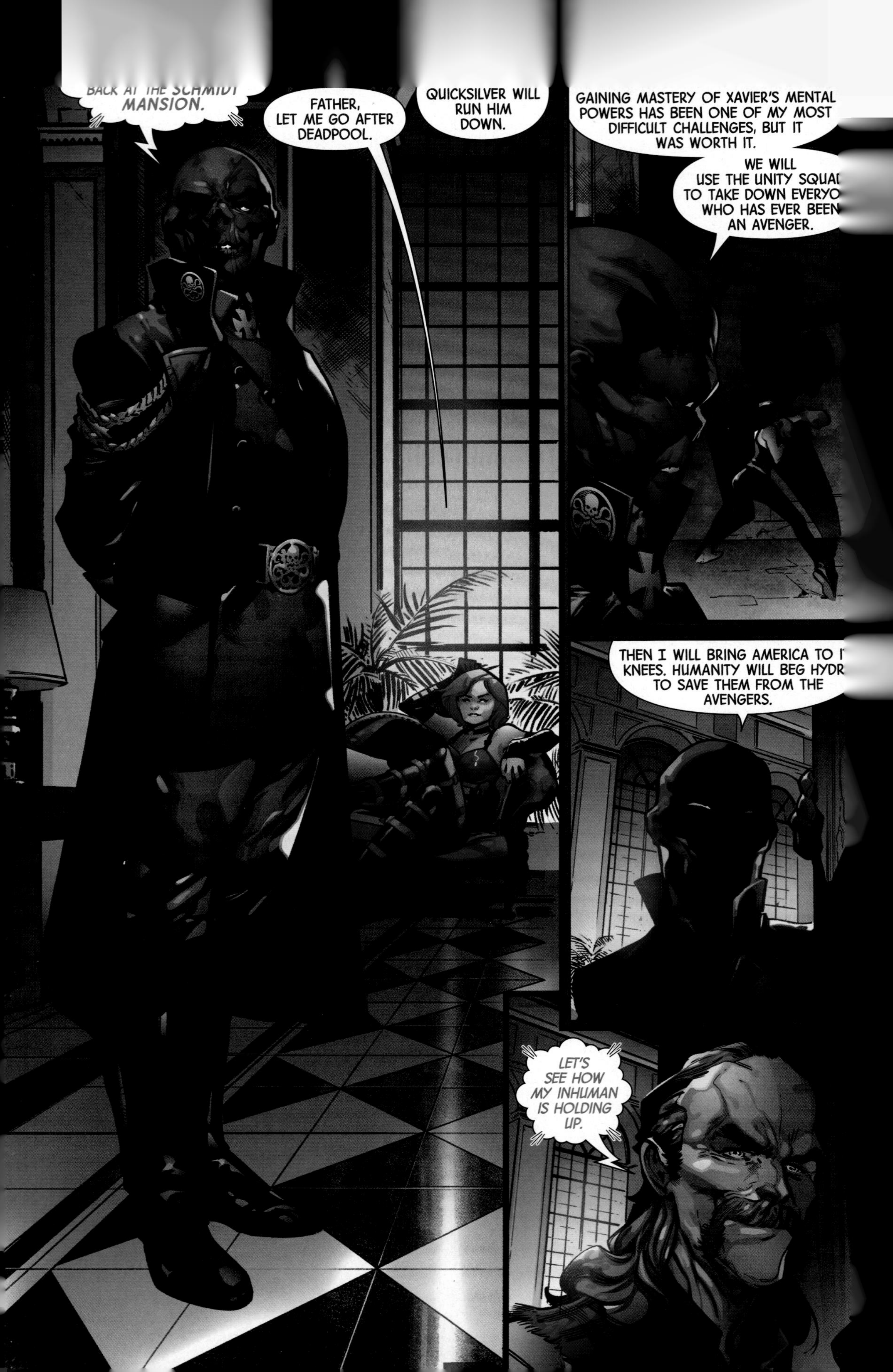
BACK AT THE SCHMIDT MANSION.
FATHER, LET ME GO AFTER DEADPOOL.
QUICKSILVER WILL RUN HIM DOWN.
GAINING MASTERY OF XAVIER'S MENTAL POWERS HAS BEEN ONE OF MY MOST DIFFICULT CHALLENGES, BUT IT WAS WORTH IT.
WE WILL USE THE UNITY SQUAD TO TAKE DOWN EVERYO WHO HAS EVER BEEN AN AVENGER.
THEN I WILL BRING AMERICA TO I KNEES. HUMANITY WILL BEG HYDR TO SAVE THEM FROM THE AVENGERS.
LET'S SEE HOW MY INHUMAN IS HOLDING UP.

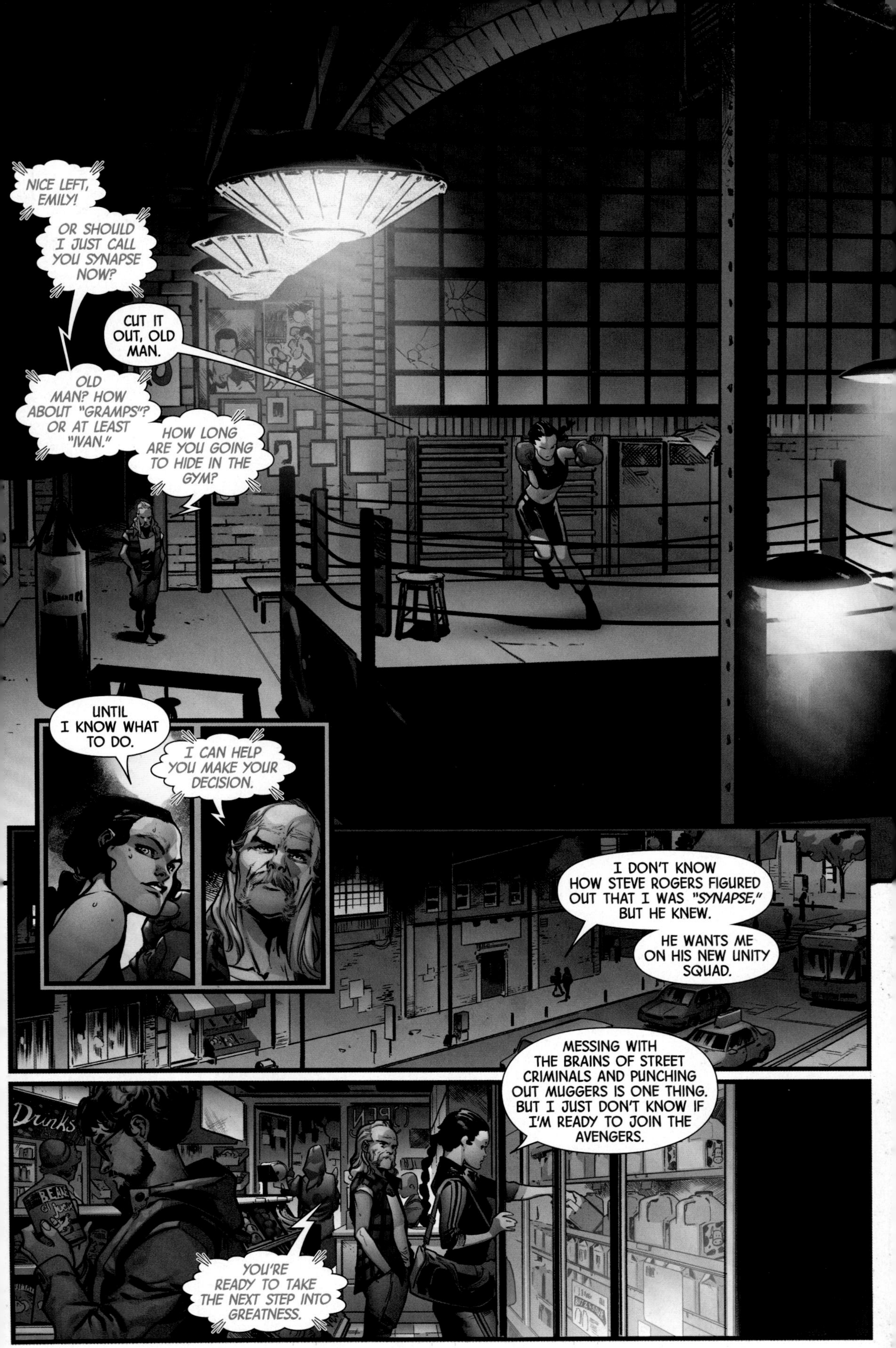
NICE LEFT, EMILY!
OR SHOULD I JUST CALL YOU SYNAPSE NOW?
CUT IT OUT, OLD MAN.
OLD MAN? HOW ABOUT "GRAMPS"? OR AT LEAST "IVAN."
HOW LONG ARE YOU GOING TO HIDE IN THE GYM?
UNTIL I KNOW WHAT TO DO.
I CAN HELP YOU MAKE YOUR DECISION.
I DON'T KNOW HOW STEVE ROGERS FIGURED OUT THAT I WAS "SYNAPSE," BUT HE KNEW.
HE WANTS ME ON HIS NEW UNITY SQUAD.
MESSING WITH THE BRAINS OF STREET CRIMINALS AND PUNCHING OUT MUGGERS IS ONE THING. BUT I JUST DON'T KNOW IF I'M READY TO JOIN THE AVENGERS.
Drinks
YOU'RE READY TO TAKE THE NEXT STEP INTO GREATNESS.

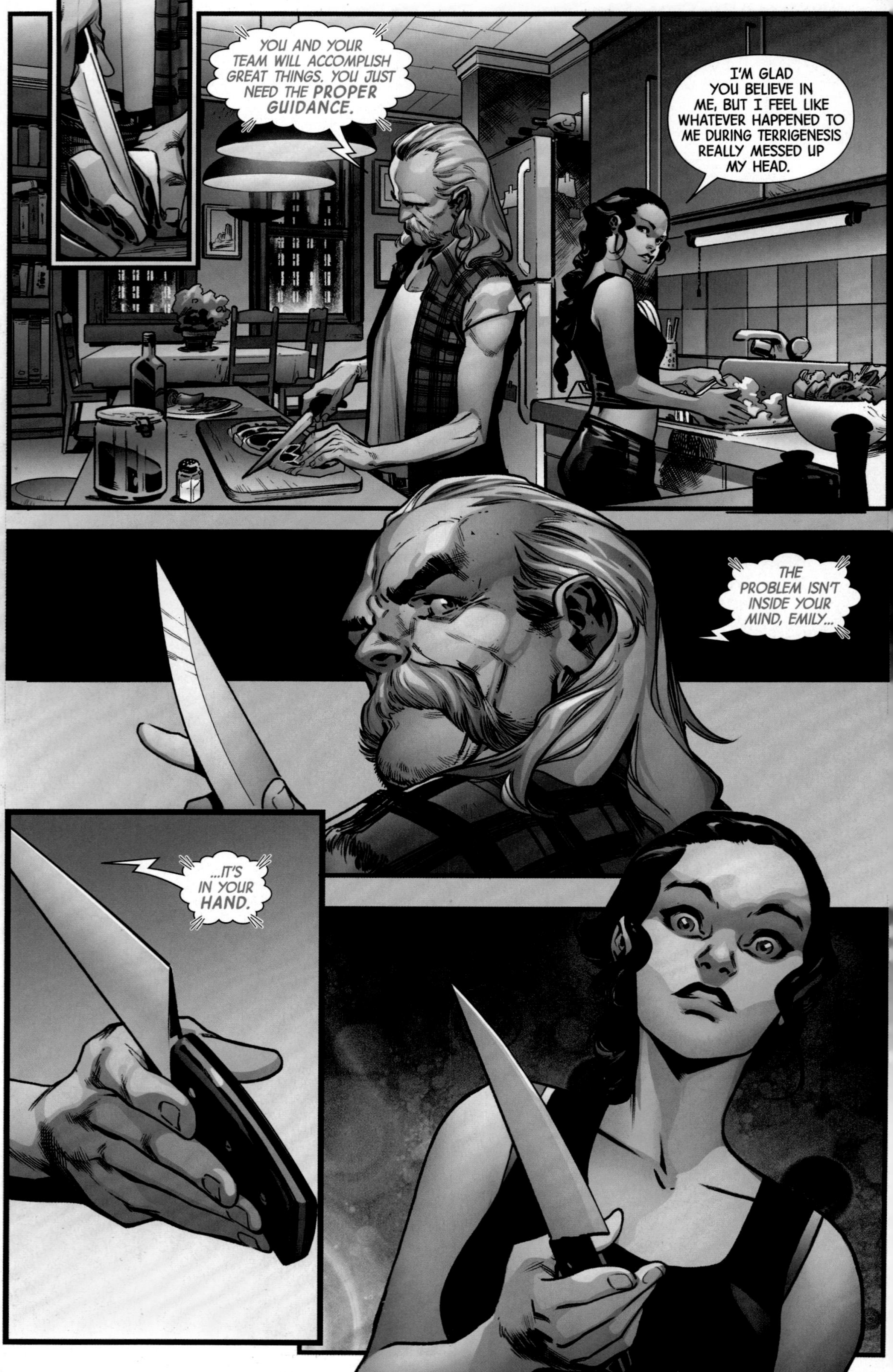
YOU AND YOUR TEAM WILL ACCOMPLISH GREAT THINGS. YOU JUST NEED THE PROPER GUIDANCE.
I'M GLAD YOU BELIEVE IN ME, BUT I FEEL LIKE WHATEVER HAPPENED TO ME DURING TERRIGENESIS REALLY MESSED UP MY HEAD.
THE PROBLEM ISN'T INSIDE YOUR MIND, EMILY...
...IT'S IN YOUR HAND.

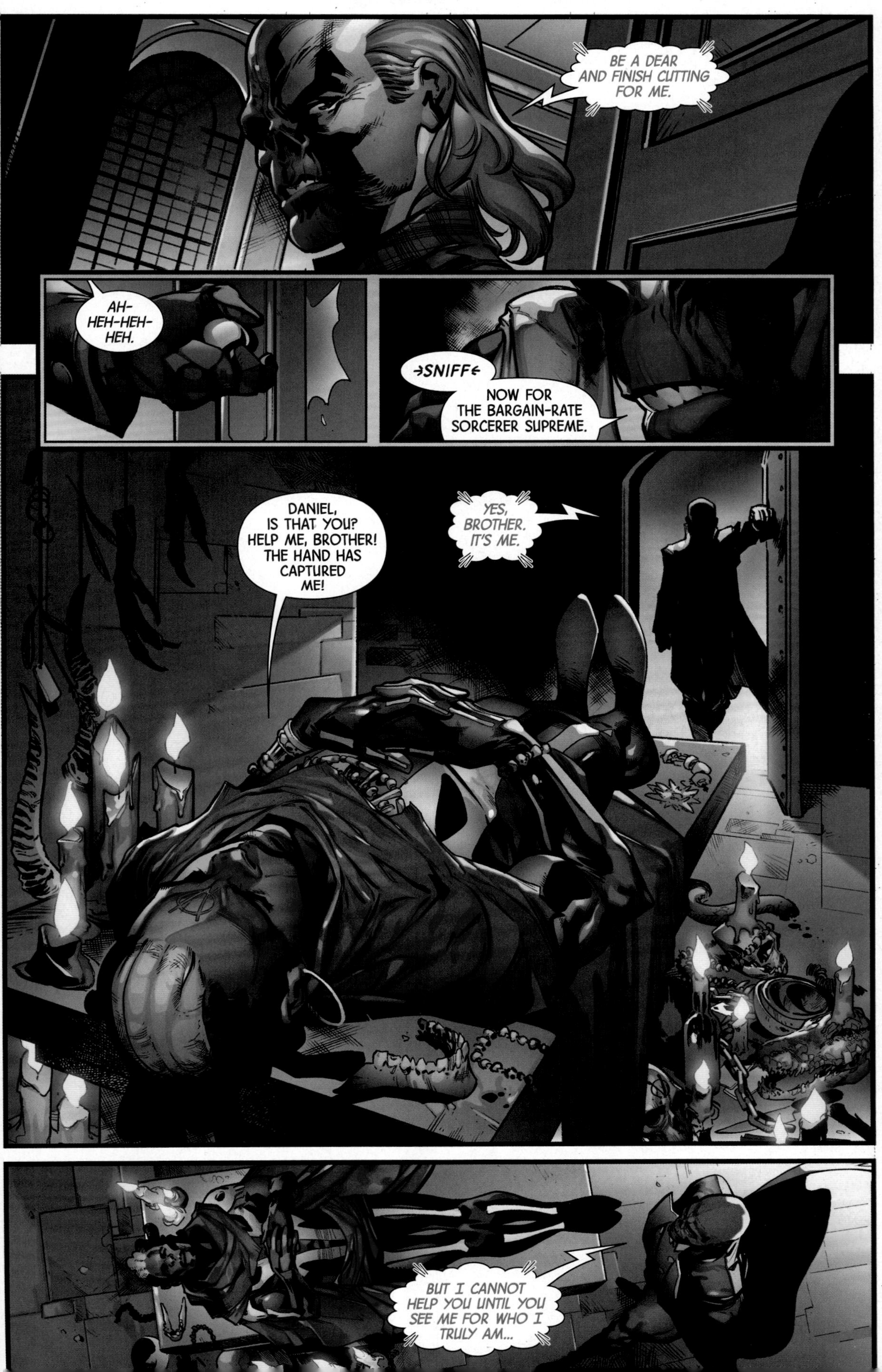
BE A DEAR AND FINISH CUTTING FOR ME.
AH-HEH-HEH-HEH.
→SNIFF←
NOW FOR THE BARGAIN-RATE SORCERER SUPREME.
DANIEL, IS THAT YOU? HELP ME, BROTHER! THE HAND HAS CAPTURED ME!
YES, BROTHER. IT'S ME.
BUT I CANNOT HELP YOU UNTIL YOU SEE ME FOR WHO I TRULY AM...

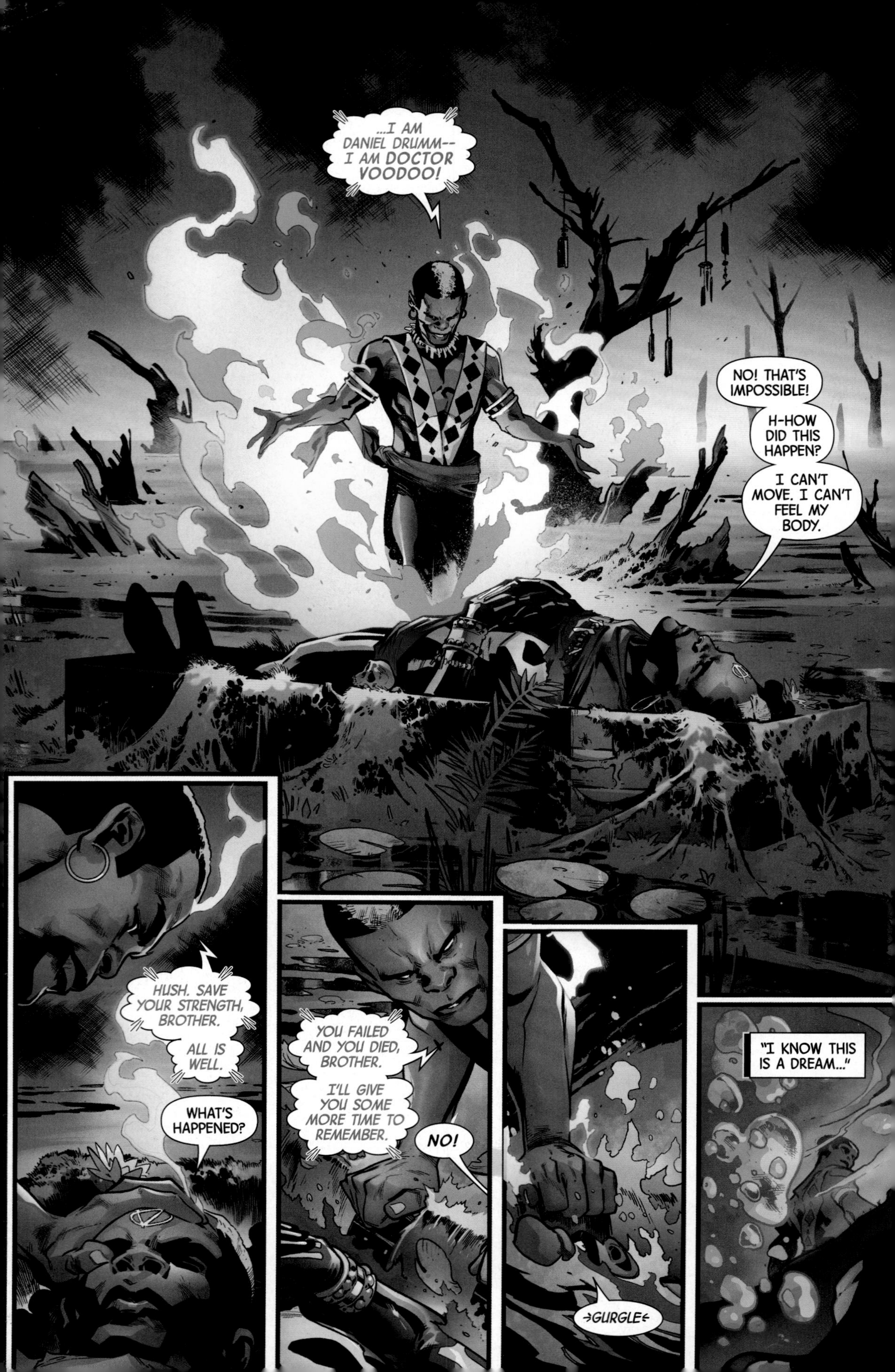

...I AM DANIEL DRUMM-- I AM DOCTOR VOODOO!
NO! THAT'S IMPOSSIBLE!
H-HOW DID THIS HAPPEN?
I CAN'T MOVE. I CAN'T FEEL MY BODY.
HUSH. SAVE YOUR STRENGTH, BROTHER.
ALL IS WELL.
WHAT'S HAPPENED?
YOU FAILED AND YOU DIED, BROTHER.
I'LL GIVE YOU SOME MORE TIME TO REMEMBER.
NO!
GURGLE
"I KNOW THIS IS A DREAM..."

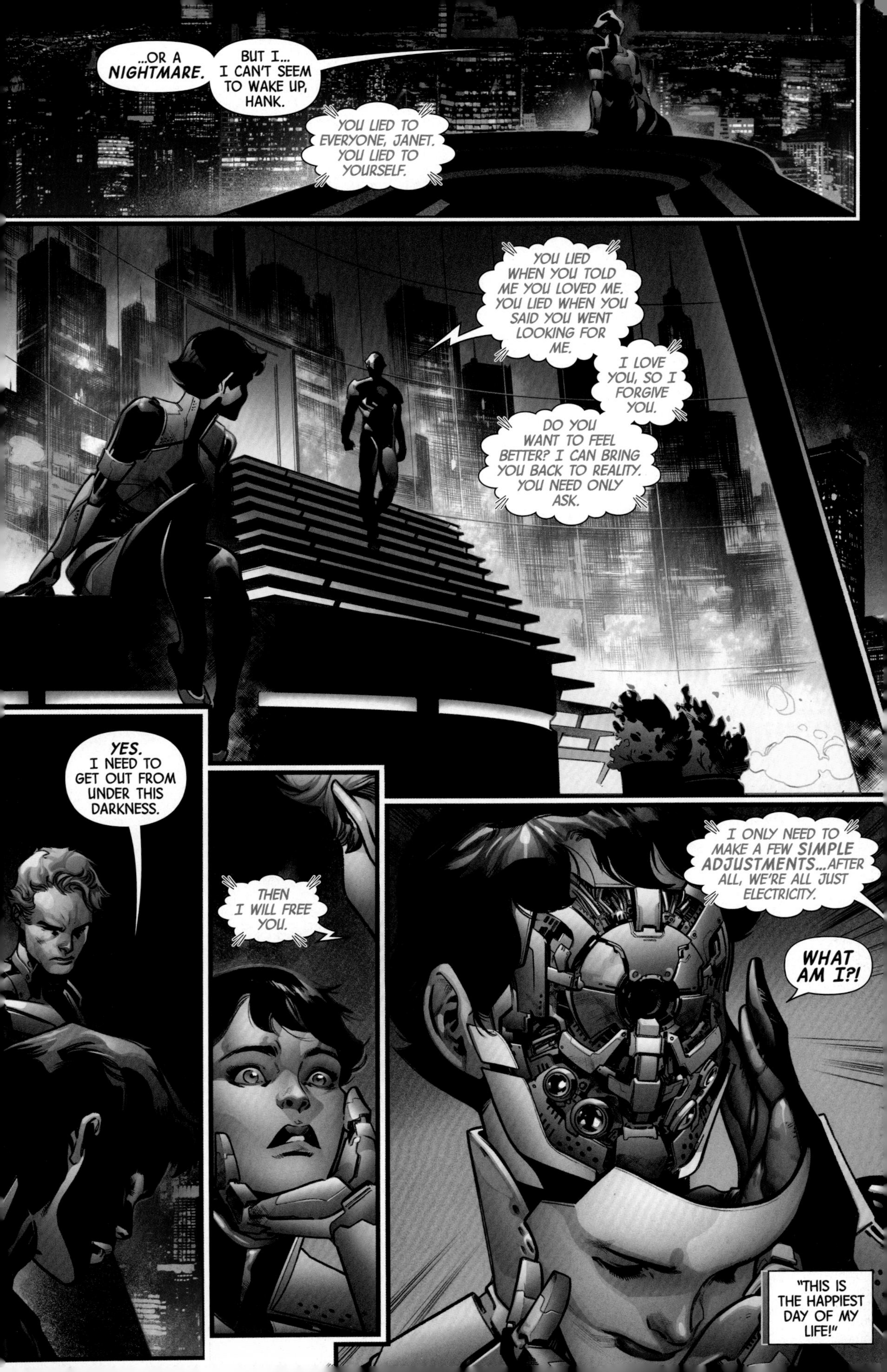

...OR A NIGHTMARE.
BUT I... I CAN'T SEEM TO WAKE UP, HANK.
YOU LIED TO EVERYONE, JANET. YOU LIED TO YOURSELF.
YOU LIED WHEN YOU TOLD ME YOU LOVED ME. YOU LIED WHEN YOU SAID YOU WENT LOOKING FOR ME.
I LOVE YOU, SO I FORGIVE YOU.
DO YOU WANT TO FEEL BETTER? I CAN BRING YOU BACK TO REALITY. YOU NEED ONLY ASK.
YES. I NEED TO GET OUT FROM UNDER THIS DARKNESS.
THEN I WILL FREE YOU.
I ONLY NEED TO MAKE A FEW SIMPLE ADJUSTMENTS...AFTER ALL, WE'RE ALL JUST ELECTRICITY.
WHAT AM I?!
"THIS IS THE HAPPIEST DAY OF MY LIFE!"

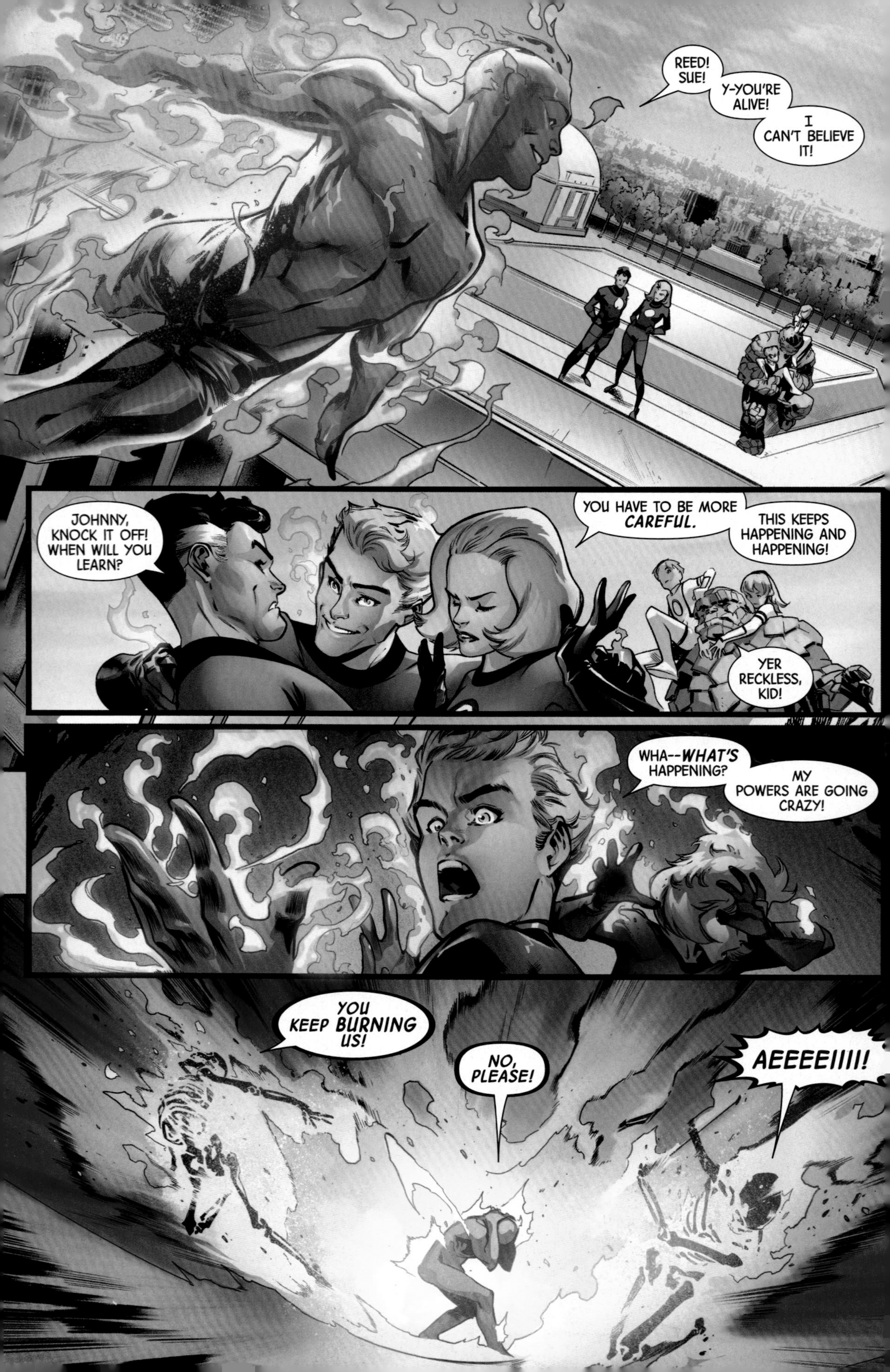
REED! SUE!
Y-YOU'RE ALIVE!
I CAN'T BELIEVE IT!
JOHNNY, KNOCK IT OFF! WHEN WILL YOU LEARN?
YOU HAVE TO BE MORE CAREFUL.
THIS KEEPS HAPPENING AND HAPPENING!
YER RECKLESS, KID!
WHA--WHAT'S HAPPENING?
MY POWERS ARE GOING CRAZY!
YOU KEEP BURNING US!
NO, PLEASE!
AEEEEIIIII!

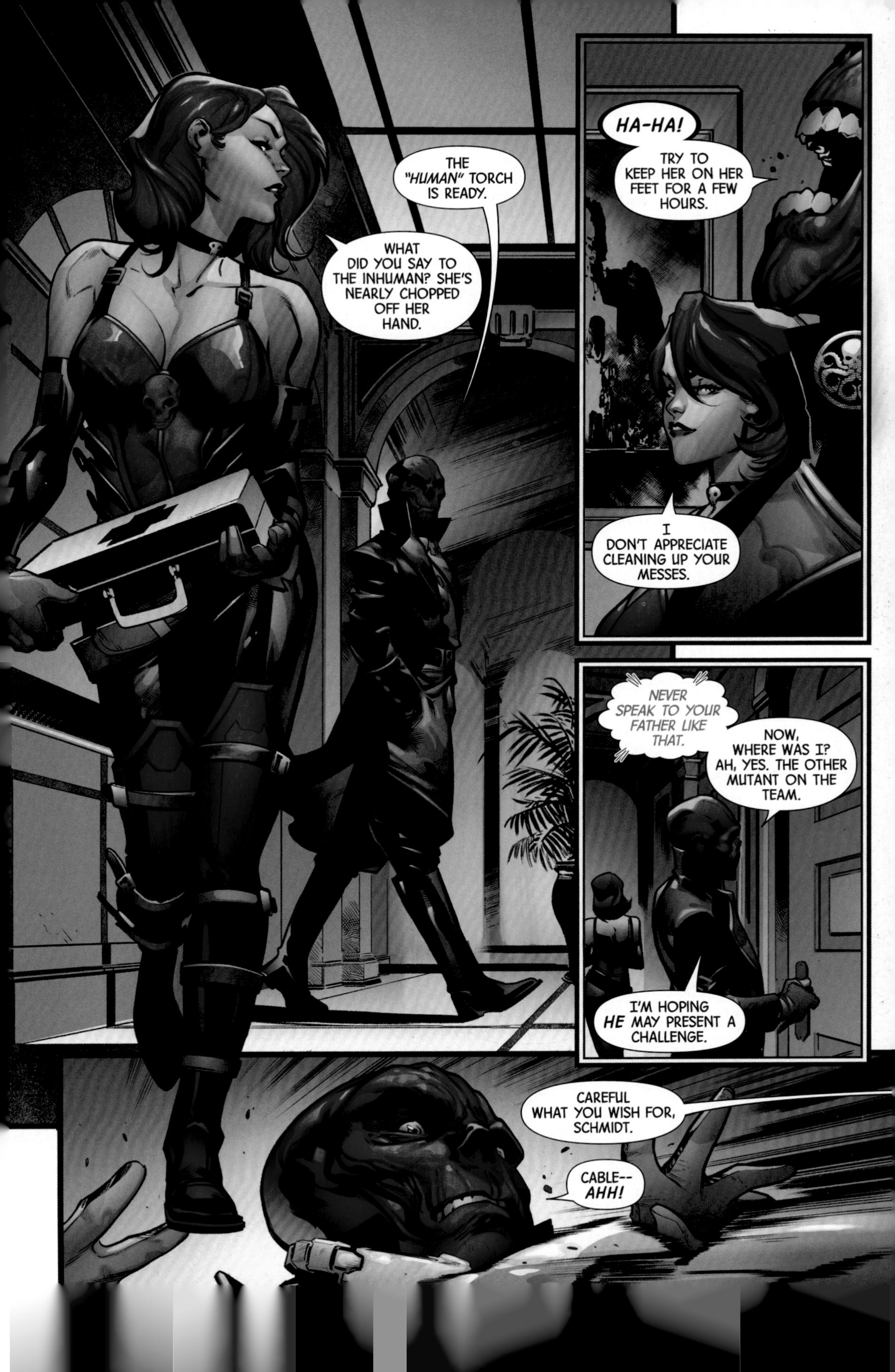
WHAT DID YOU SAY TO THE INHUMAN? SHE'S NEARLY CHOPPED OFF HER HAND.
THE "HUMAN" TORCH IS READY.
HA-HA!
TRY TO KEEP HER ON HER FEET FOR A FEW HOURS.
I DON'T APPRECIATE CLEANING UP YOUR MESSES.
NEVER SPEAK TO YOUR FATHER LIKE THAT.
NOW, WHERE WAS I? AH, YES. THE OTHER MUTANT ON THE TEAM.
I'M HOPING HE MAY PRESENT A CHALLENGE.
CAREFUL WHAT YOU WISH FOR, SCHMIDT.
CABLE-- AHH!

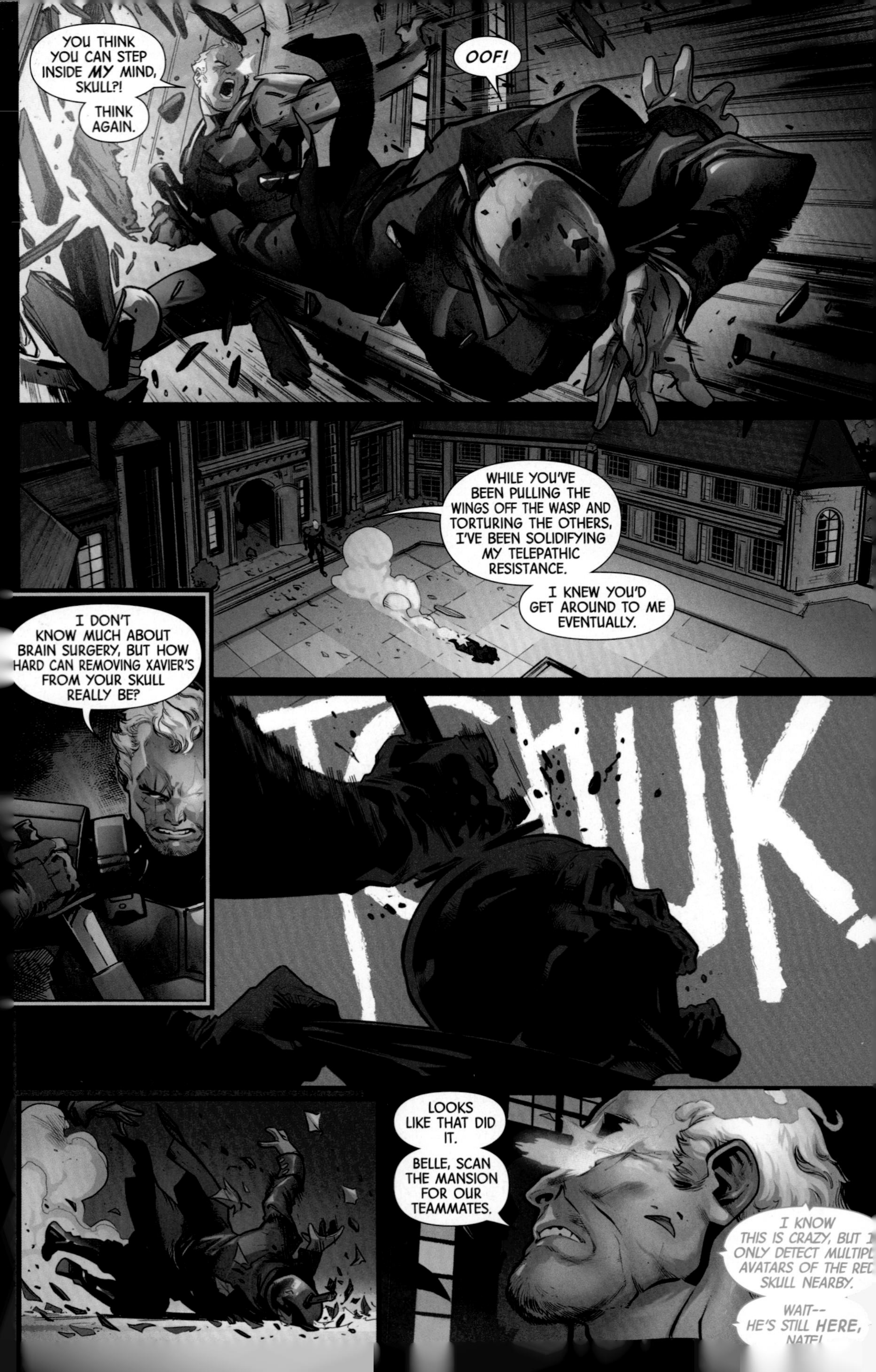
YOU THINK YOU CAN STEP INSIDE MY MIND, SKULL?!
THINK AGAIN.
OOF!
WHILE YOU'VE BEEN PULLING THE WINGS OFF THE WASP AND TORTURING THE OTHERS, I'VE BEEN SOLIDIFYING MY TELEPATHIC RESISTANCE.
I KNEW YOU'D GET AROUND TO ME EVENTUALLY.
I DON'T KNOW MUCH ABOUT BRAIN SURGERY, BUT HOW HARD CAN REMOVING XAVIER'S FROM YOUR SKULL REALLY BE?
TCHUK!
LOOKS LIKE THAT DID IT.
BELLE, SCAN THE MANSION FOR OUR TEAMMATES.
I KNOW THIS IS CRAZY, BUT I ONLY DETECT MULTIPL AVATARS OF THE RED SKULL NEARBY.
WAIT-- HE'S STILL HERE, NATE!

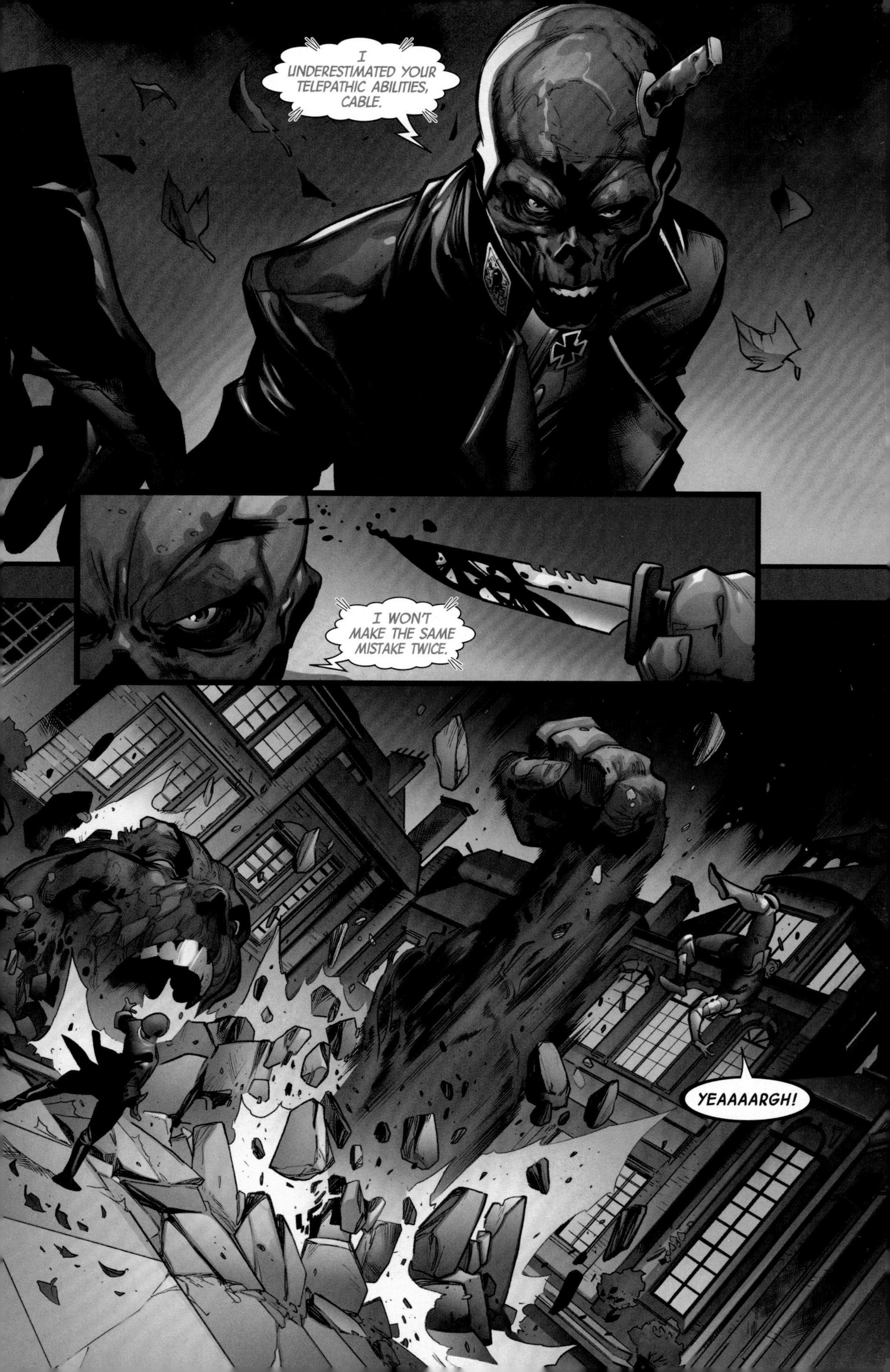
I UNDERESTIMATED YOUR TELEPATHIC ABILITIES, CABLE.
I WON'T MAKE THE SAME MISTAKE TWICE.
YEAAAARGH!

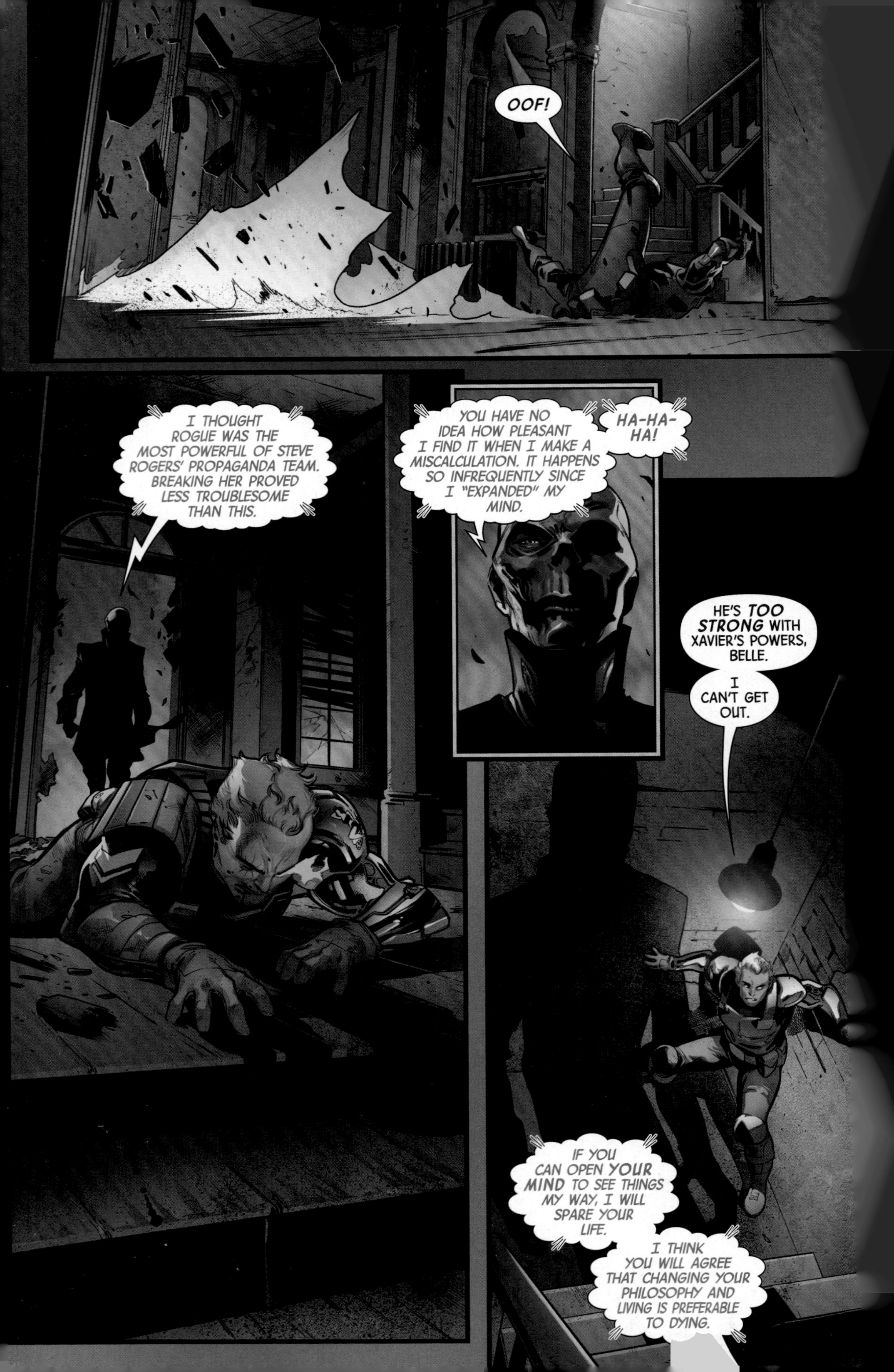
OOF!
I THOUGHT ROGUE WAS THE MOST POWERFUL OF STEVE ROGERS' PROPAGANDA TEAM. BREAKING HER PROVED LESS TROUBLESOME THAN THIS.
YOU HAVE NO IDEA HOW PLEASANT I FIND IT WHEN I MAKE A MISCALCULATION. IT HAPPENS SO INFREQUENTLY SINCE I "EXPANDED" MY MIND.
HA-HA-HA!
HE'S TOO STRONG WITH XAVIER'S POWERS, BELLE.
I CAN'T GET OUT.
IF YOU CAN OPEN YOUR MIND TO SEE THINGS MY WAY, I WILL SPARE YOUR LIFE.
I THINK YOU WILL AGREE THAT CHANGING YOUR PHILOSOPHY AND LIVING IS PREFERABLE TO DYING.

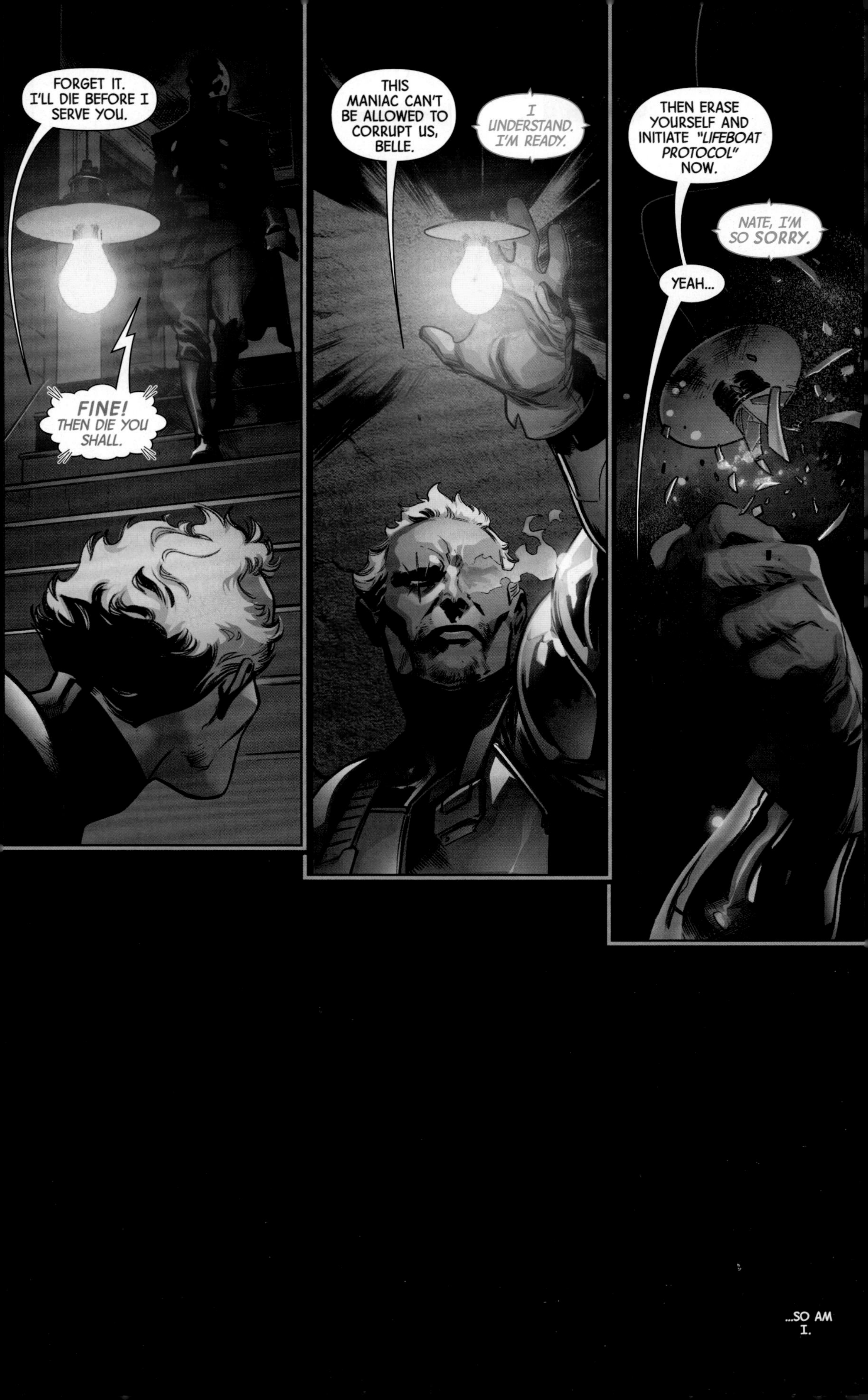

FORGET IT. I'LL DIE BEFORE I SERVE YOU.
FINE! THEN DIE YOU SHALL.
THIS MANIAC CAN'T BE ALLOWED TO CORRUPT US, BELLE.
I UNDERSTAND. I'M READY.
THEN ERASE YOURSELF AND INITIATE "LIFEBOAT PROTOCOL" NOW.
NATE, I'M SO SORRY.
YEAH...
...SO AM I.

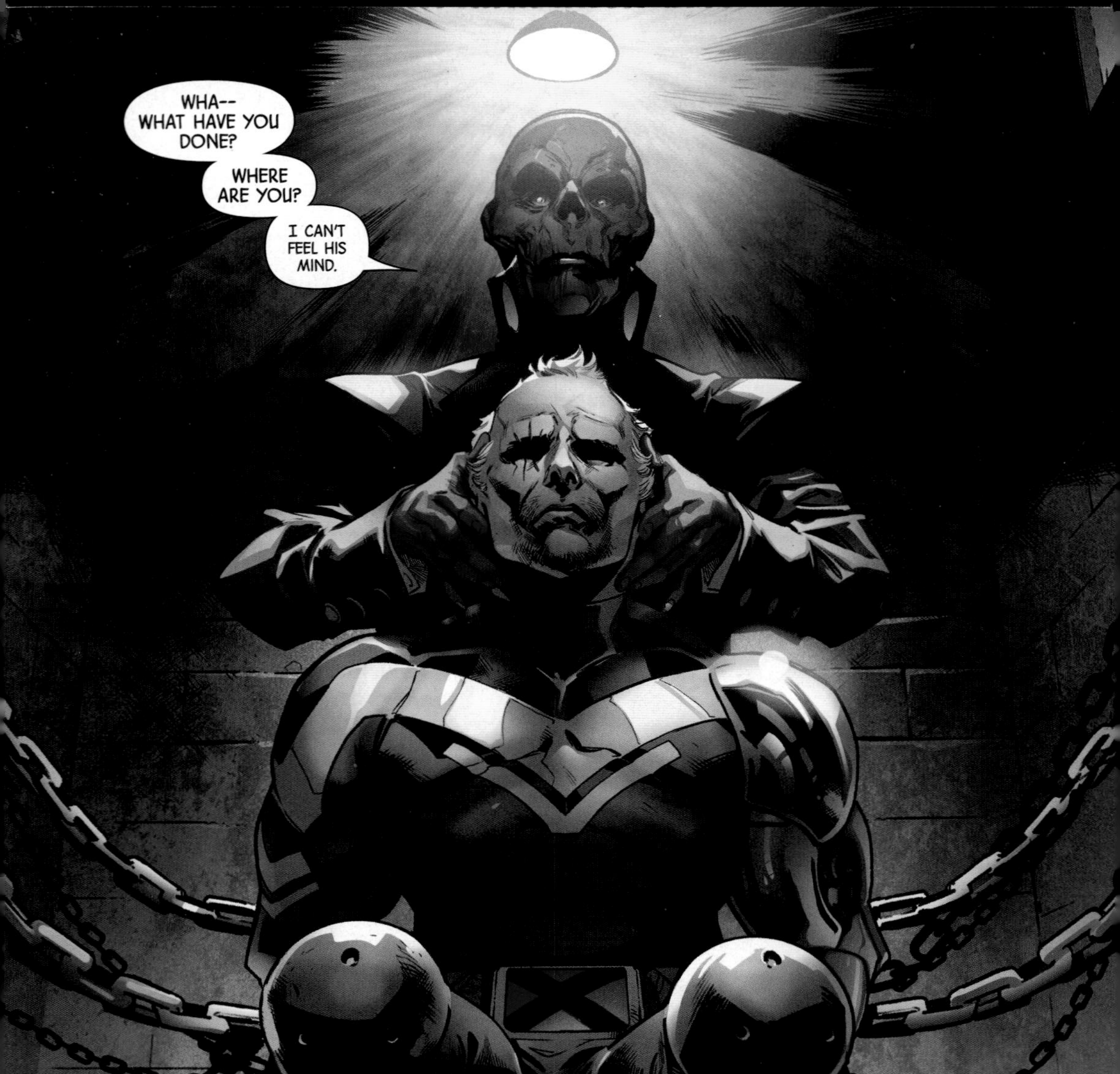
WHA--
WHAT HAVE YOU DONE?
WHERE ARE YOU?
I CAN'T FEEL HIS MIND.

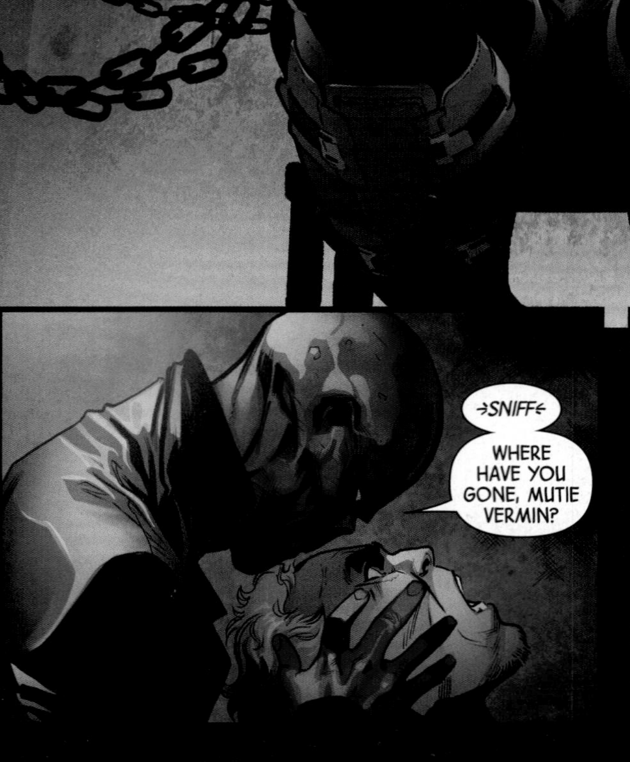
SNIFF
WHERE HAVE YOU GONE, MUTIE VERMIN?

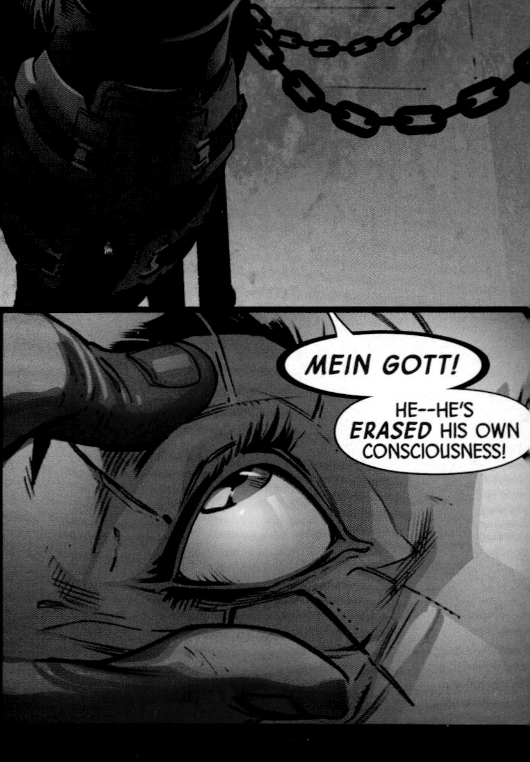
MEIN GOTT!
HE--HE'S ERASED HIS OWN CONSCIOUSNESS!

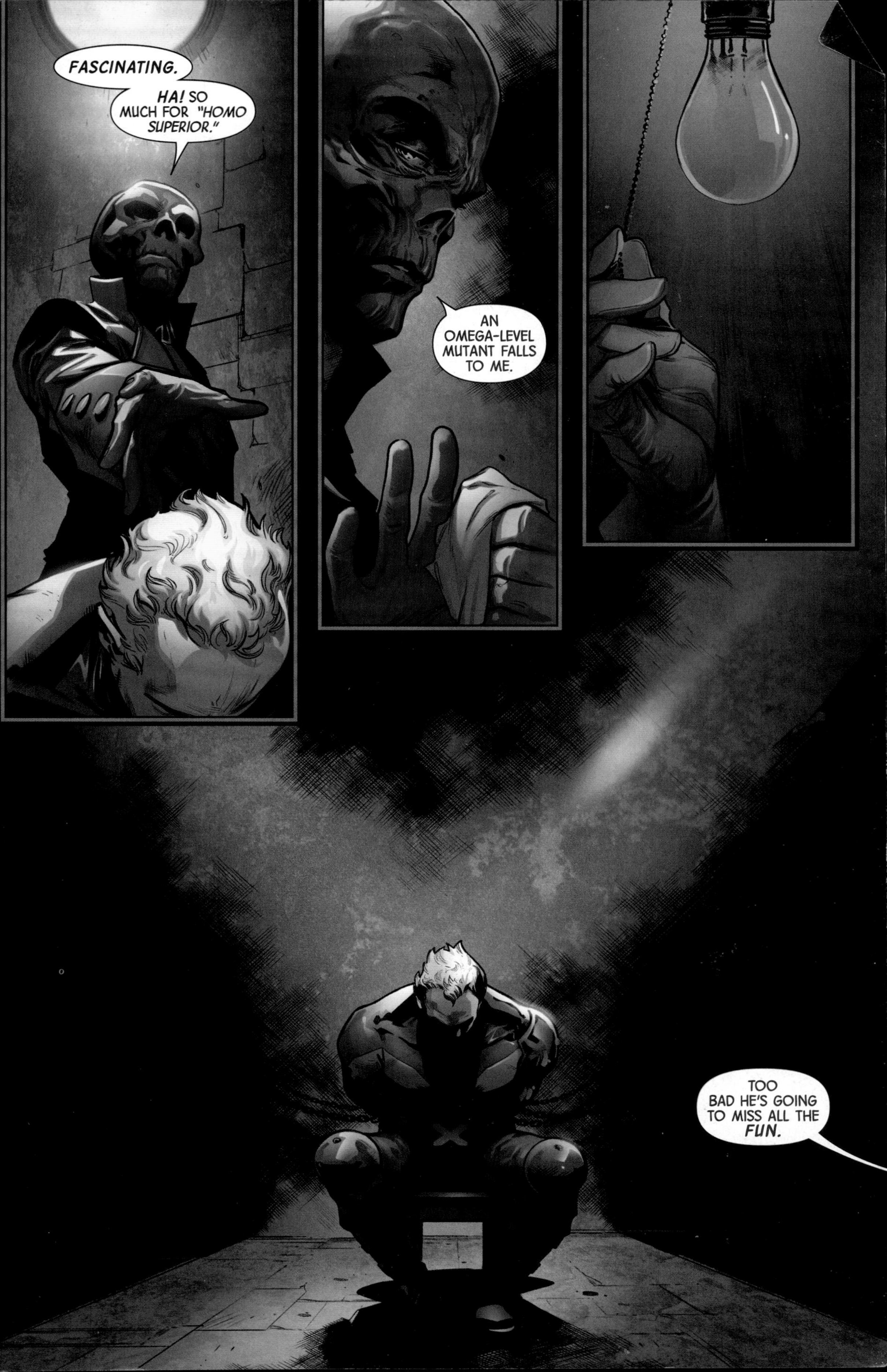
FASCINATING.
HA! SO MUCH FOR "HOMO SUPERIOR."
AN OMEGA-LEVEL MUTANT FALLS TO ME.
TOO BAD HE'S GOING TO MISS ALL THE FUN.

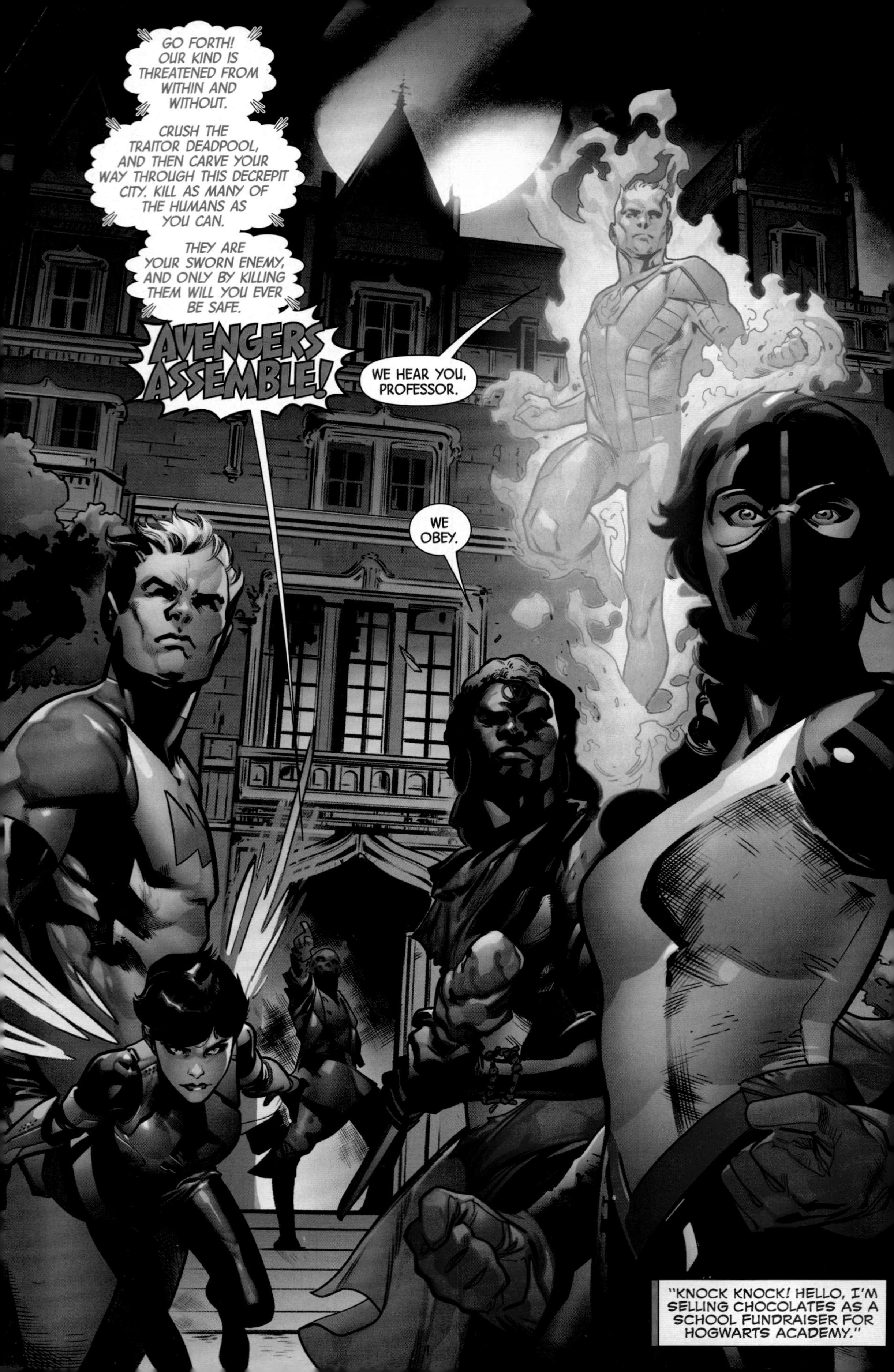
GO FORTH! OUR KIND IS THREATENED FROM WITHIN AND WITHOUT.
CRUSH THE TRAITOR DEADPOOL, AND THEN CARVE YOUR WAY THROUGH THIS DECREPIT CITY. KILL AS MANY OF THE HUMANS AS YOU CAN.
THEY ARE YOUR SWORN ENEMY, AND ONLY BY KILLING THEM WILL YOU EVER BE SAFE.
AVENGERS ASSEMBLE!
WE HEAR YOU, PROFESSOR.
WE OBEY.
"KNOCK KNOCK! HELLO, I'M SELLING CHOCOLATES AS A SCHOOL FUNDRAISER FOR HOGWARTS ACADEMY."

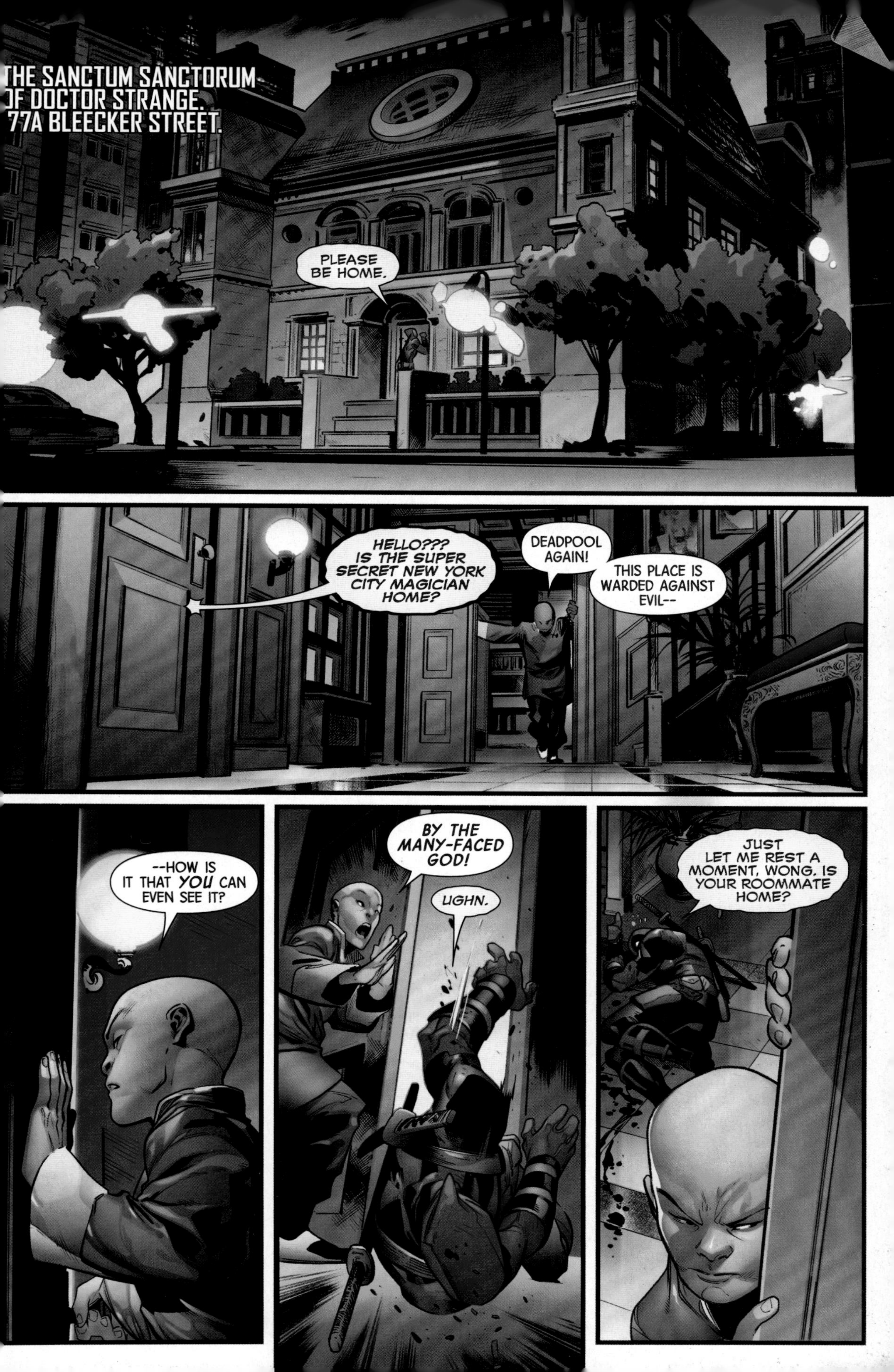
THE SANCTUM SANCTORUM OF DOCTOR STRANGE. 77A BLEECKER STREET.
PLEASE BE HOME.
HELLO??? IS THE SUPER SECRET NEW YORK CITY MAGICIAN HOME?
DEADPOOL AGAIN!
THIS PLACE IS WARDED AGAINST EVIL--
--HOW IS IT THAT YOU CAN EVEN SEE IT?
BY THE MANY-FACED GOD!
UGHN.
JUST LET ME REST A MOMENT, WONG. IS YOUR ROOMMATE HOME?

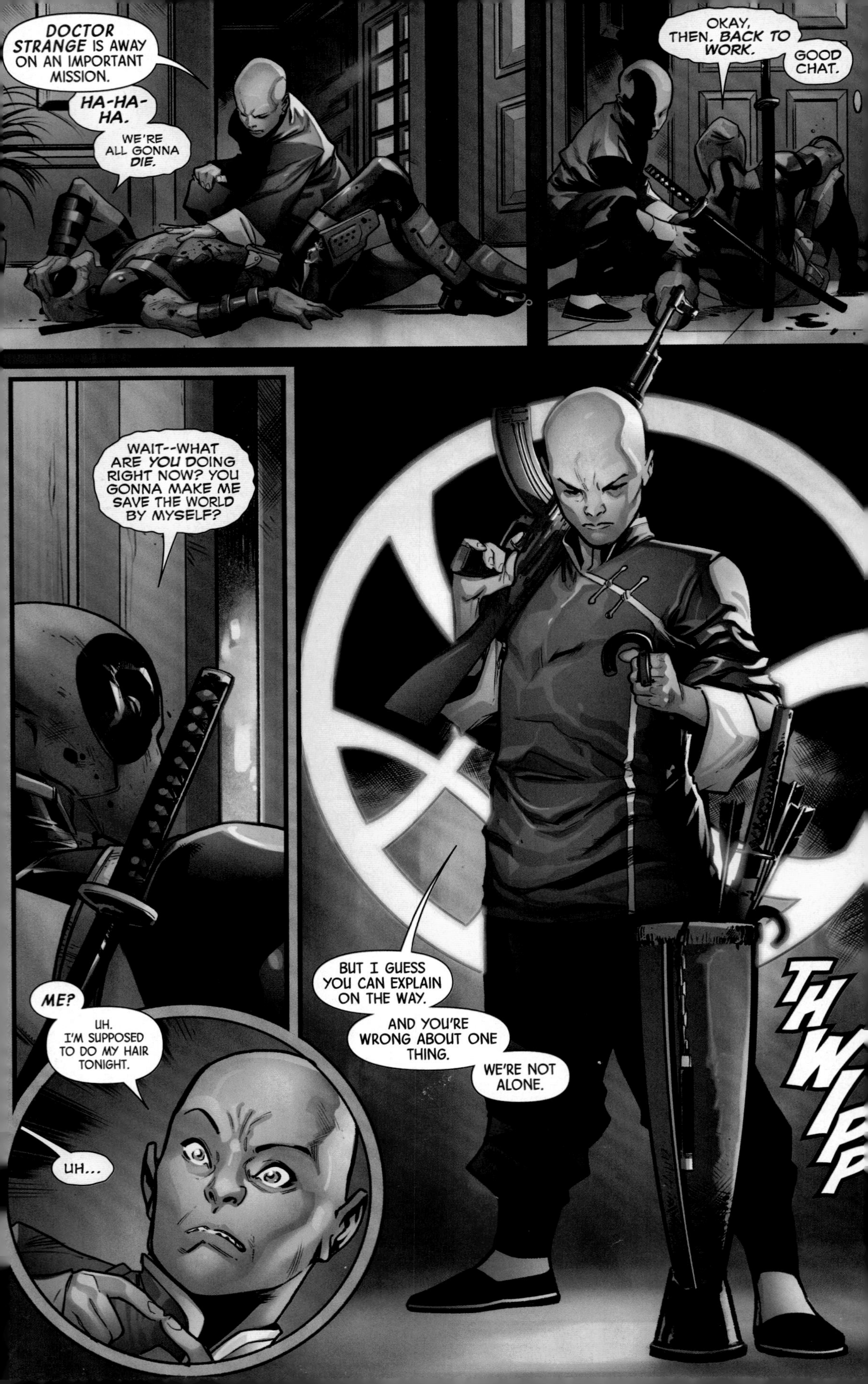
DOCTOR STRANGE IS AWAY ON AN IMPORTANT MISSION.
HA-HA-HA.
WE'RE ALL GONNA DIE.
OKAY, THEN. BACK TO WORK.
GOOD CHAT.
WAIT--WHAT ARE YOU DOING RIGHT NOW? YOU GONNA MAKE ME SAVE THE WORLD BY MYSELF?
ME?
UH. I'M SUPPOSED TO DO MY HAIR TONIGHT.
UH...
BUT I GUESS YOU CAN EXPLAIN ON THE WAY.
AND YOU'RE WRONG ABOUT ONE THING.
WE'RE NOT ALONE.
THWIPP

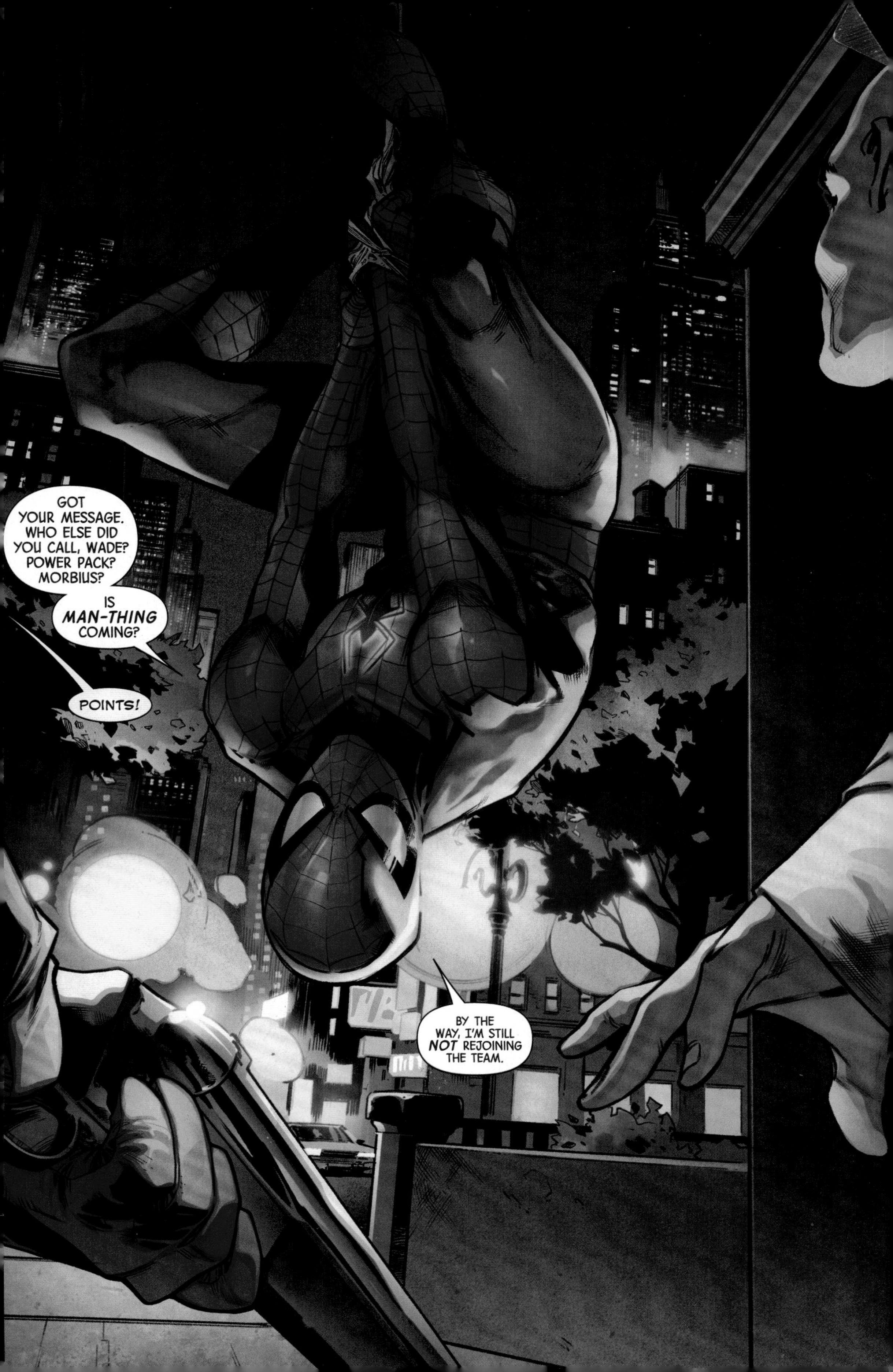
GOT YOUR MESSAGE. WHO ELSE DID YOU CALL, WADE? POWER PACK? MORBIUS?
IS MAN-THING COMING?
POINTS!
BY THE WAY, I'M STILL NOT REJOINING THE TEAM.

20

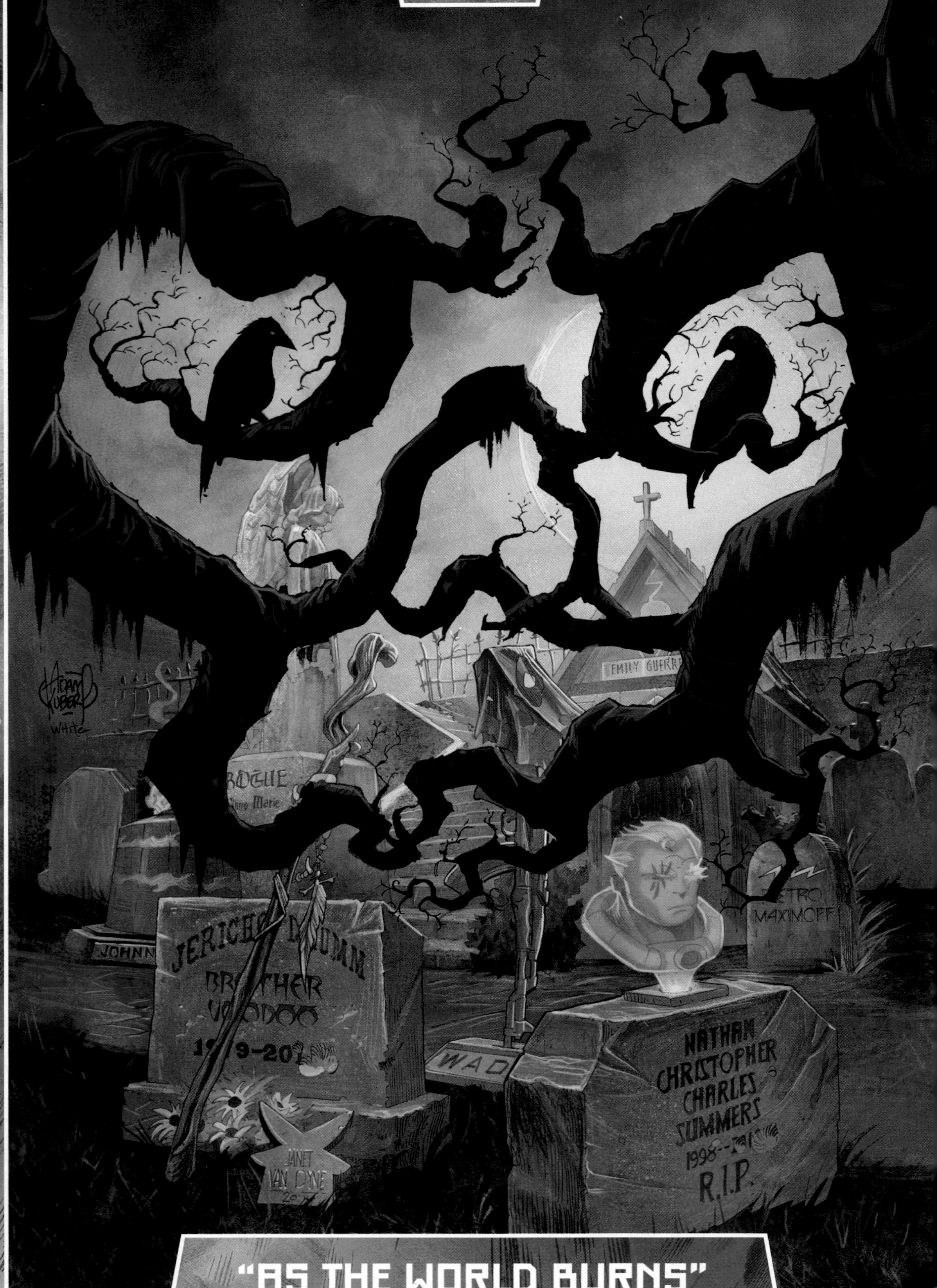
ROGUE
Anna Marie
EMILY GUERR
JOHNN
MAXIMOFF
WAD
NATHAN CHRISTOPHER CHARLES SUMMERS
R.I.P.
JANET VAN DYNE

"AS THE WORLD BURNS"

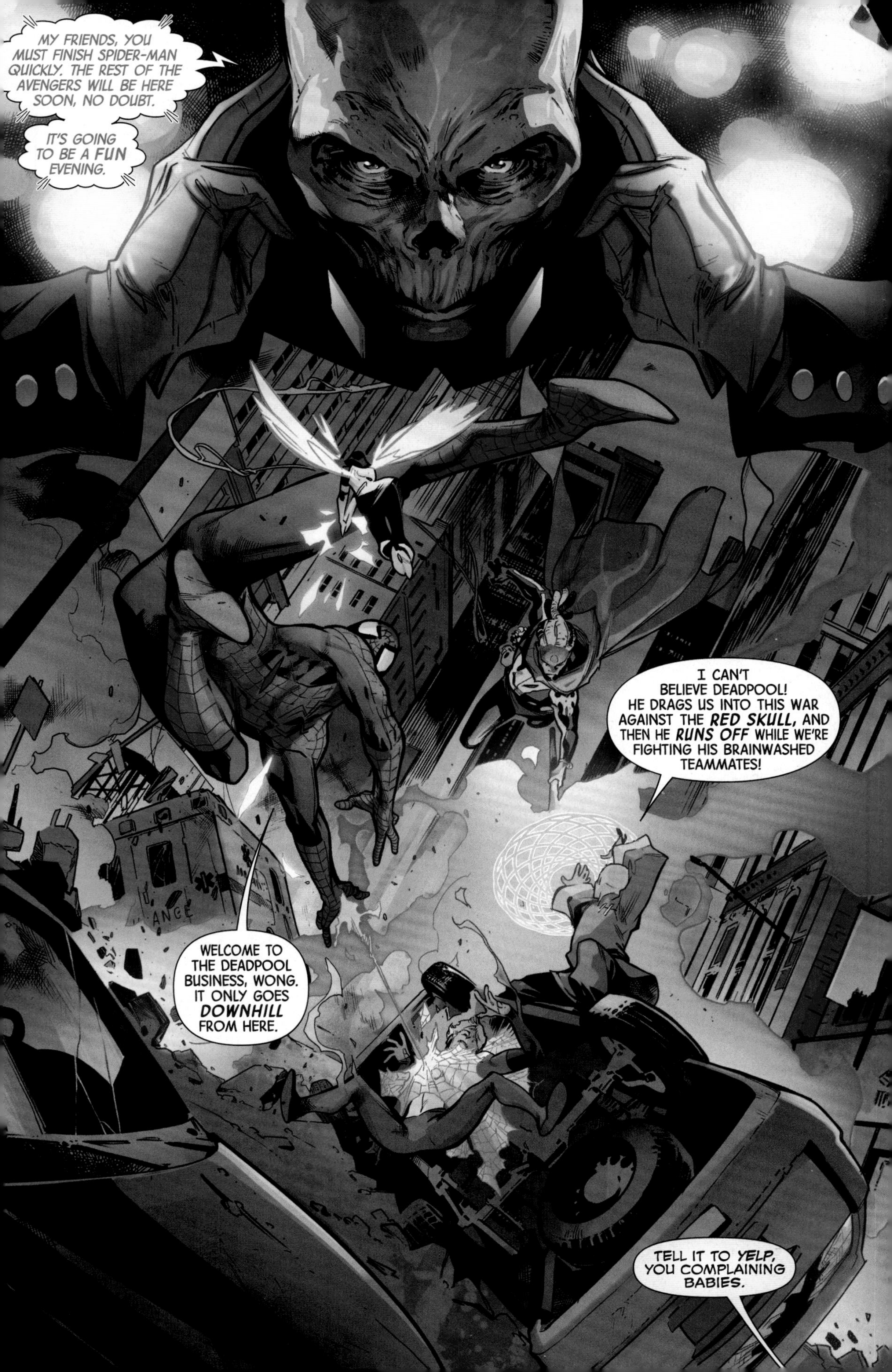
MY FRIENDS, YOU MUST FINISH SPIDER-MAN QUICKLY. THE REST OF THE AVENGERS WILL BE HERE SOON, NO DOUBT.
IT'S GOING TO BE A FUN EVENING.
I CAN'T BELIEVE DEADPOOL! HE DRAGS US INTO THIS WAR AGAINST THE RED SKULL, AND THEN HE RUNS OFF WHILE WE'RE FIGHTING HIS BRAINWASHED TEAMMATES!
WELCOME TO THE DEADPOOL BUSINESS, WONG. IT ONLY GOES DOWNHILL FROM HERE.
TELL IT TO YELP, YOU COMPLAINING BABIES.

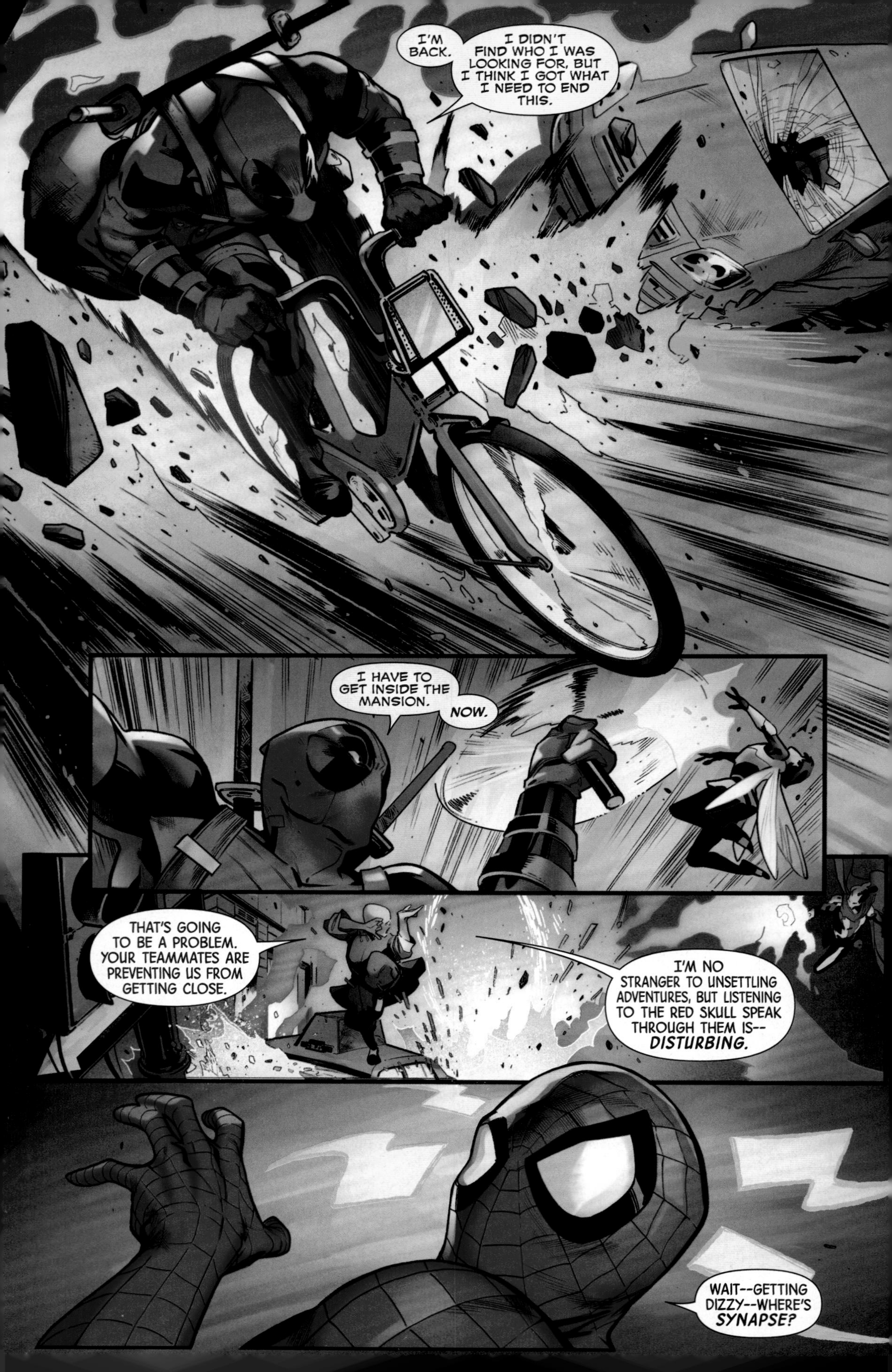
I'M BACK.
I DIDN'T FIND WHO I WAS LOOKING FOR, BUT I THINK I GOT WHAT I NEED TO END THIS.
I HAVE TO GET INSIDE THE MANSION.
NOW.
THAT'S GOING TO BE A PROBLEM. YOUR TEAMMATES ARE PREVENTING US FROM GETTING CLOSE.
I'M NO STRANGER TO UNSETTLING ADVENTURES, BUT LISTENING TO THE RED SKULL SPEAK THROUGH THEM IS-- DISTURBING.
WAIT--GETTING DIZZY--WHERE'S SYNAPSE?

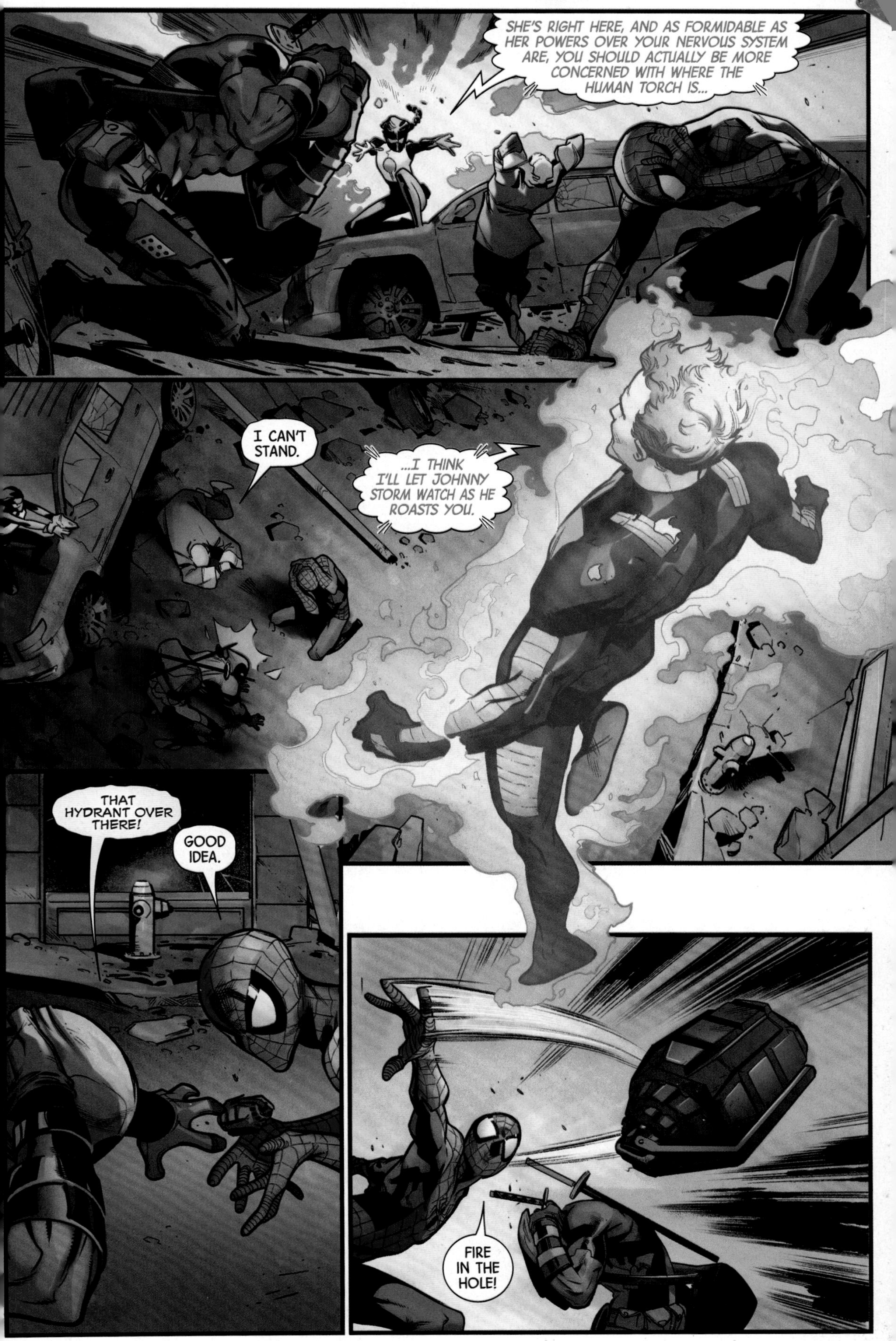

SHE'S RIGHT HERE, AND AS FORMIDABLE AS HER POWERS OVER YOUR NERVOUS SYSTEM ARE, YOU SHOULD ACTUALLY BE MORE CONCERNED WITH WHERE THE HUMAN TORCH IS...
I CAN'T STAND.
...I THINK I'LL LET JOHNNY STORM WATCH AS HE ROASTS YOU.
THAT HYDRANT OVER THERE!
GOOD IDEA.
FIRE IN THE HOLE!

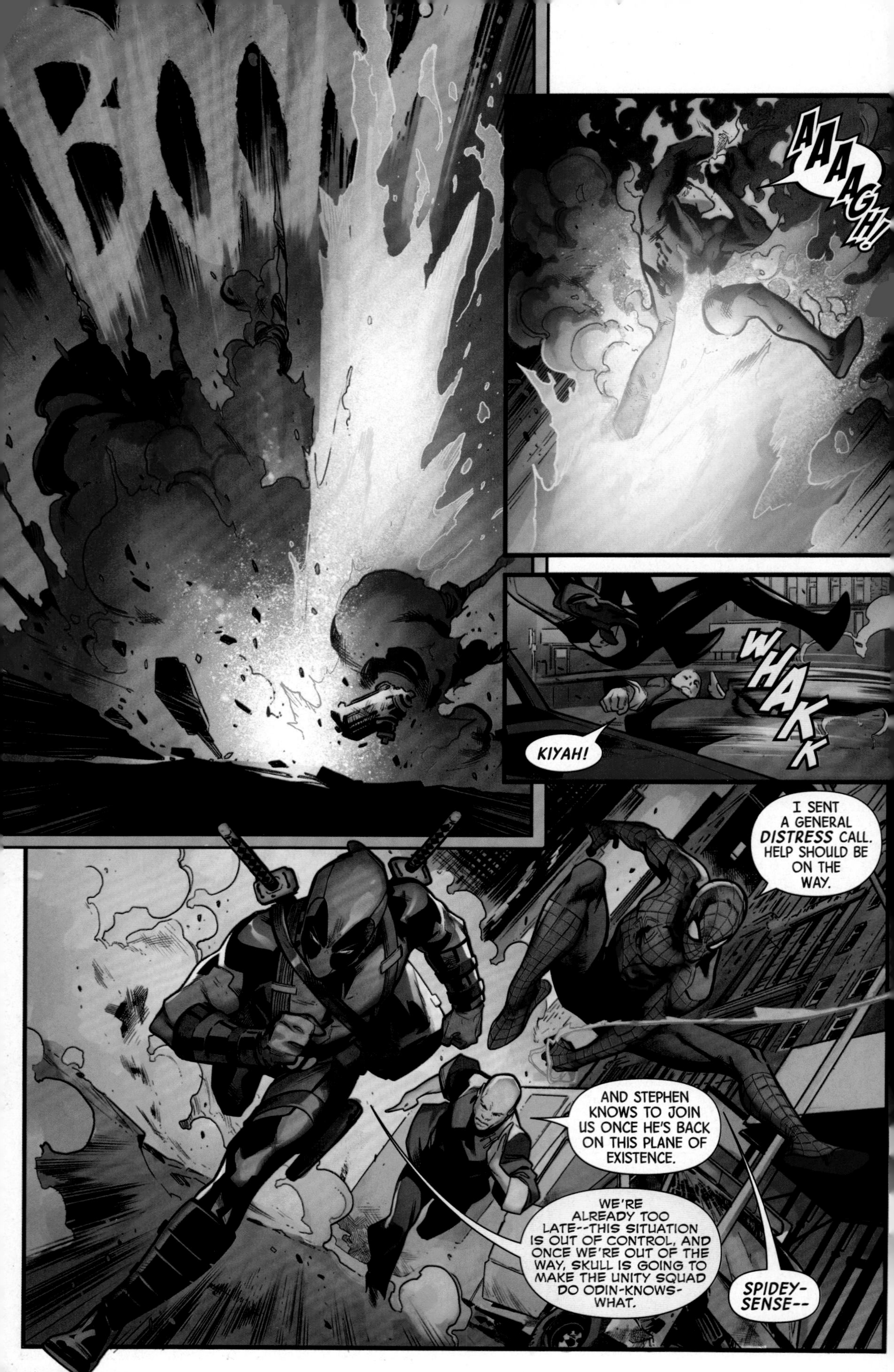
BOOM
AAAAAGH!
KIYAH!
WHAKK
I SENT A GENERAL DISTRESS CALL. HELP SHOULD BE ON THE WAY.
AND STEPHEN KNOWS TO JOIN US ONCE HE'S BACK ON THIS PLANE OF EXISTENCE.
WE'RE ALREADY TOO LATE--THIS SITUATION IS OUT OF CONTROL, AND ONCE WE'RE OUT OF THE WAY, SKULL IS GOING TO MAKE THE UNITY SQUAD DO ODIN-KNOWS-WHAT.
SPIDEY-SENSE--

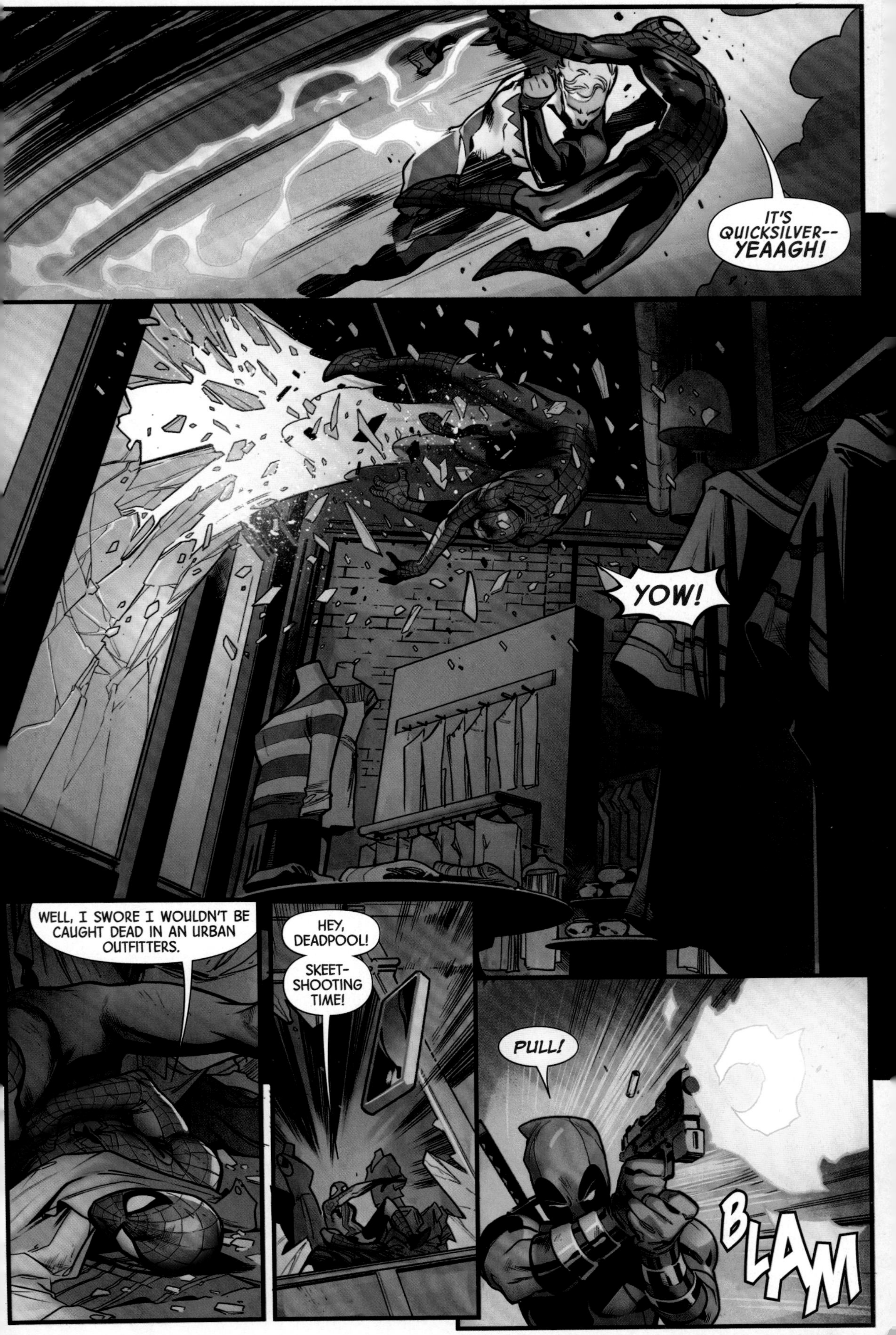
IT'S QUICKSILVER-- YEAAGH!
YOW!
WELL, I SWORE I WOULDN'T BE CAUGHT DEAD IN AN URBAN OUTFITTERS.
HEY, DEADPOOL!
SKEET-SHOOTING TIME!
PULL!
BLAM

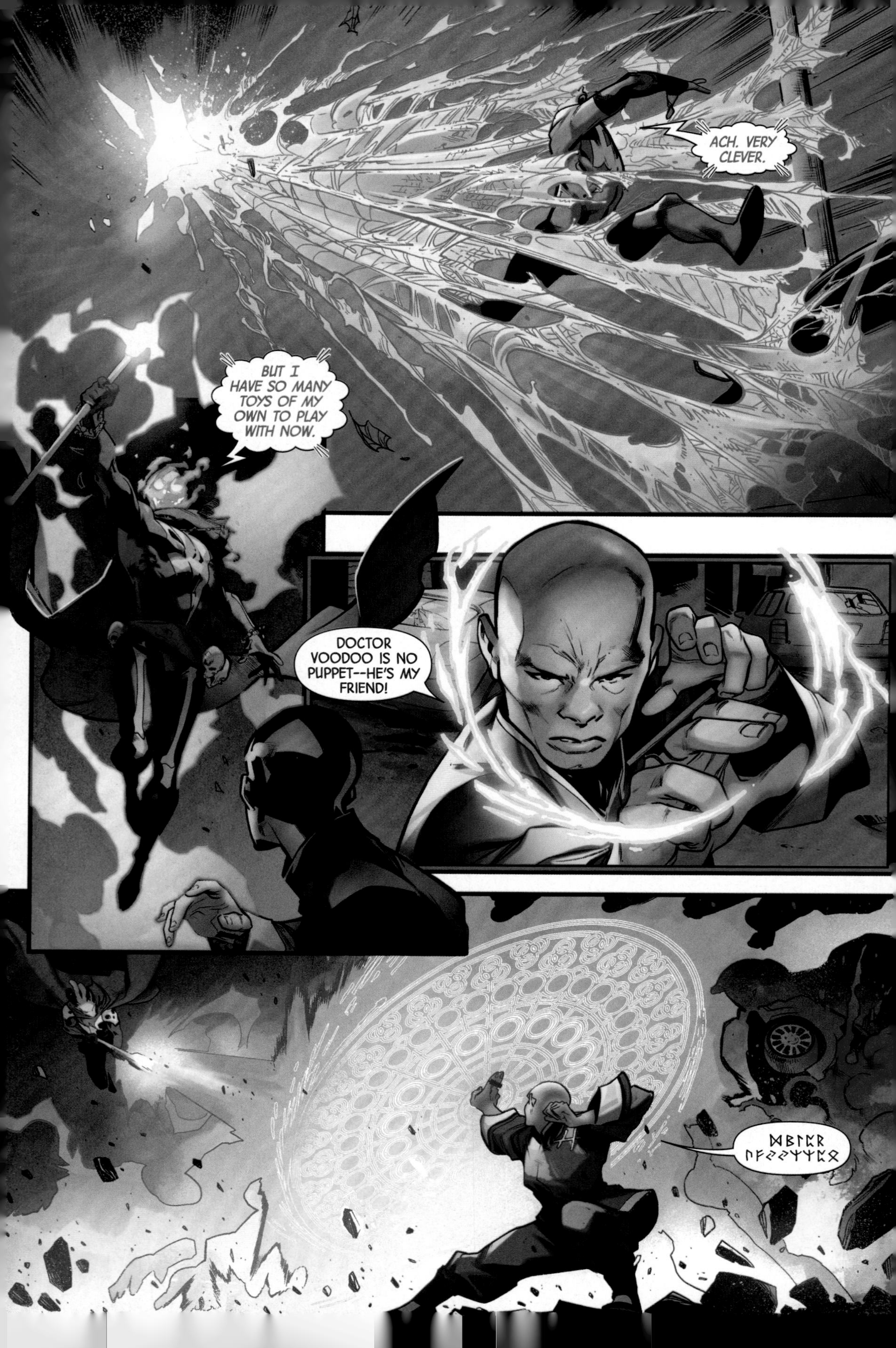
ACH. VERY CLEVER.
BUT I HAVE SO MANY TOYS OF MY OWN TO PLAY WITH NOW.
DOCTOR VOODOO IS NO PUPPET--HE'S MY FRIEND!

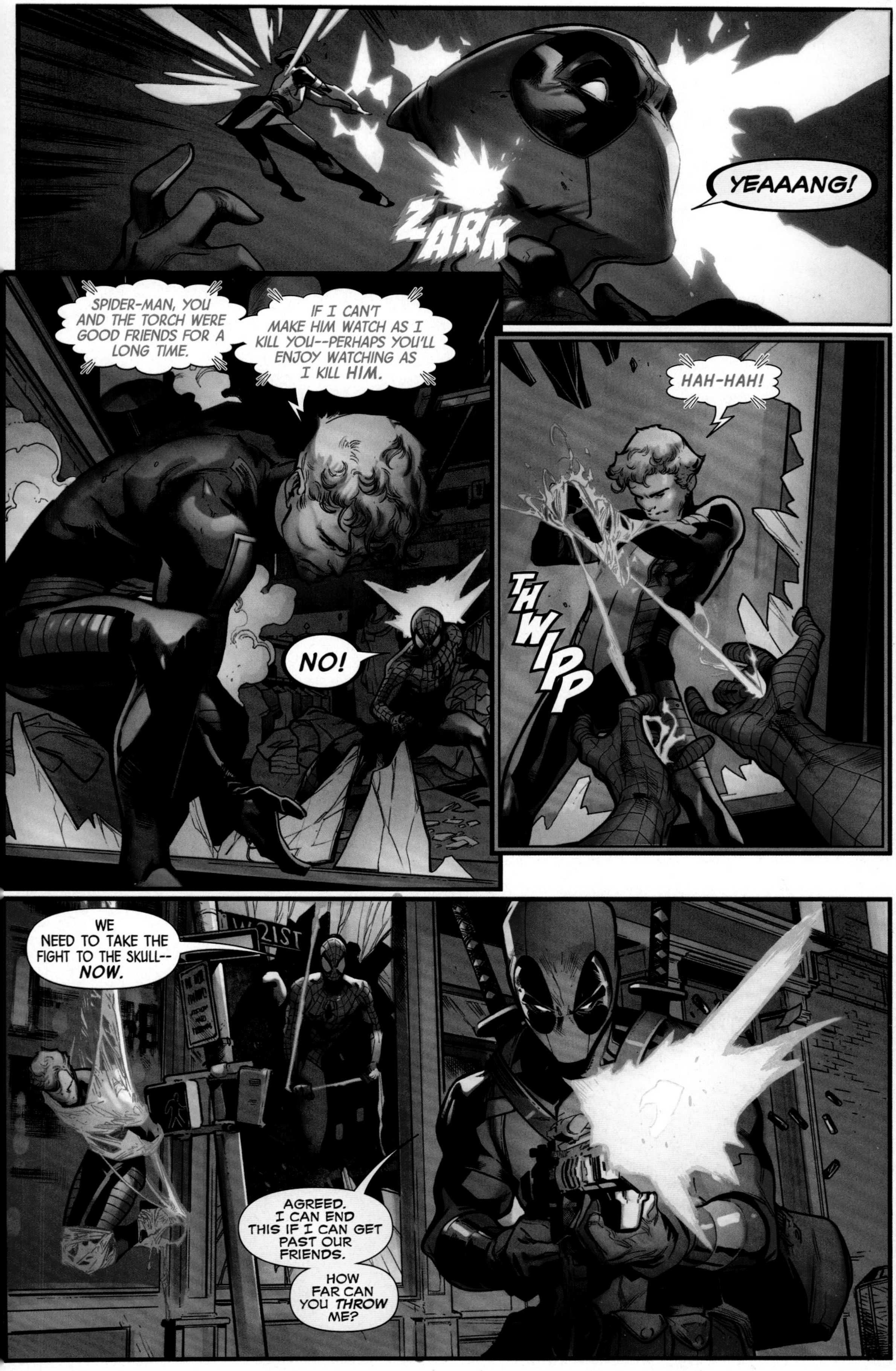

ZARK
YEAAANG!
SPIDER-MAN, YOU AND THE TORCH WERE GOOD FRIENDS FOR A LONG TIME.
IF I CAN'T MAKE HIM WATCH AS I KILL YOU--PERHAPS YOU'LL ENJOY WATCHING AS I KILL HIM.
NO!
HAH-HAH!
THWIPP
WE NEED TO TAKE THE FIGHT TO THE SKULL-- NOW.
AGREED. I CAN END THIS IF I CAN GET PAST OUR FRIENDS.
HOW FAR CAN YOU THROW ME?

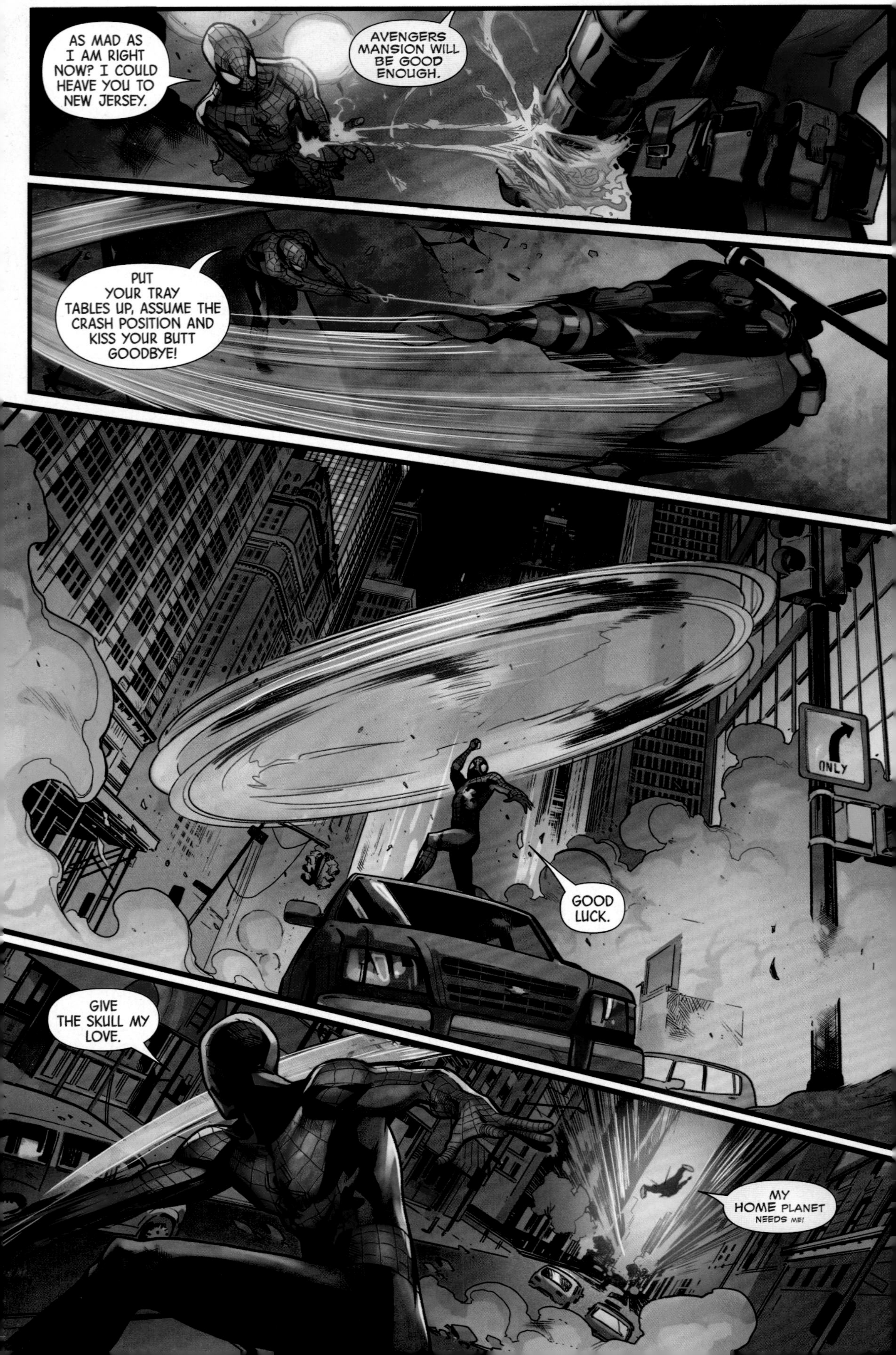
AS MAD AS I AM RIGHT NOW? I COULD HEAVE YOU TO NEW JERSEY.
AVENGERS MANSION WILL BE GOOD ENOUGH.
PUT YOUR TRAY TABLES UP, ASSUME THE CRASH POSITION AND KISS YOUR BUTT GOODBYE!
ONLY
GOOD LUCK.
GIVE THE SKULL MY LOVE.
MY HOME PLANET NEEDS ME!

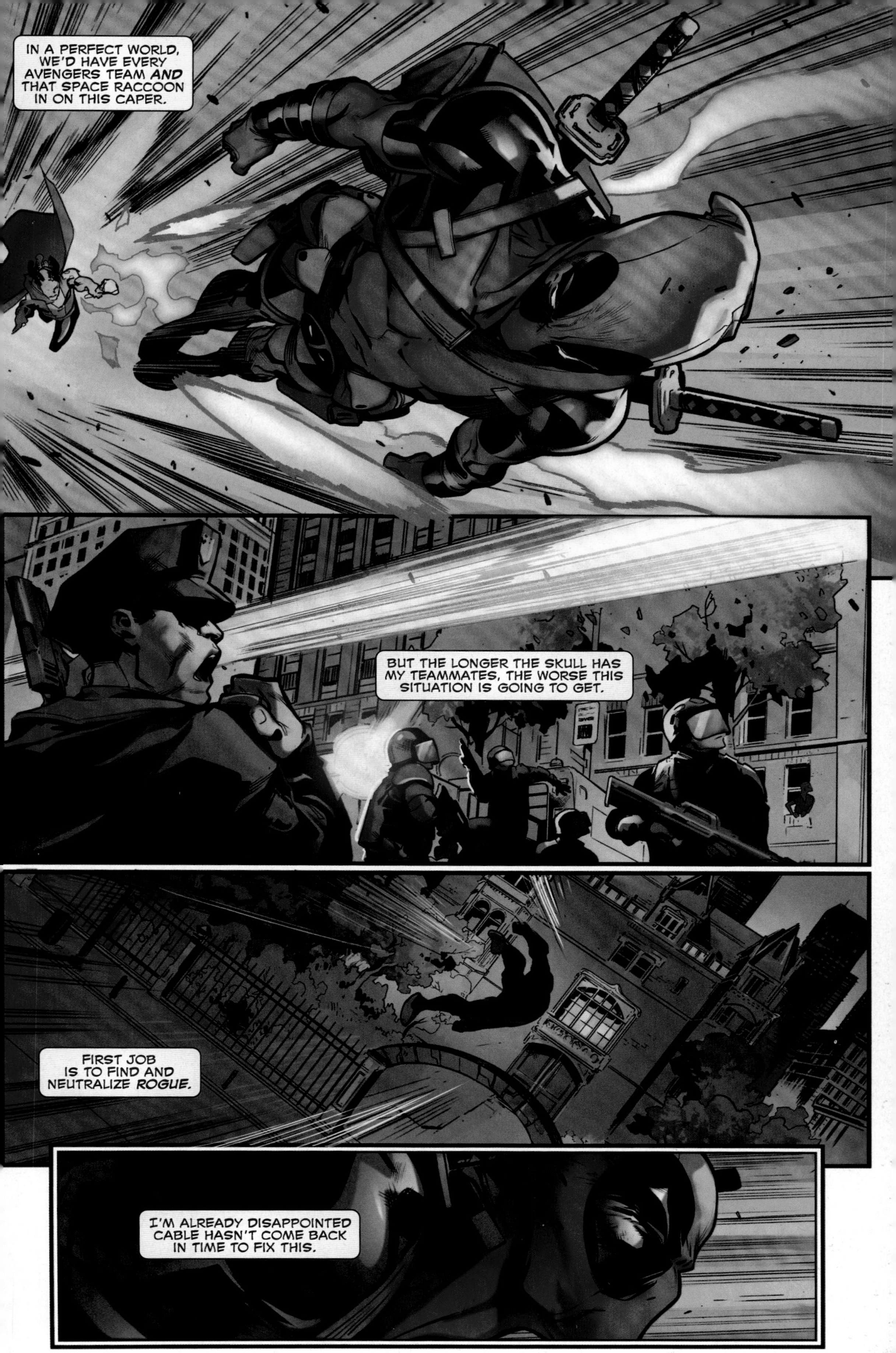
IN A PERFECT WORLD, WE'D HAVE EVERY AVENGERS TEAM *AND* THAT SPACE RACCOON IN ON THIS CAPER.
BUT THE LONGER THE SKULL HAS MY TEAMMATES, THE WORSE THIS SITUATION IS GOING TO GET.
FIRST JOB IS TO FIND AND NEUTRALIZE *ROGUE.*
I'M ALREADY DISAPPOINTED CABLE HASN'T COME BACK IN TIME TO FIX THIS.

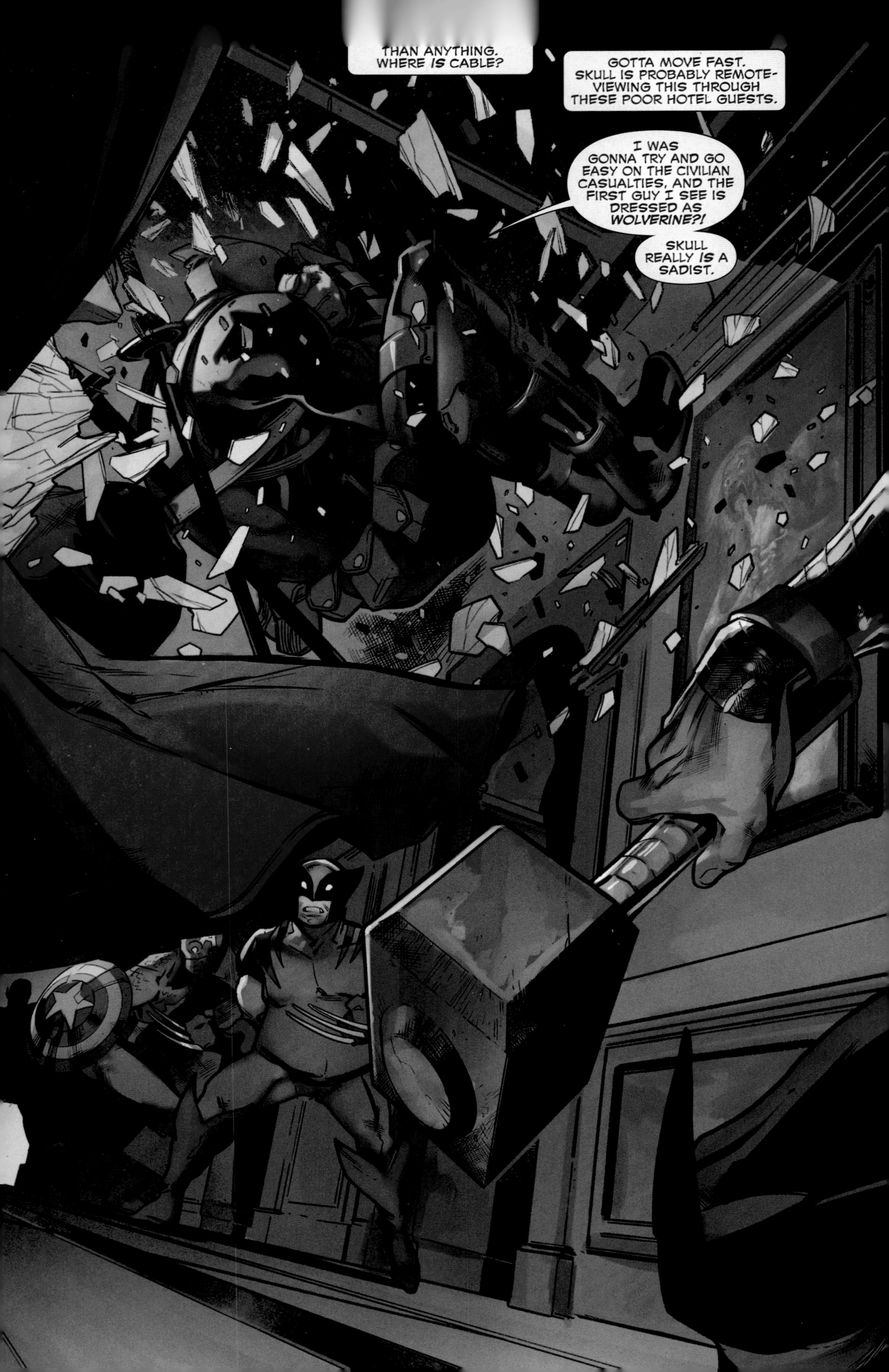
THAN ANYTHING. WHERE IS CABLE?
GOTTA MOVE FAST. SKULL IS PROBABLY REMOTE-VIEWING THIS THROUGH THESE POOR HOTEL GUESTS.
I WAS GONNA TRY AND GO EASY ON THE CIVILIAN CASUALTIES, AND THE FIRST GUY I SEE IS DRESSED AS WOLVERINE?!
SKULL REALLY IS A SADIST.

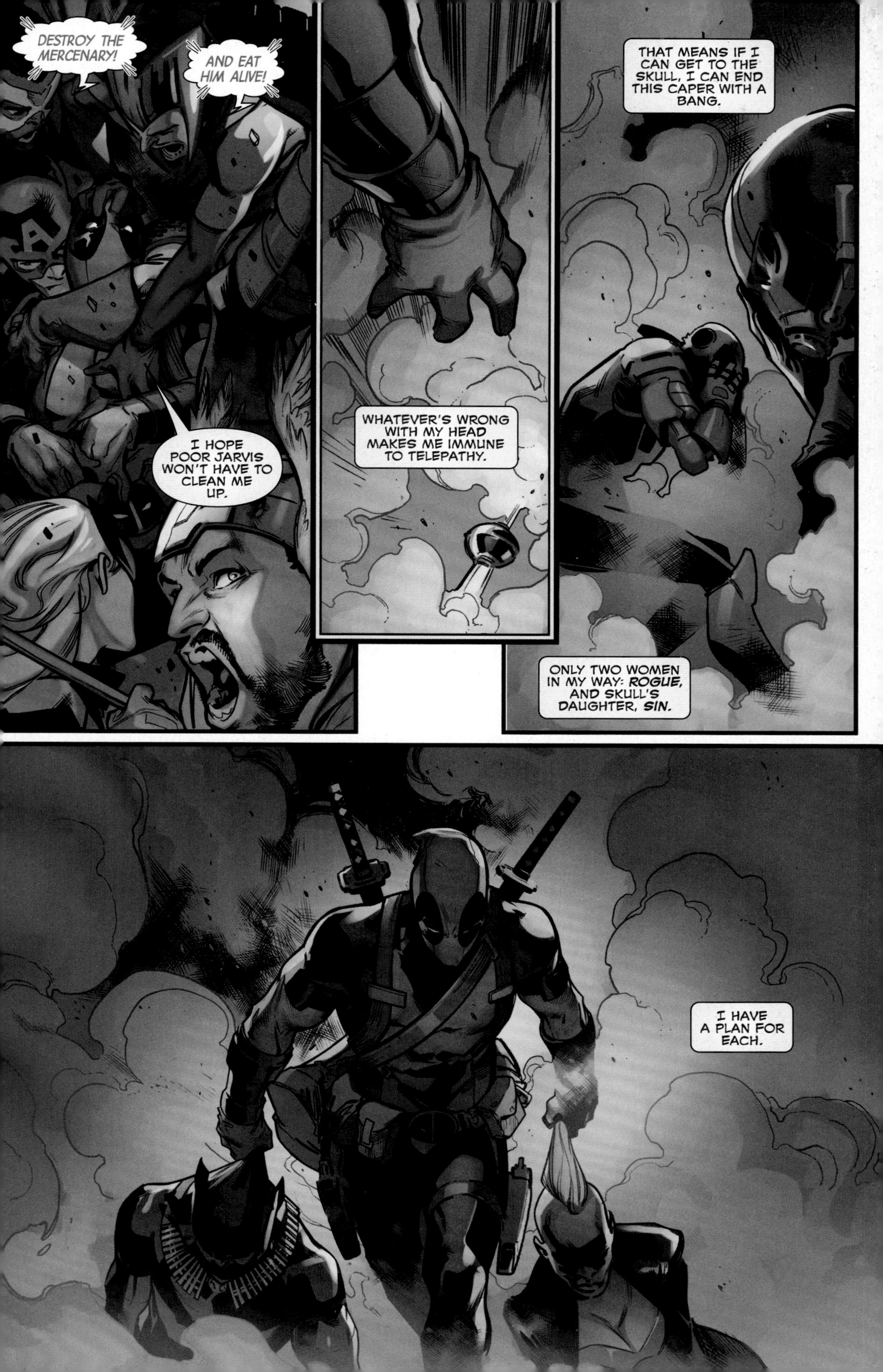
DESTROY THE MERCENARY!
AND EAT HIM ALIVE!
I HOPE POOR JARVIS WON'T HAVE TO CLEAN ME UP.
WHATEVER'S WRONG WITH MY HEAD MAKES ME IMMUNE TO TELEPATHY.
THAT MEANS IF I CAN GET TO THE SKULL, I CAN END THIS CAPER WITH A BANG.
ONLY TWO WOMEN IN MY WAY: *ROGUE*, AND SKULL'S DAUGHTER, *SIN*.
I HAVE A PLAN FOR EACH.

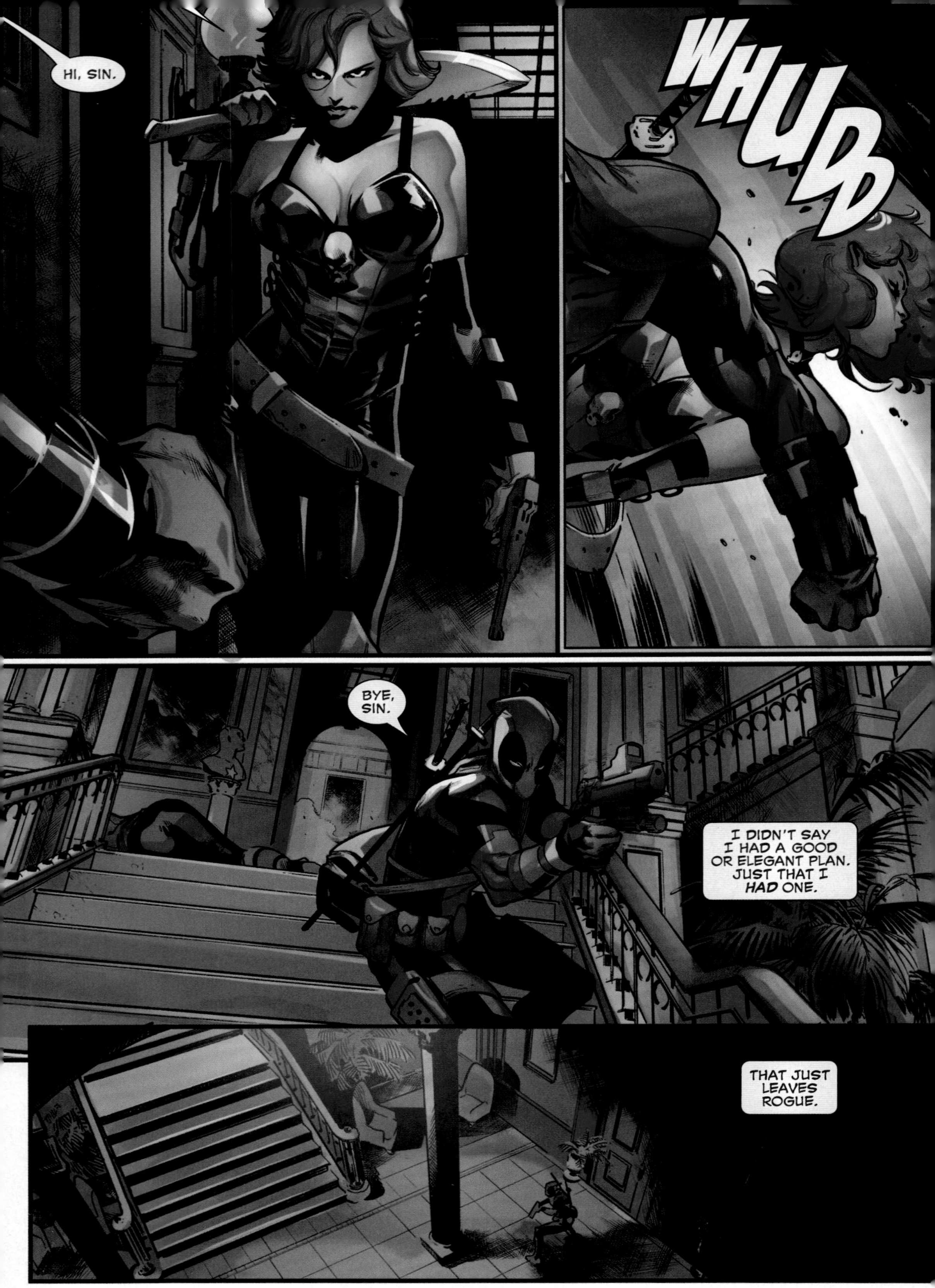
HI, SIN.
WHUDD
BYE, SIN.
I DIDN'T SAY I HAD A GOOD OR ELEGANT PLAN. JUST THAT I HAD ONE.
THAT JUST LEAVES ROGUE.

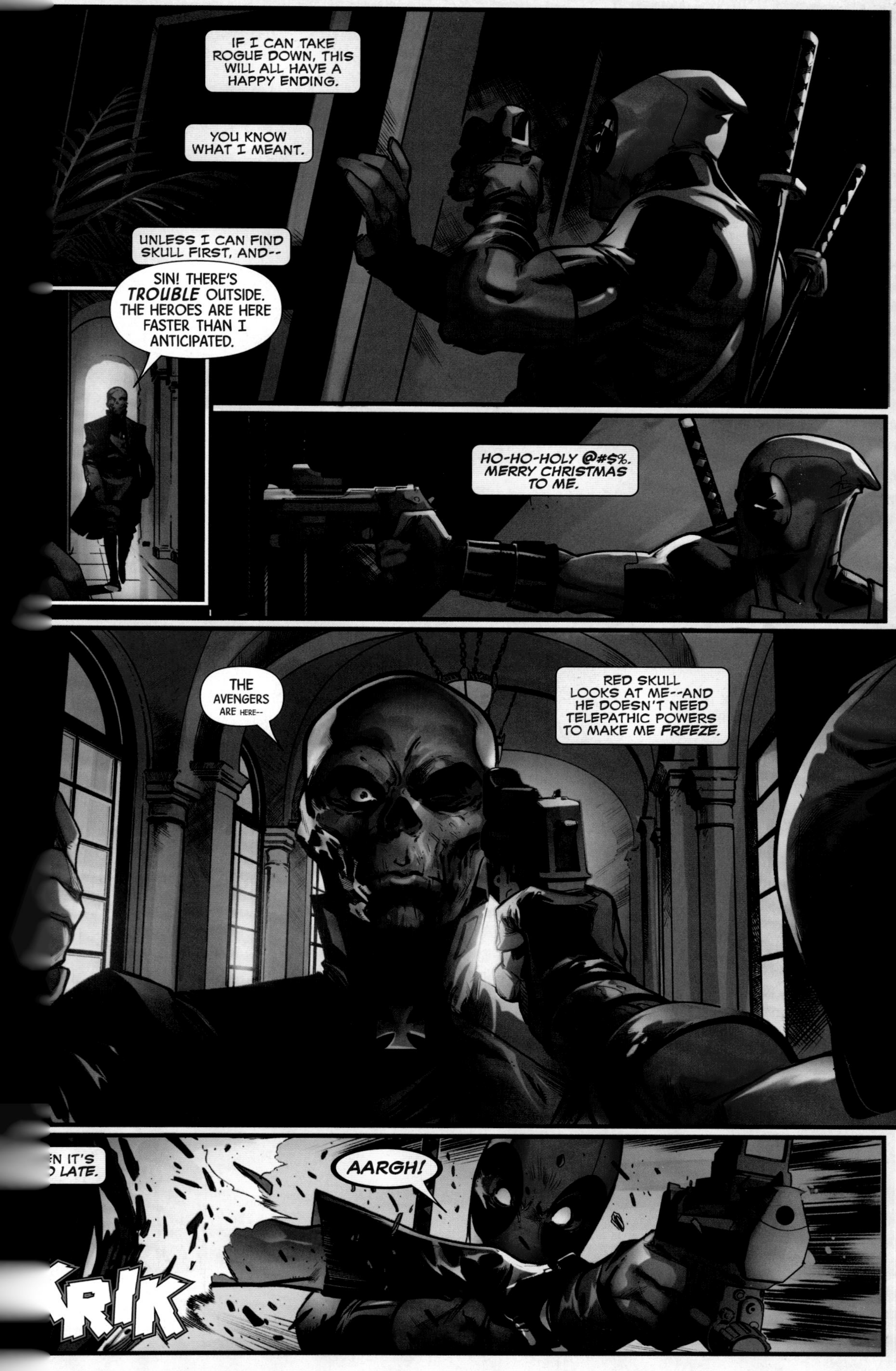
IF I CAN TAKE ROGUE DOWN, THIS WILL ALL HAVE A HAPPY ENDING.
YOU KNOW WHAT I MEANT.
UNLESS I CAN FIND SKULL FIRST, AND--
SIN! THERE'S TROUBLE OUTSIDE. THE HEROES ARE HERE FASTER THAN I ANTICIPATED.
HO-HO-HOLY @#$%. MERRY CHRISTMAS TO ME.
THE AVENGERS ARE HERE--
RED SKULL LOOKS AT ME--AND HE DOESN'T NEED TELEPATHIC POWERS TO MAKE ME FREEZE.
EN IT'S
D LATE.
AARGH!
RIK

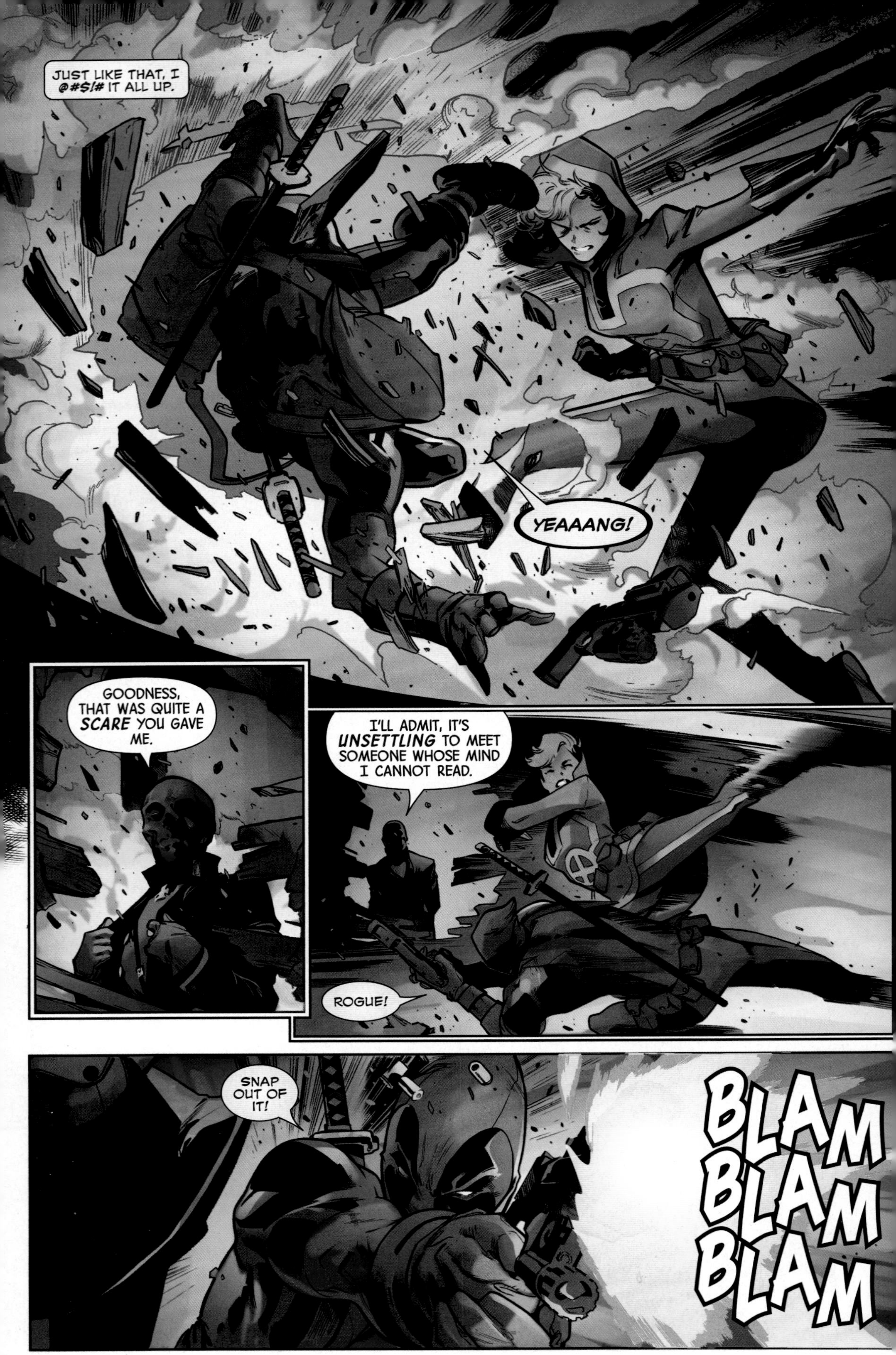
JUST LIKE THAT, I @#$!# IT ALL UP.
YEAAANG!
GOODNESS, THAT WAS QUITE A SCARE YOU GAVE ME.
I'LL ADMIT, IT'S UNSETTLING TO MEET SOMEONE WHOSE MIND I CANNOT READ.
ROGUE!
SNAP OUT OF IT!
BLAM BLAM BLAM

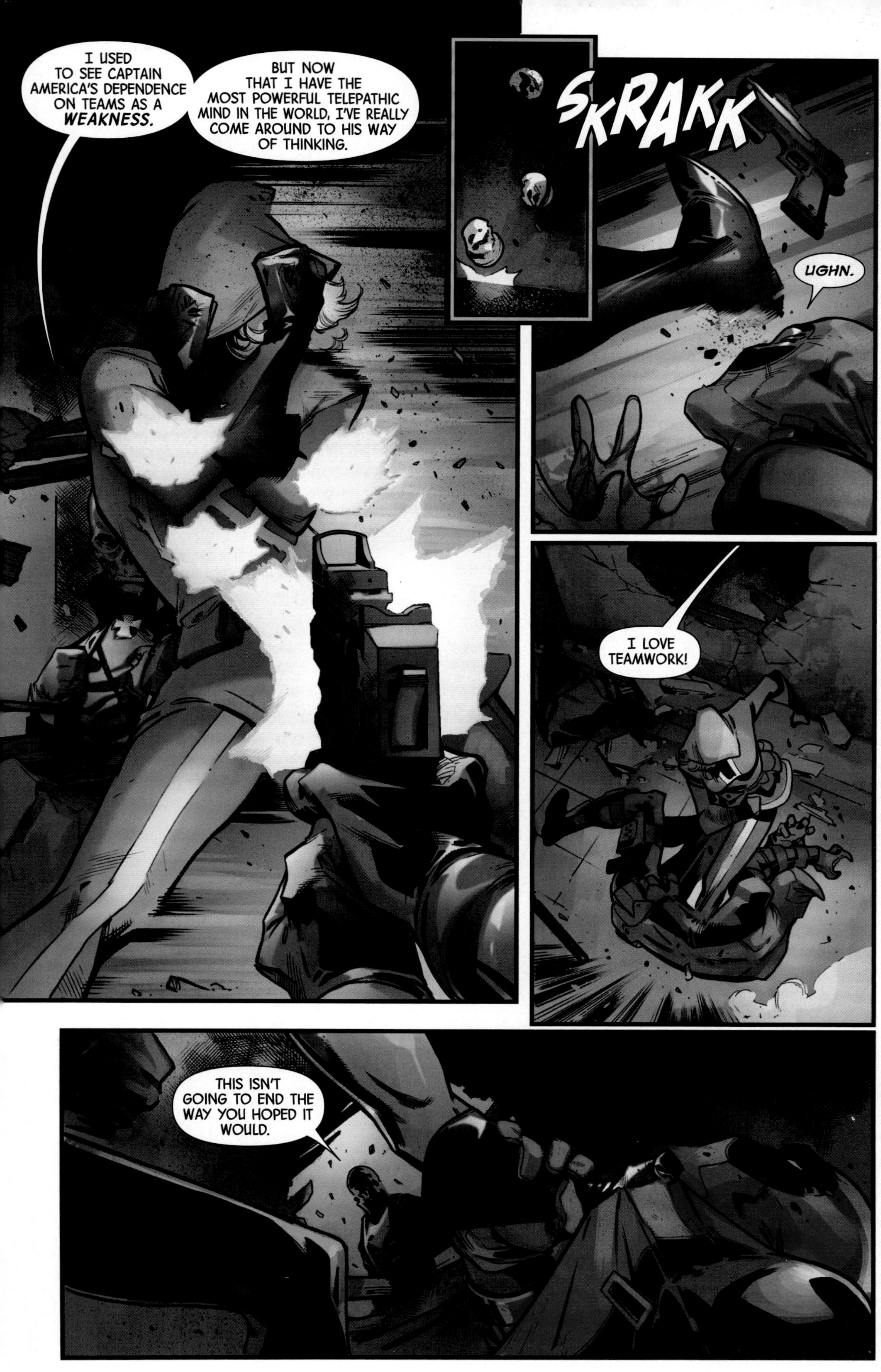
I USED TO SEE CAPTAIN AMERICA'S DEPENDENCE ON TEAMS AS A *WEAKNESS.*
BUT NOW THAT I HAVE THE MOST POWERFUL TELEPATHIC MIND IN THE WORLD, I'VE REALLY COME AROUND TO HIS WAY OF THINKING.
SKRAKK
UGHN.
I LOVE TEAMWORK!
THIS ISN'T GOING TO END THE WAY YOU HOPED IT WOULD.

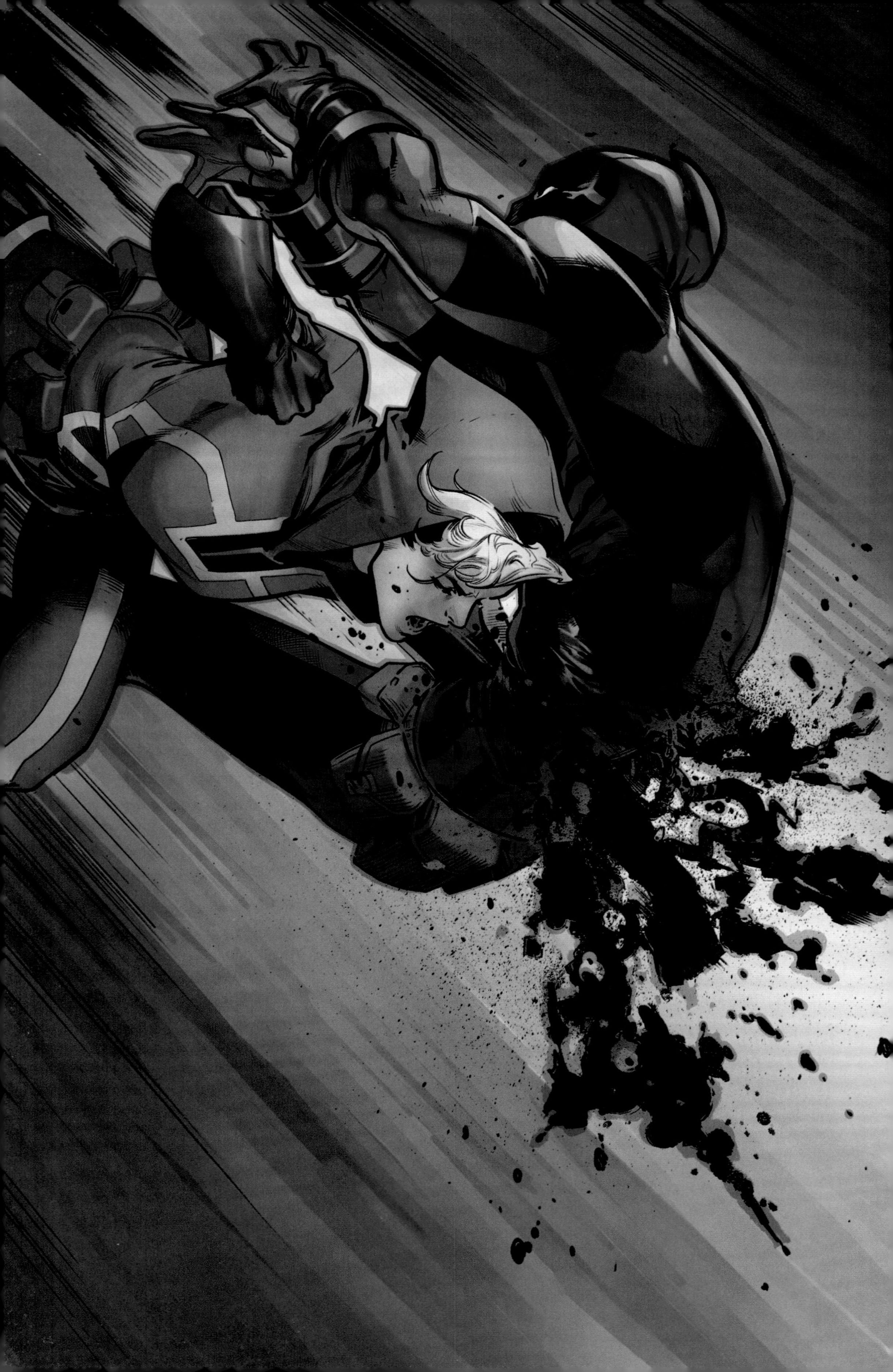

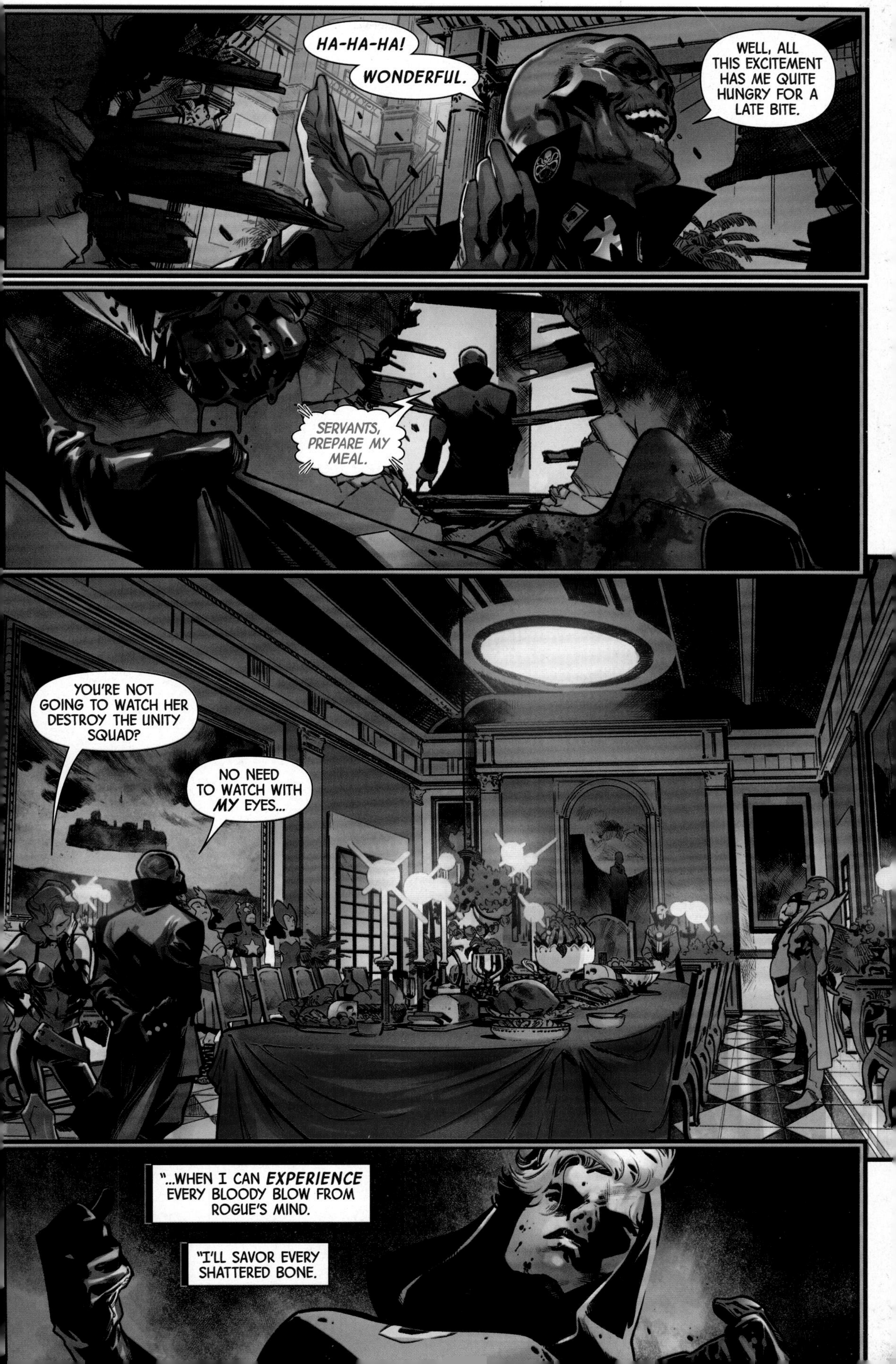
HA-HA-HA!
WONDERFUL.
WELL, ALL THIS EXCITEMENT HAS ME QUITE HUNGRY FOR A LATE BITE.
SERVANTS, PREPARE MY MEAL.
YOU'RE NOT GOING TO WATCH HER DESTROY THE UNITY SQUAD?
NO NEED TO WATCH WITH MY EYES...
"...WHEN I CAN EXPERIENCE EVERY BLOODY BLOW FROM ROGUE'S MIND.
"I'LL SAVOR EVERY SHATTERED BONE.

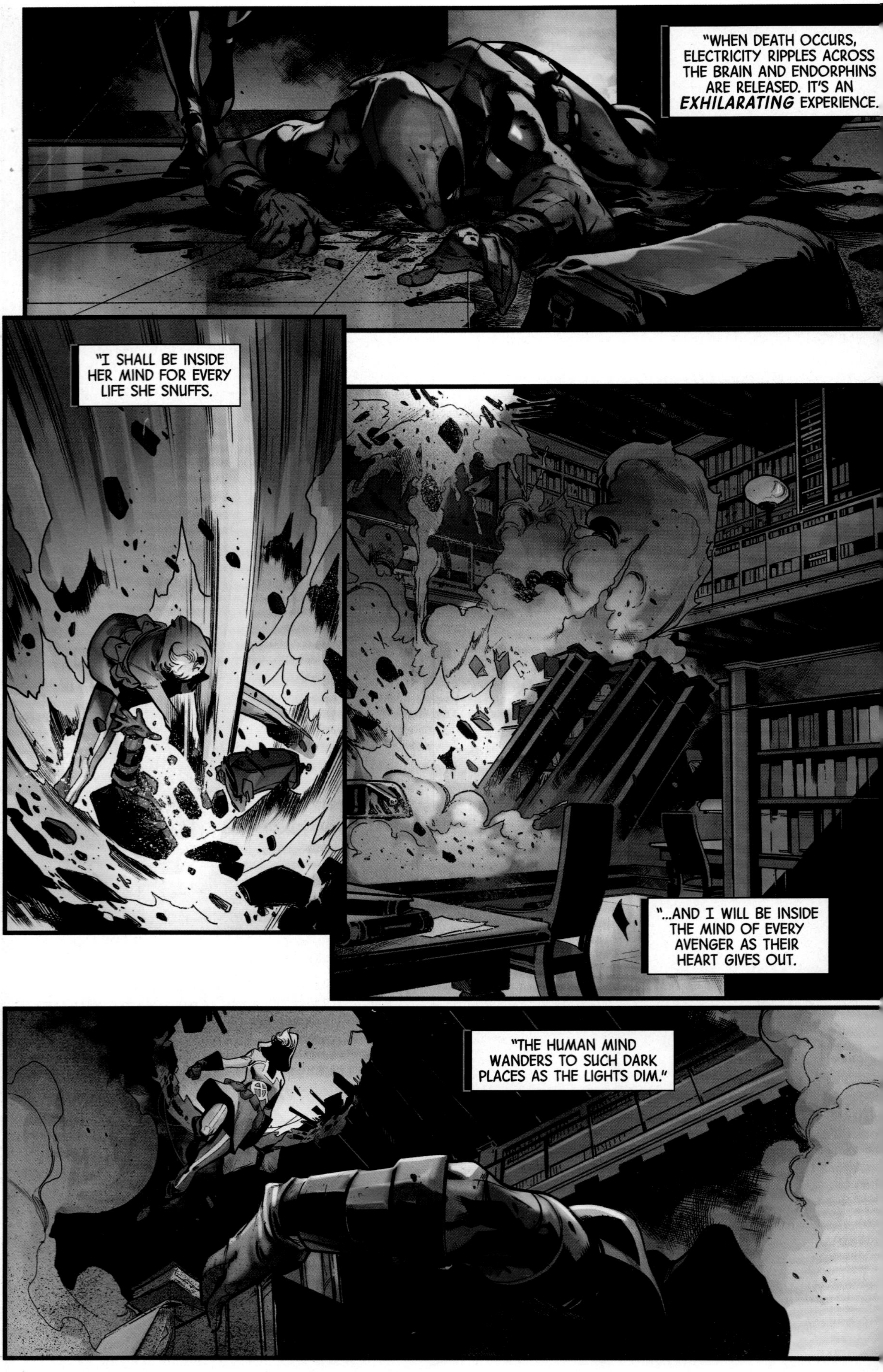
"WHEN DEATH OCCURS, ELECTRICITY RIPPLES ACROSS THE BRAIN AND ENDORPHINS ARE RELEASED. IT'S AN *EXHILARATING* EXPERIENCE.
"I SHALL BE INSIDE HER MIND FOR EVERY LIFE SHE SNUFFS.
"...AND I WILL BE INSIDE THE MIND OF EVERY AVENGER AS THEIR HEART GIVES OUT.
"THE HUMAN MIND WANDERS TO SUCH DARK PLACES AS THE LIGHTS DIM."

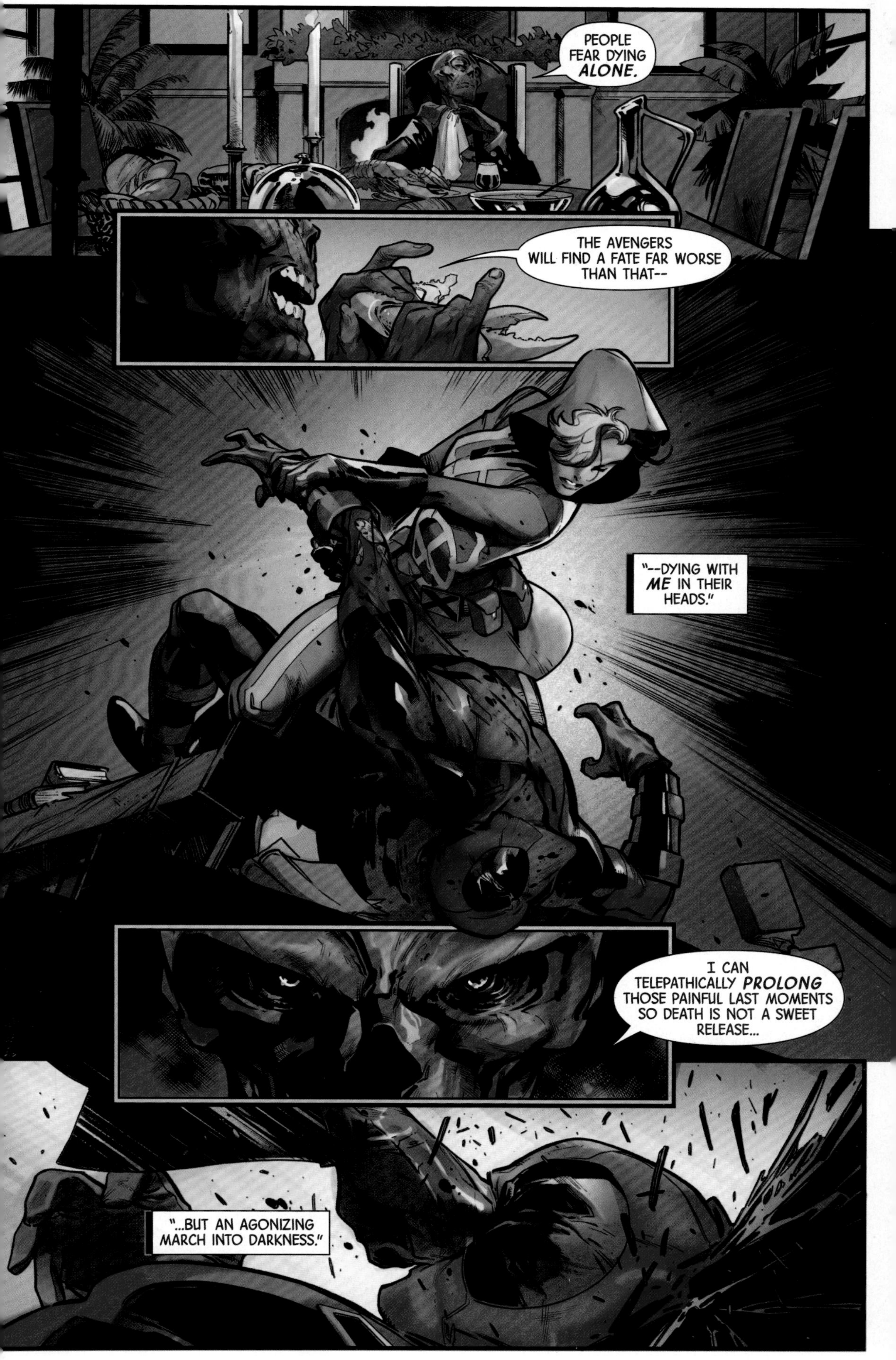
PEOPLE FEAR DYING *ALONE.*
THE AVENGERS WILL FIND A FATE FAR WORSE THAN THAT--
"--DYING WITH *ME* IN THEIR HEADS."
I CAN TELEPATHICALLY *PROLONG* THOSE PAINFUL LAST MOMENTS SO DEATH IS NOT A SWEET RELEASE...
"...BUT AN AGONIZING MARCH INTO DARKNESS."

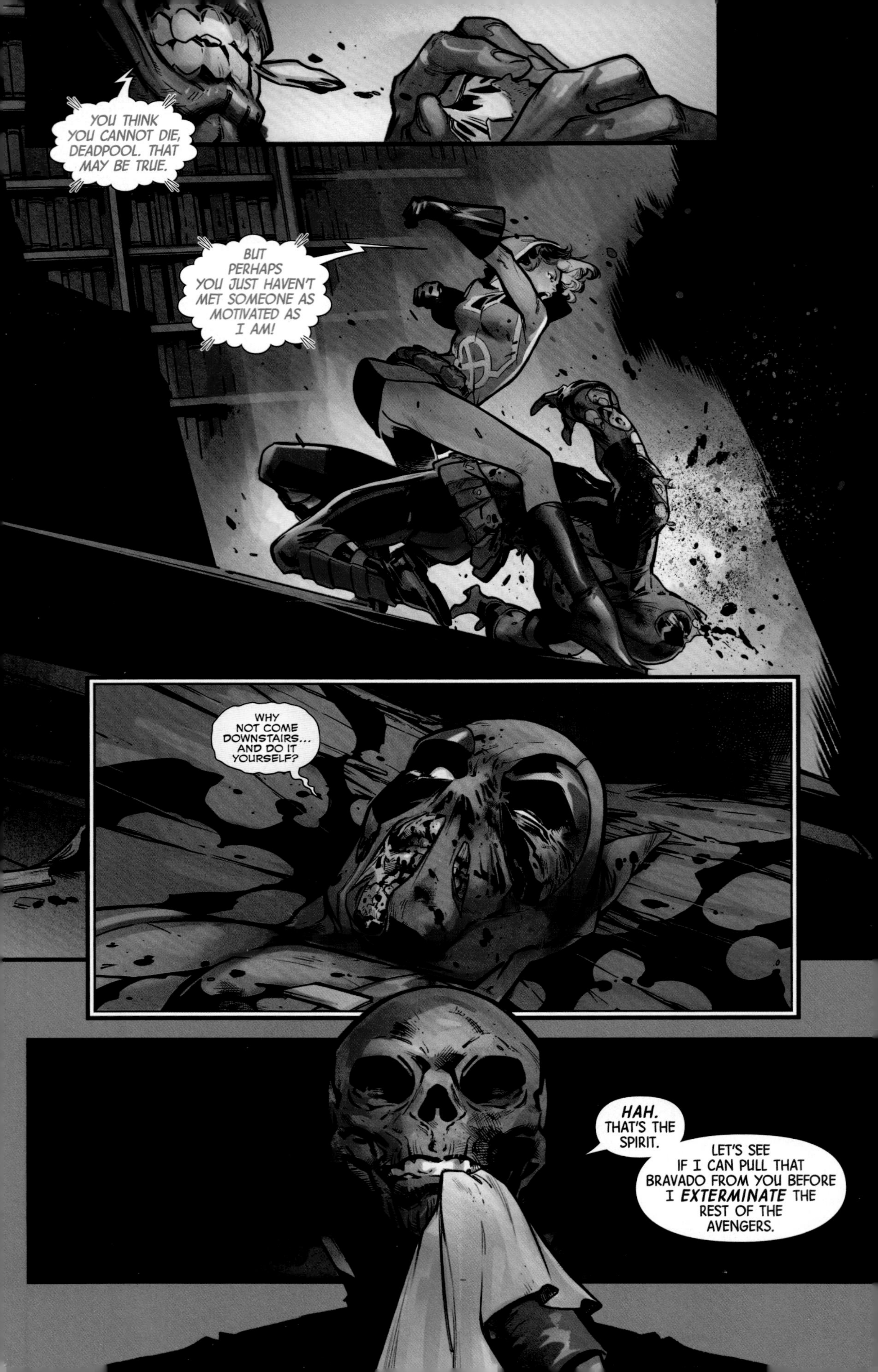
YOU THINK YOU CANNOT DIE, DEADPOOL. THAT MAY BE TRUE.
BUT PERHAPS YOU JUST HAVEN'T MET SOMEONE AS MOTIVATED AS I AM!
WHY NOT COME DOWNSTAIRS... AND DO IT YOURSELF?
HAH. THAT'S THE SPIRIT.
LET'S SEE IF I CAN PULL THAT BRAVADO FROM YOU BEFORE I EXTERMINATE THE REST OF THE AVENGERS.

21

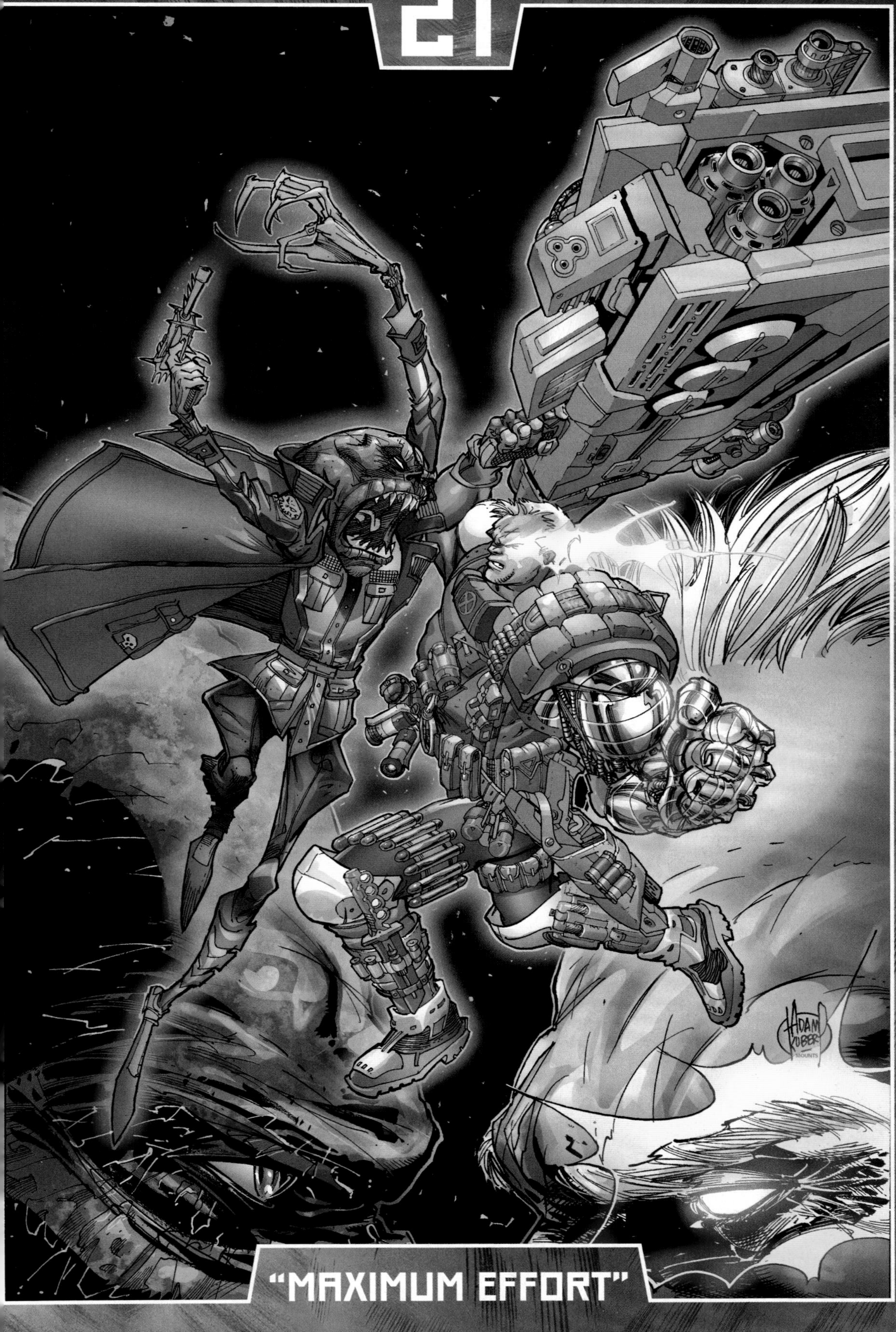

“MAXIMUM EFFORT”

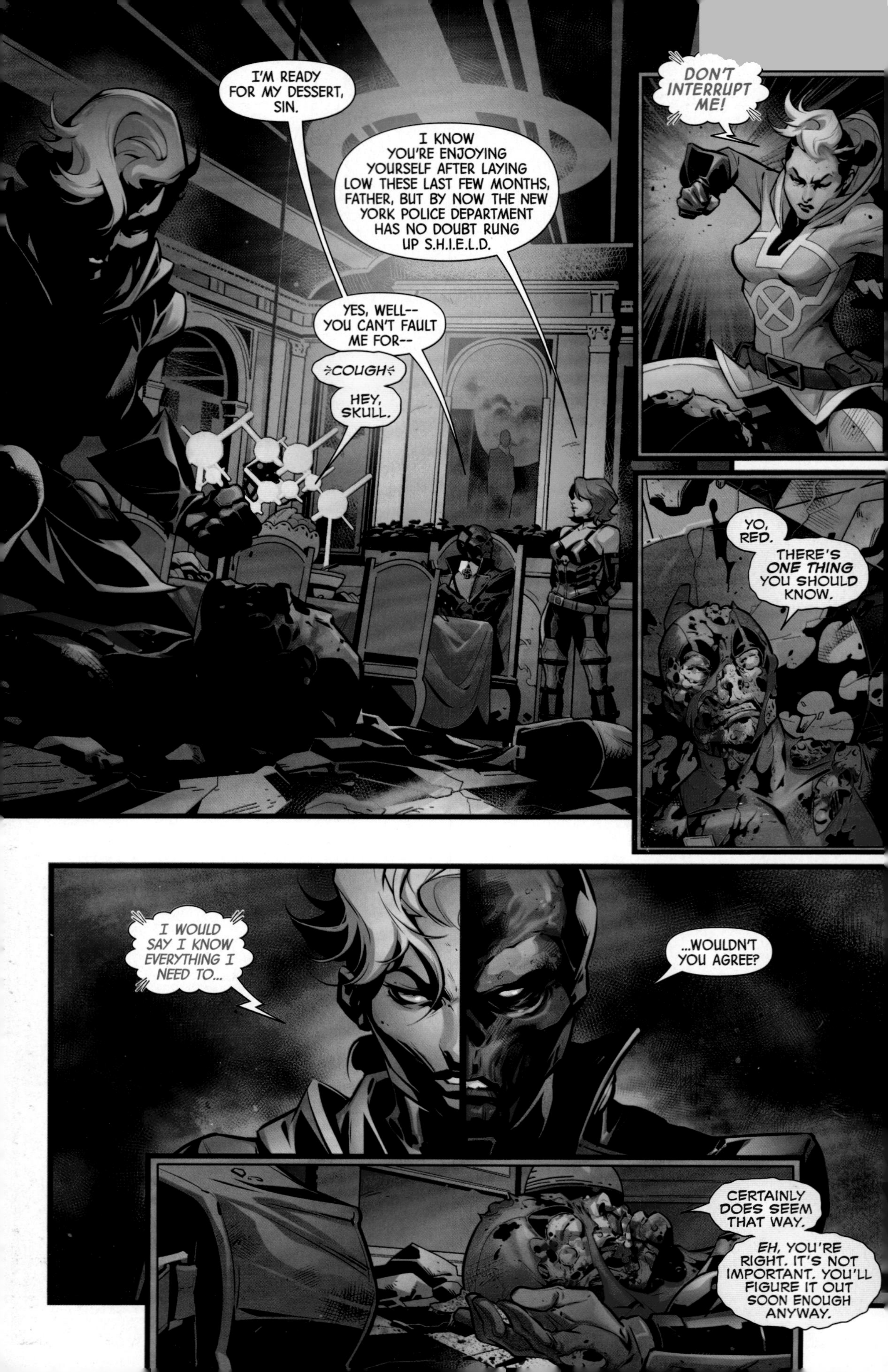
I'M READY FOR MY DESSERT, SIN.
I KNOW YOU'RE ENJOYING YOURSELF AFTER LAYING LOW THESE LAST FEW MONTHS, FATHER, BUT BY NOW THE NEW YORK POLICE DEPARTMENT HAS NO DOUBT RUNG UP S.H.I.E.L.D.
YES, WELL-- YOU CAN'T FAULT ME FOR--
COUGH
HEY, SKULL.
DON'T INTERRUPT ME!
YO, RED. THERE'S ONE THING YOU SHOULD KNOW.
I WOULD SAY I KNOW EVERYTHING I NEED TO...
...WOULDN'T YOU AGREE?
CERTAINLY DOES SEEM THAT WAY.
EH, YOU'RE RIGHT. IT'S NOT IMPORTANT. YOU'LL FIGURE IT OUT SOON ENOUGH ANYWAY.

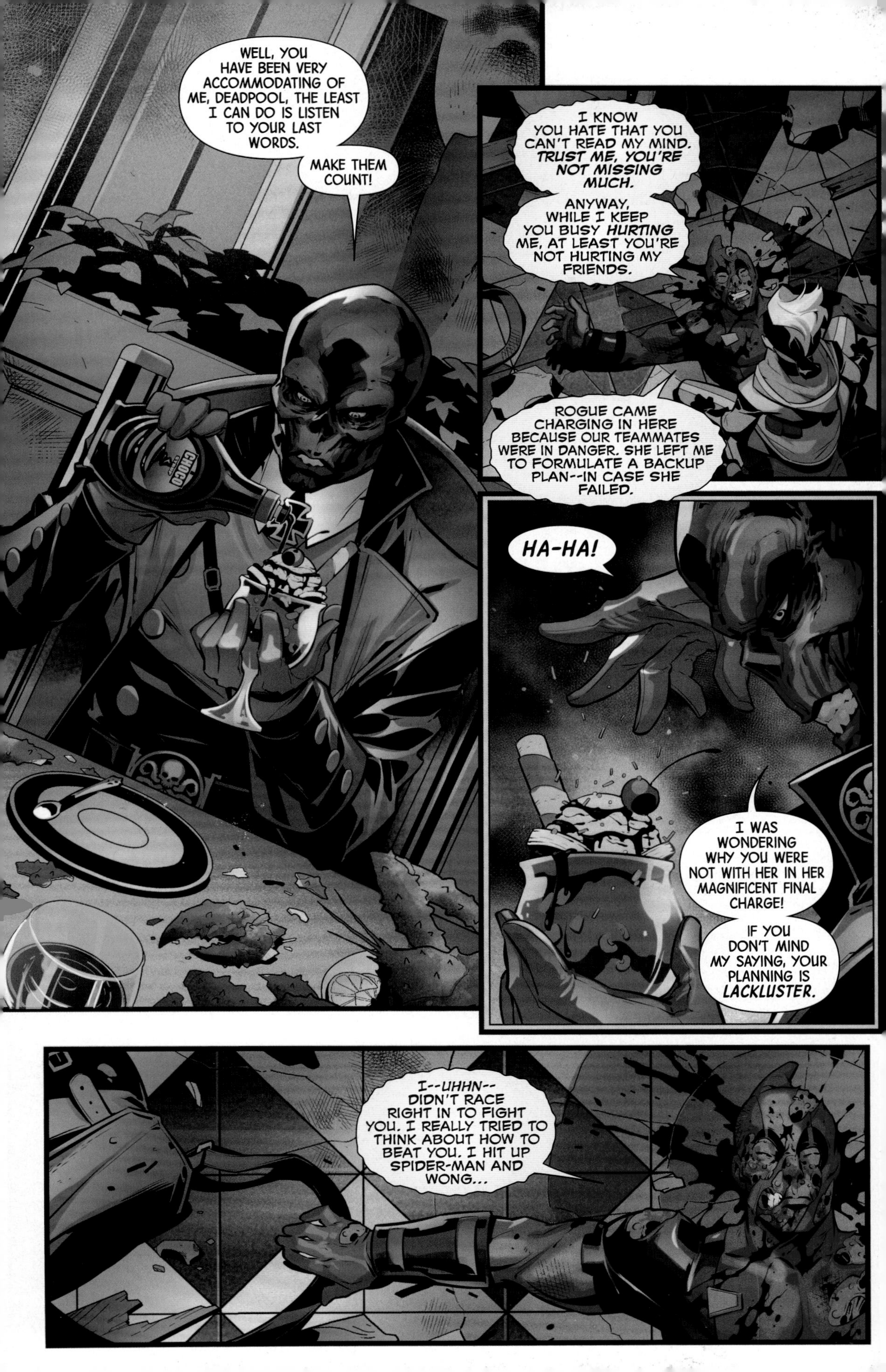

WELL, YOU HAVE BEEN VERY ACCOMMODATING OF ME, DEADPOOL, THE LEAST I CAN DO IS LISTEN TO YOUR LAST WORDS.
MAKE THEM COUNT!
CHOCO
I KNOW YOU HATE THAT YOU CAN'T READ MY MIND. TRUST ME, YOU'RE NOT MISSING MUCH.
ANYWAY, WHILE I KEEP YOU BUSY HURTING ME, AT LEAST YOU'RE NOT HURTING MY FRIENDS.
ROGUE CAME CHARGING IN HERE BECAUSE OUR TEAMMATES WERE IN DANGER. SHE LEFT ME TO FORMULATE A BACKUP PLAN--IN CASE SHE FAILED.
HA-HA!
I WAS WONDERING WHY YOU WERE NOT WITH HER IN HER MAGNIFICENT FINAL CHARGE!
IF YOU DON'T MIND MY SAYING, YOUR PLANNING IS LACKLUSTER.
I--UHHN-- DIDN'T RACE RIGHT IN TO FIGHT YOU. I REALLY TRIED TO THINK ABOUT HOW TO BEAT YOU. I HIT UP SPIDER-MAN AND WONG...

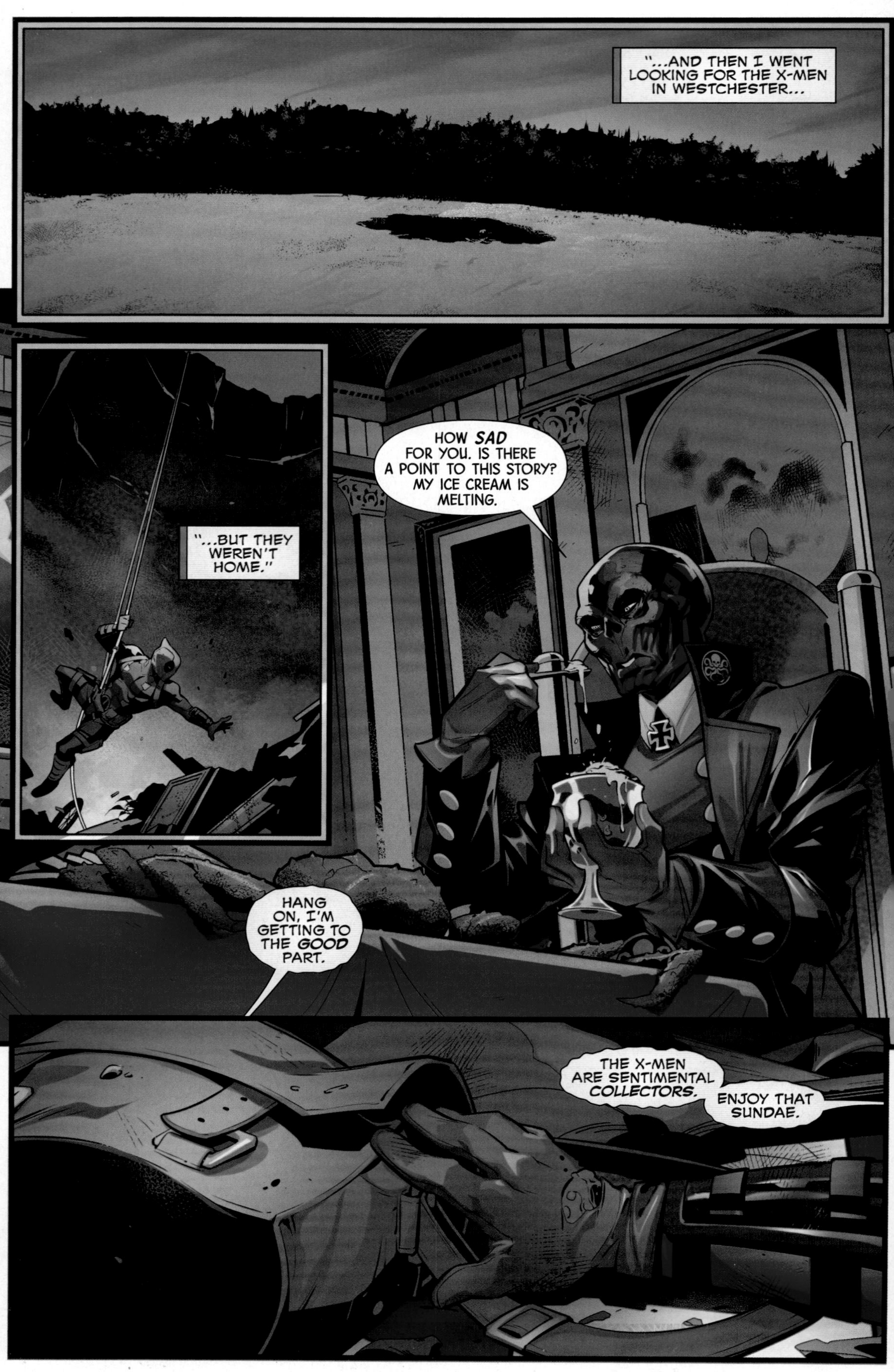
"...AND THEN I WENT LOOKING FOR THE X-MEN IN WESTCHESTER...
"...BUT THEY WEREN'T HOME."
HOW SAD FOR YOU. IS THERE A POINT TO THIS STORY? MY ICE CREAM IS MELTING.
HANG ON, I'M GETTING TO THE GOOD PART.
THE X-MEN ARE SENTIMENTAL COLLECTORS.
ENJOY THAT SUNDAE.

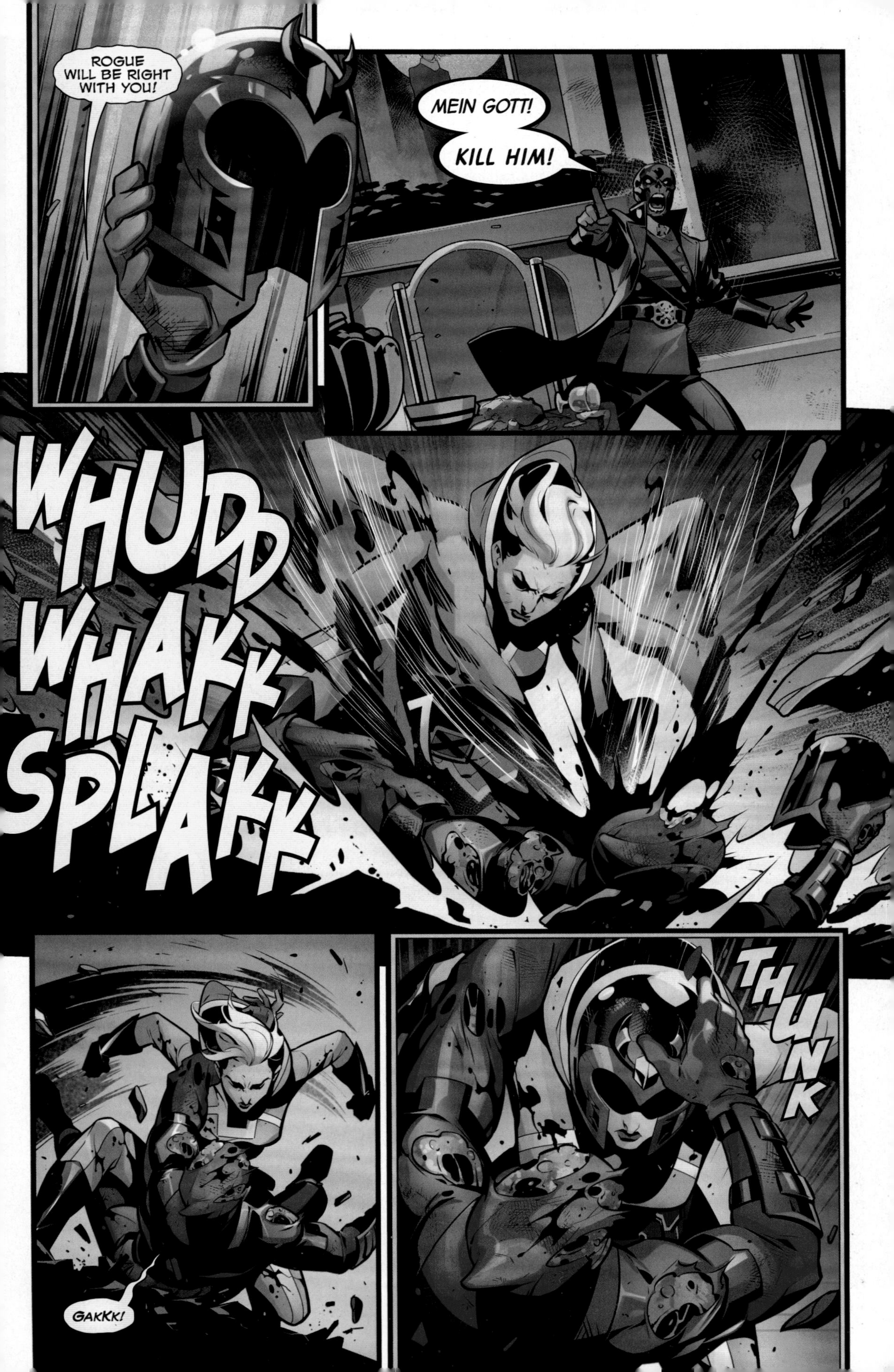
ROGUE WILL BE RIGHT WITH YOU!
MEIN GOTT!
KILL HIM!
WHUDD
WHAKK
SPLAKK
GAKKK!
THUNK

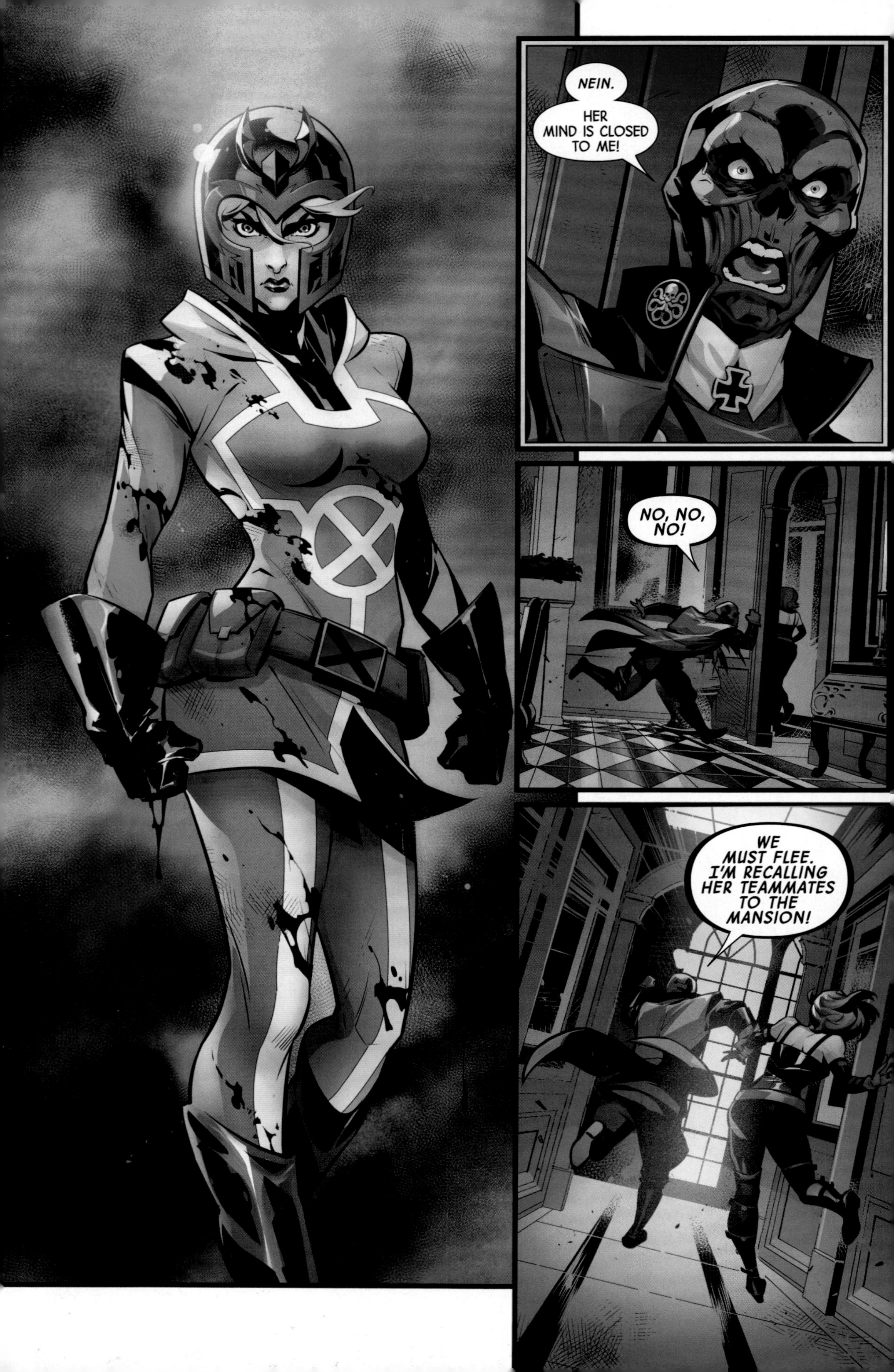
NEIN.
HER MIND IS CLOSED TO ME!
NO, NO, NO!
WE MUST FLEE. I'M RECALLING HER TEAMMATES TO THE MANSION!

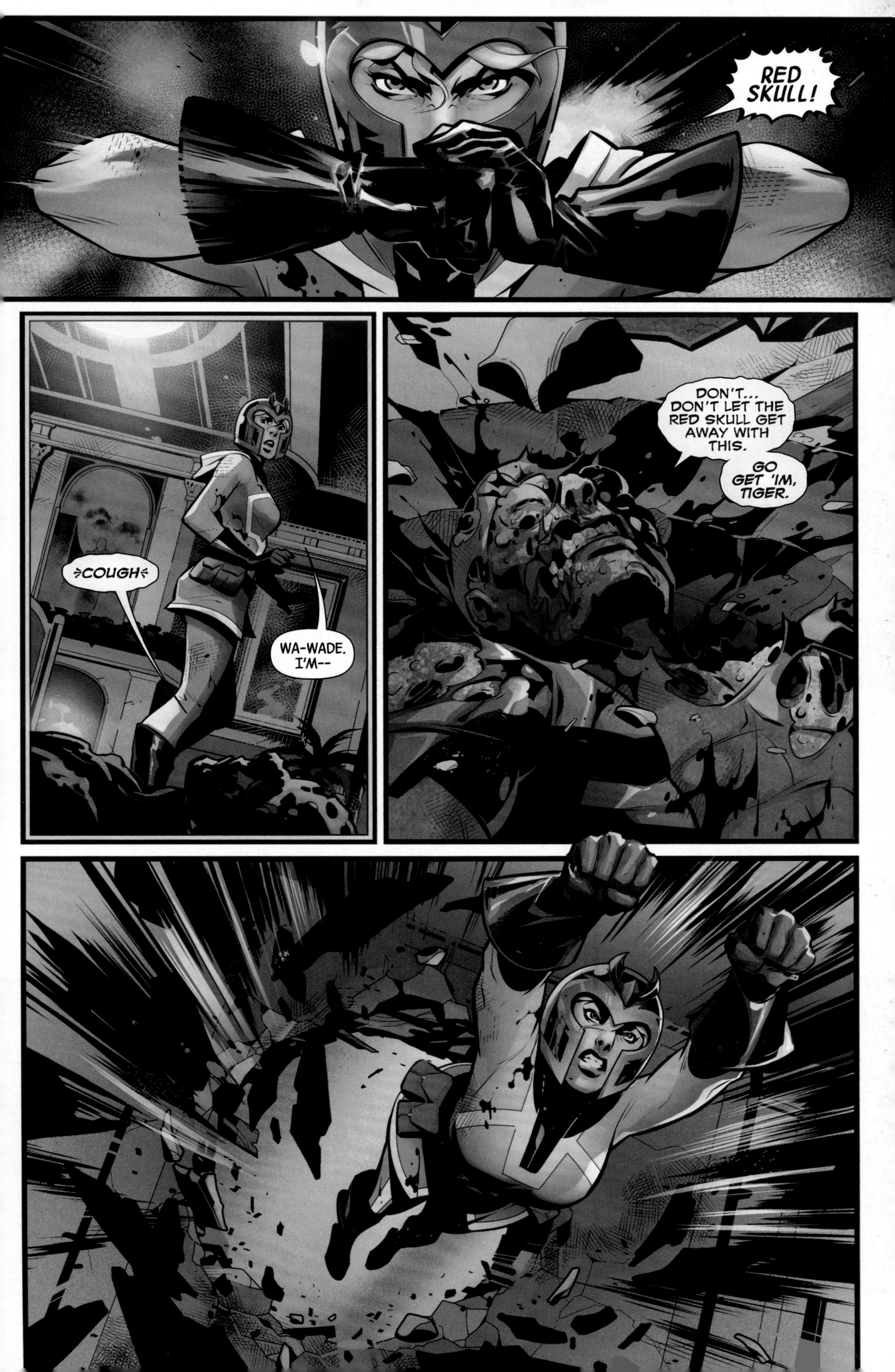
RED SKULL!
COUGH
WA-WADE. I'M--
DON'T... DON'T LET THE RED SKULL GET AWAY WITH THIS.
GO GET 'IM, TIGER.

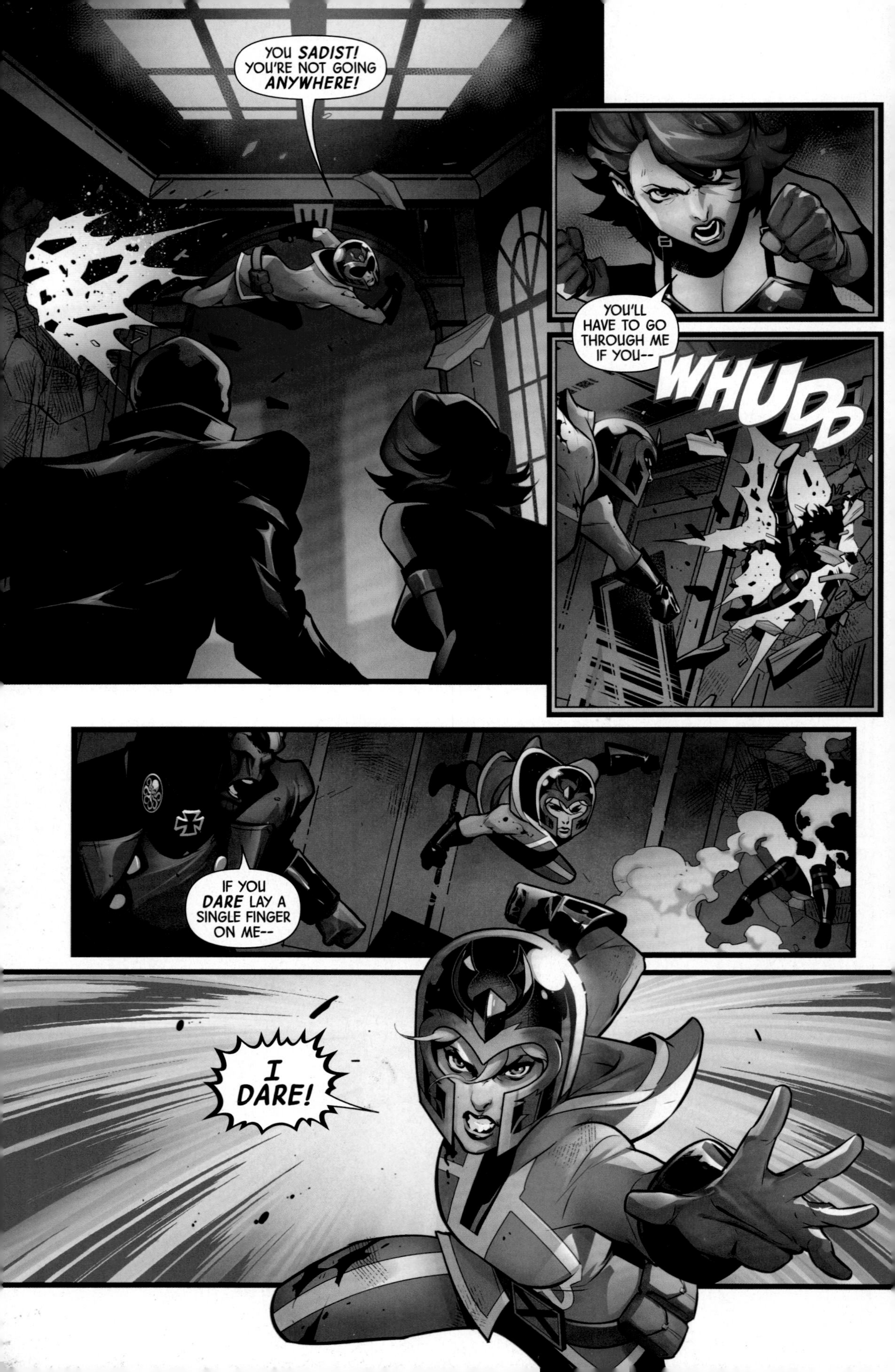
YOU SADIST! YOU'RE NOT GOING ANYWHERE!
YOU'LL HAVE TO GO THROUGH ME IF YOU--
WHUDD
IF YOU DARE LAY A SINGLE FINGER ON ME--
I DARE!

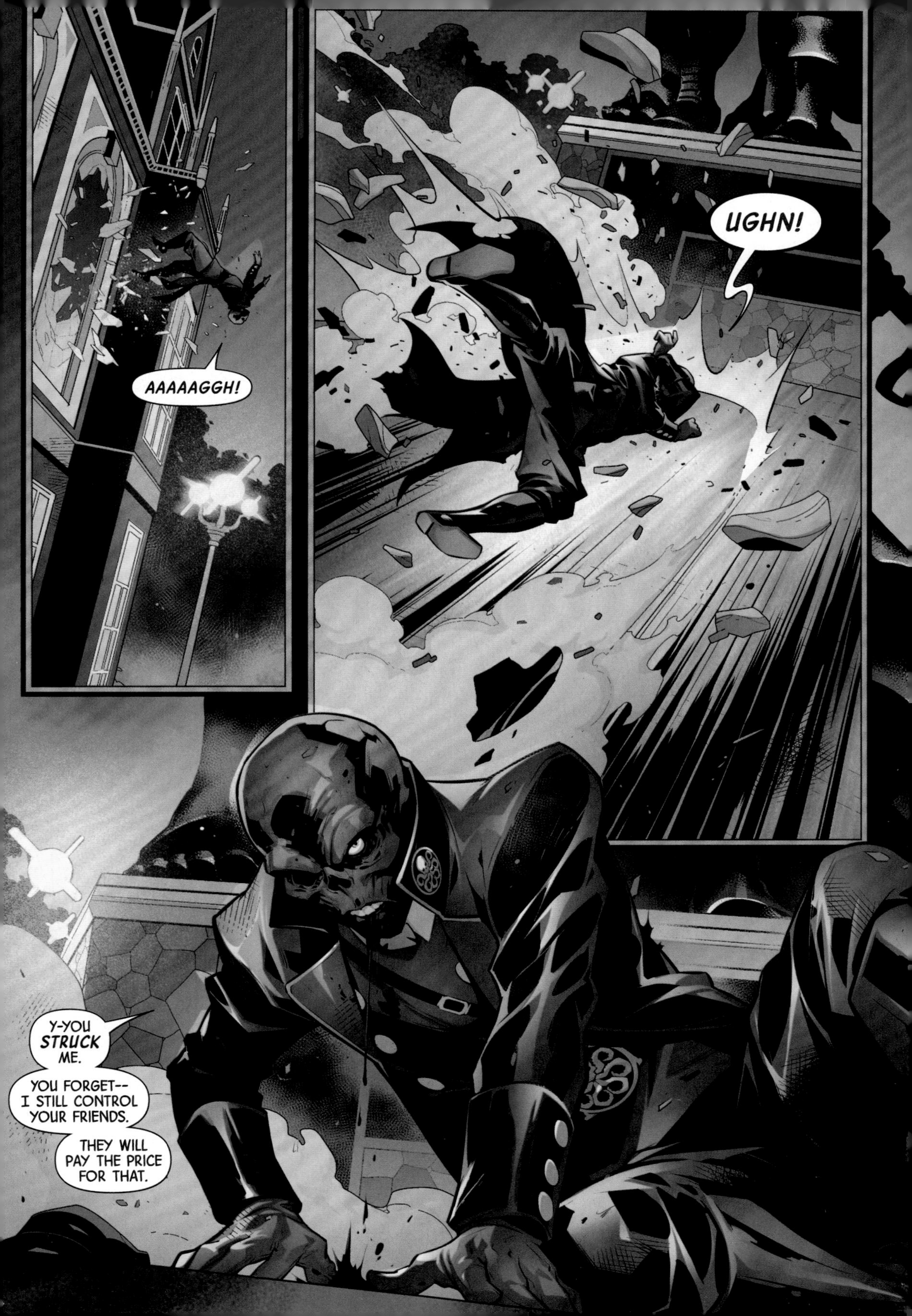
AAAAAGGH!
UGHN!
Y-YOU STRUCK ME.
YOU FORGET-- I STILL CONTROL YOUR FRIENDS.
THEY WILL PAY THE PRICE FOR THAT.

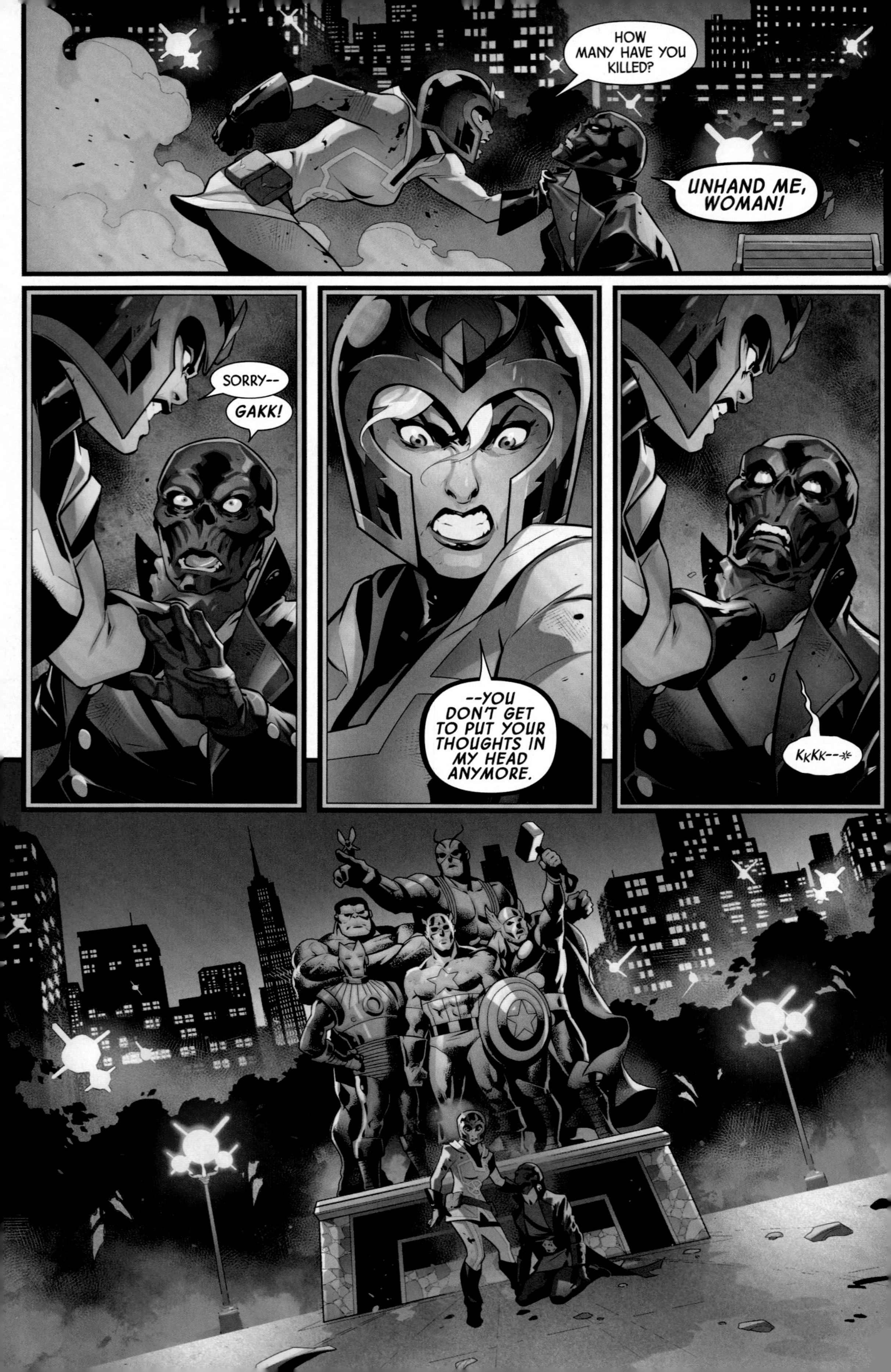
HOW MANY HAVE YOU KILLED?
UNHAND ME, WOMAN!
SORRY--
GAKK!
--YOU DON'T GET TO PUT YOUR THOUGHTS IN MY HEAD ANYMORE.
KKKK--

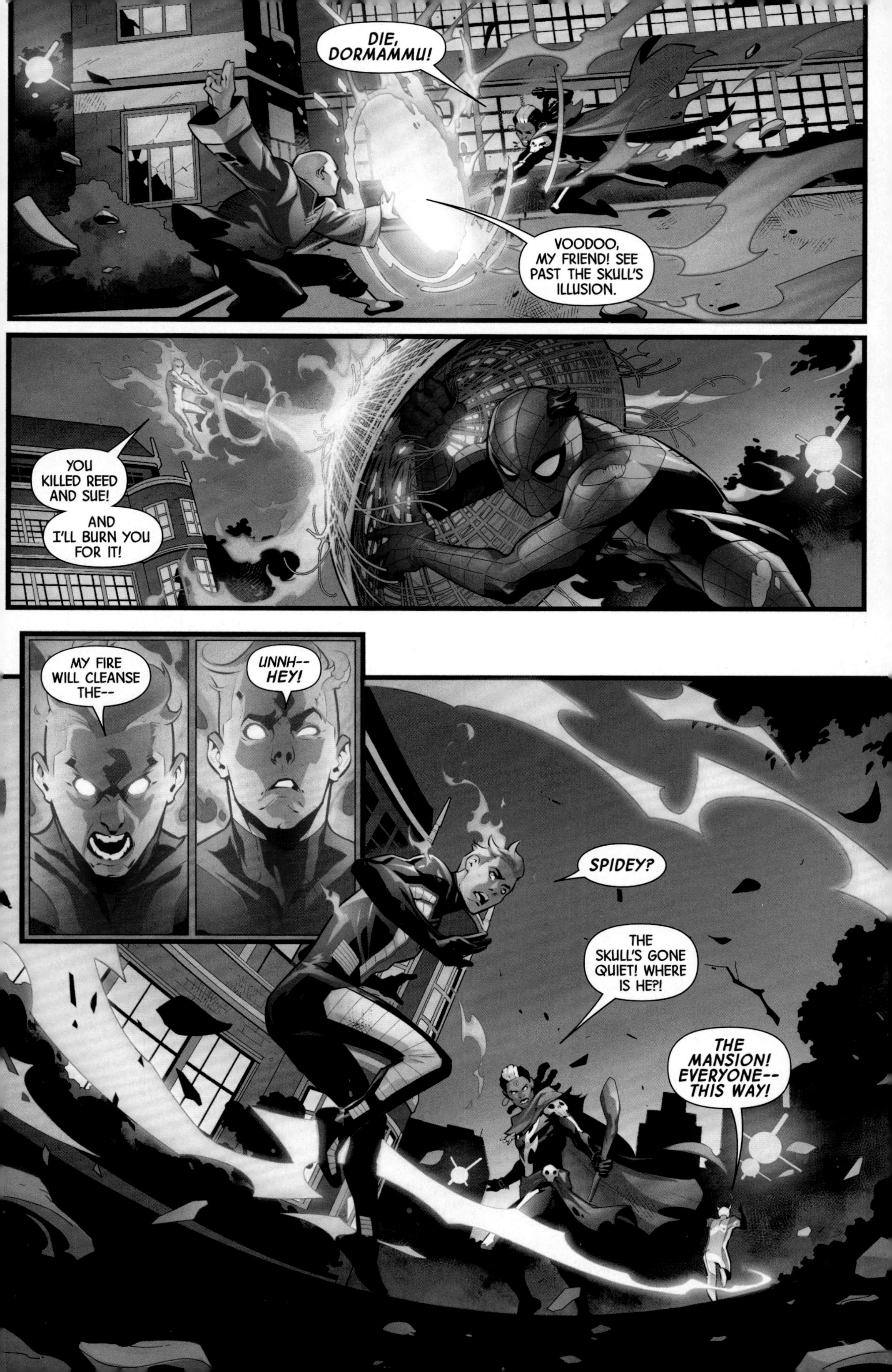
DIE, DORMAMMU!
VOODOO, MY FRIEND! SEE PAST THE SKULL'S ILLUSION.
YOU KILLED REED AND SUE!
AND I'LL BURN YOU FOR IT!
MY FIRE WILL CLEANSE THE--
UNNH-- HEY!
SPIDEY?
THE SKULL'S GONE QUIET! WHERE IS HE?!
THE MANSION! EVERYONE-- THIS WAY!

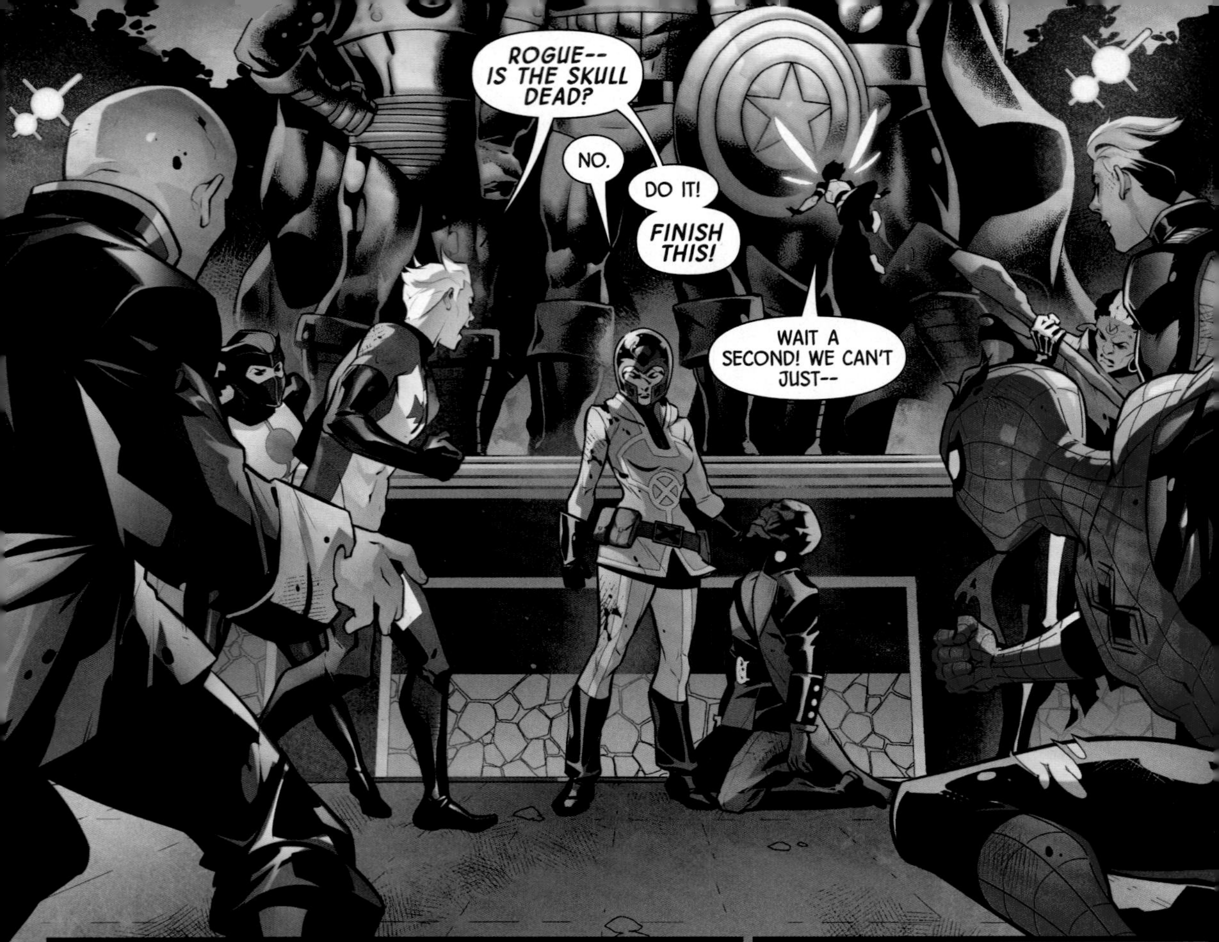
ROGUE-- IS THE SKULL DEAD?
NO.
DO IT!
FINISH THIS!
WAIT A SECOND! WE CAN'T JUST--

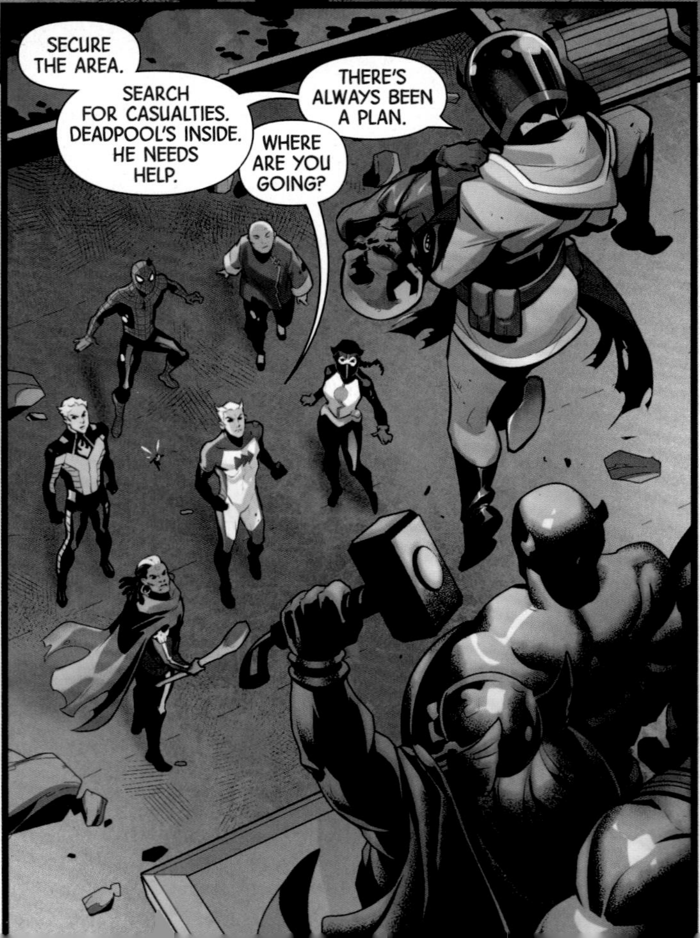
SECURE THE AREA.
SEARCH FOR CASUALTIES. DEADPOOL'S INSIDE. HE NEEDS HELP.
WHERE ARE YOU GOING?
THERE'S ALWAYS BEEN A PLAN.

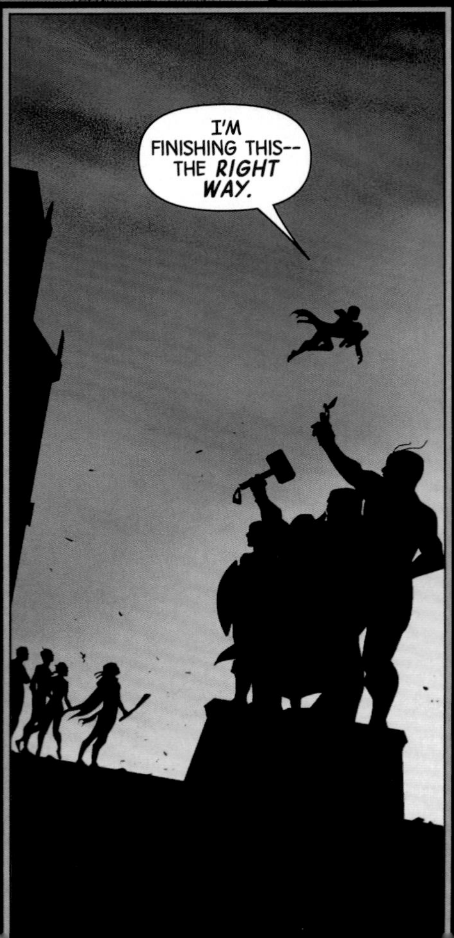
I'M FINISHING THIS-- THE RIGHT WAY.

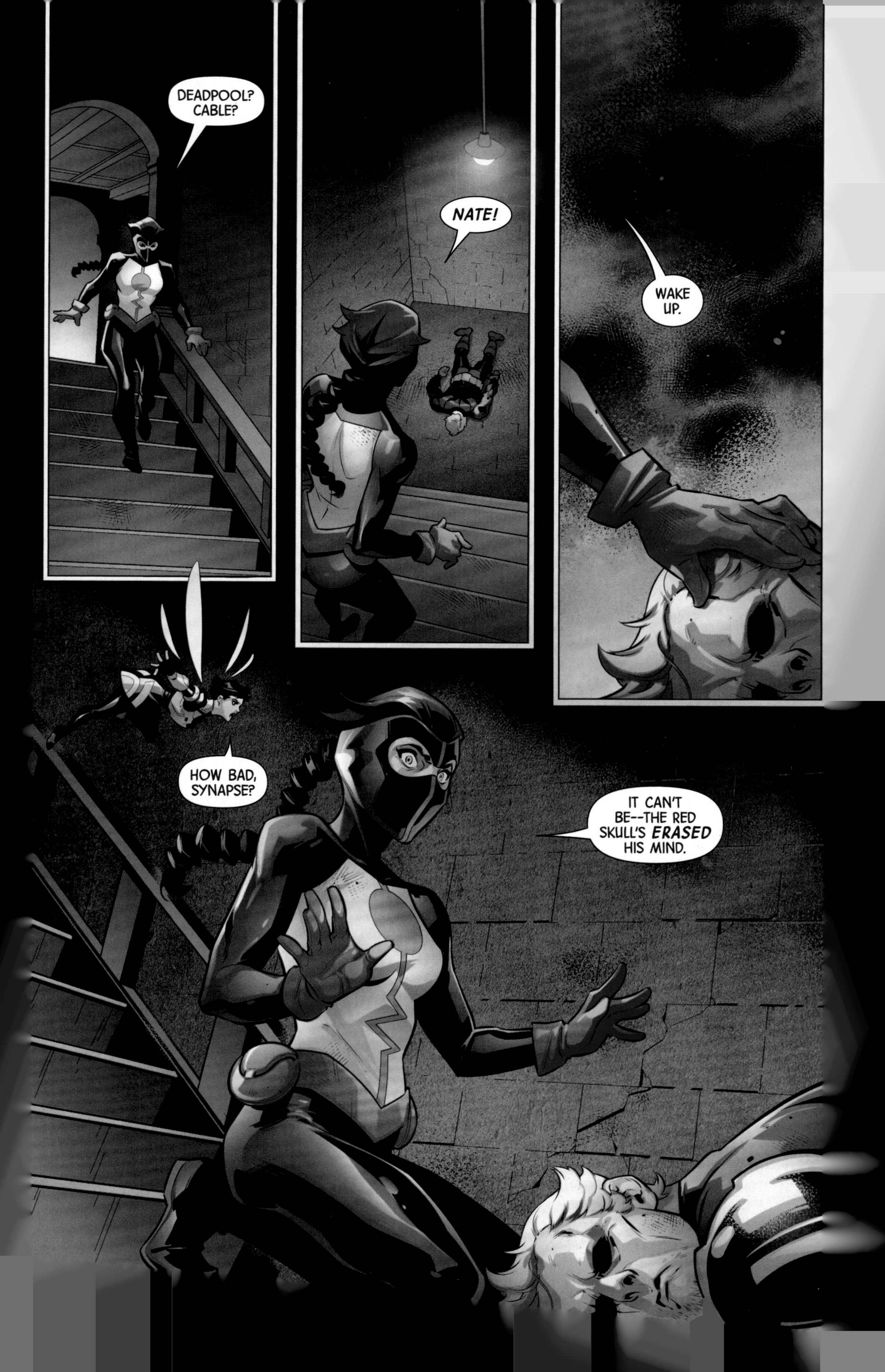
DEADPOOL? CABLE?
NATE!
WAKE UP.
HOW BAD, SYNAPSE?
IT CAN'T BE--THE RED SKULL'S ERASED HIS MIND.

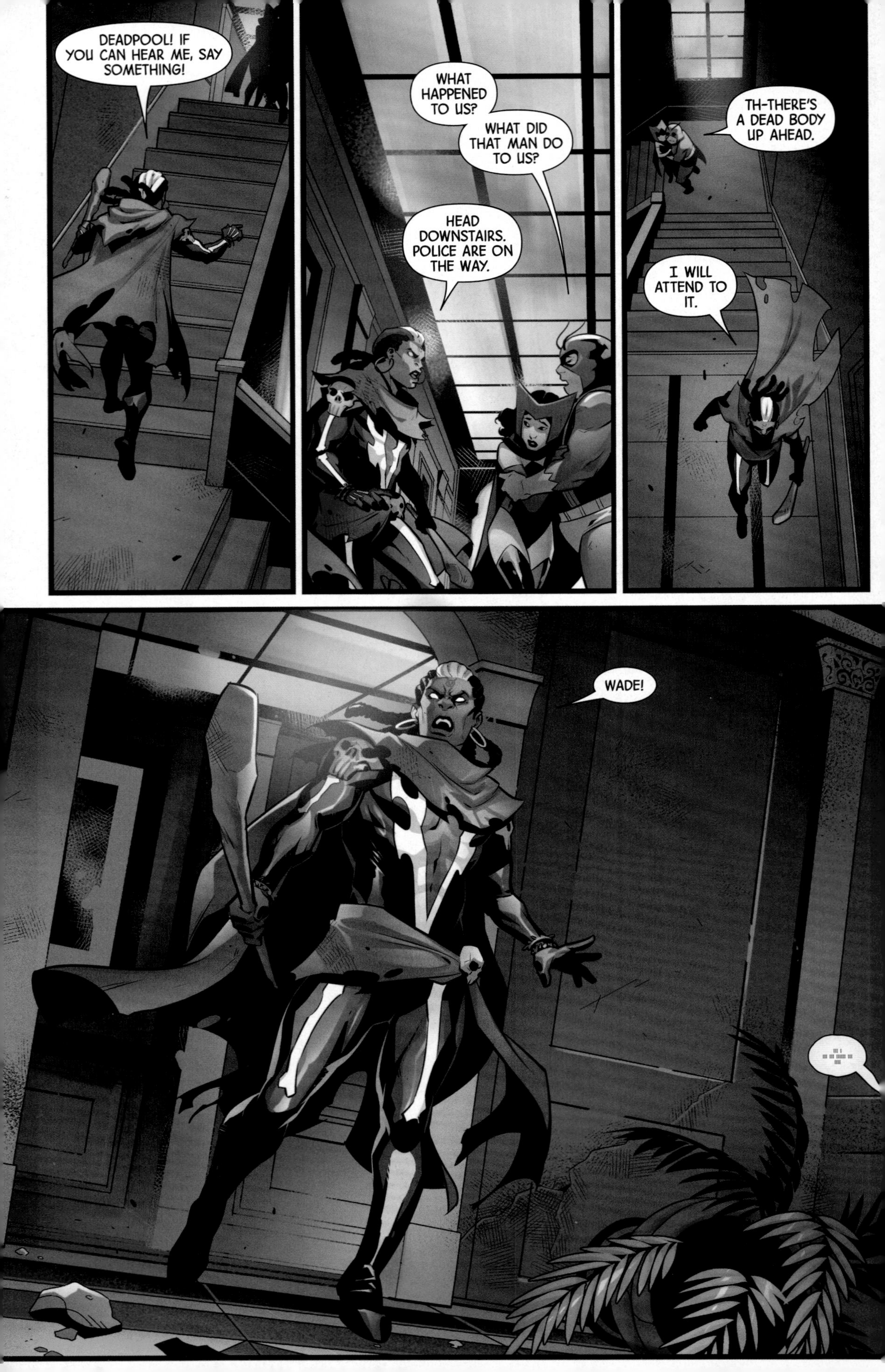
DEADPOOL! IF YOU CAN HEAR ME, SAY SOMETHING!
WHAT HAPPENED TO US?
WHAT DID THAT MAN DO TO US?
HEAD DOWNSTAIRS. POLICE ARE ON THE WAY.
TH-THERE'S A DEAD BODY UP AHEAD.
I WILL ATTEND TO IT.
WADE!

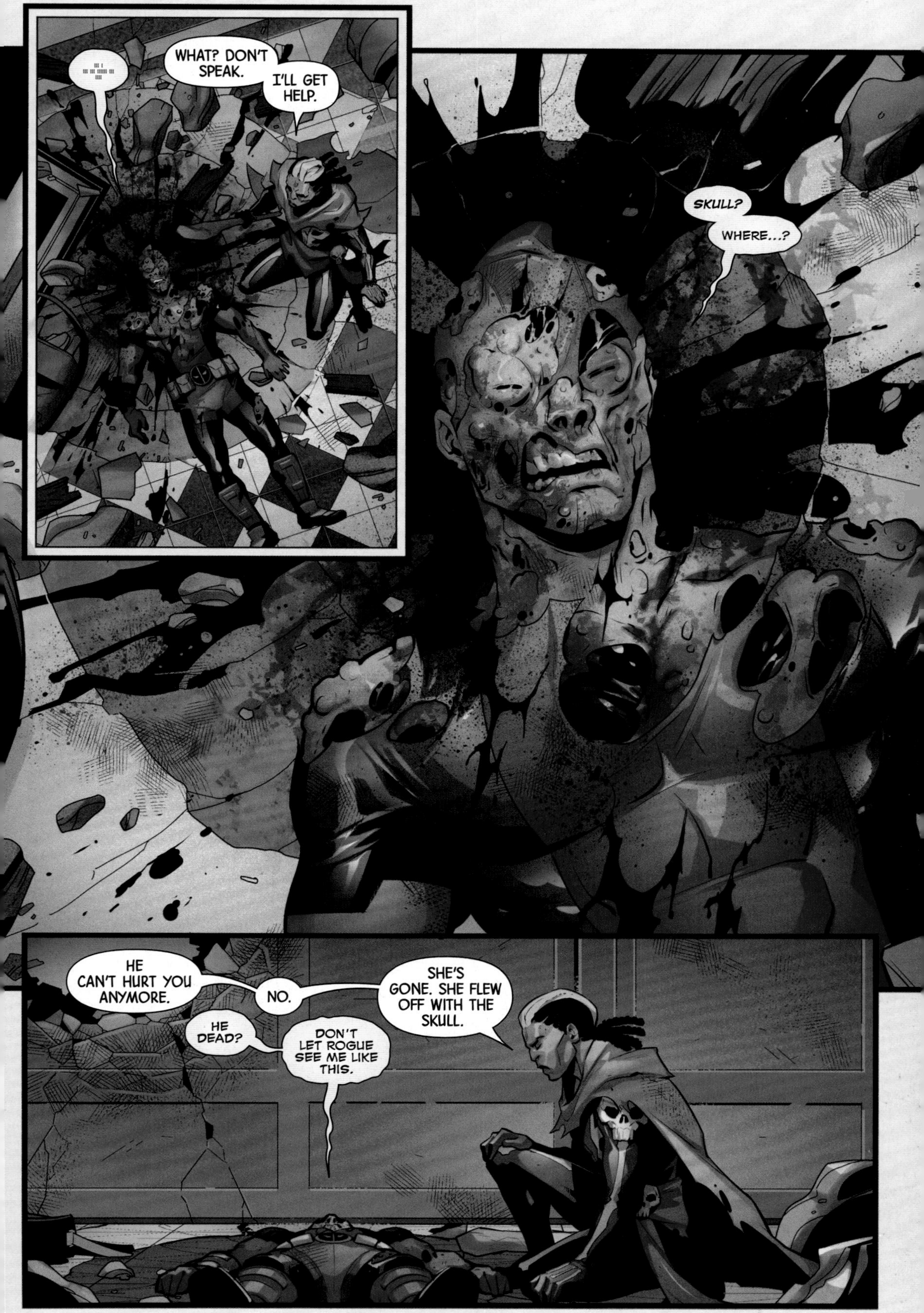

WHAT? DON'T SPEAK.
I'LL GET HELP.
SKULL?
WHERE...?
HE CAN'T HURT YOU ANYMORE.
NO.
SHE'S GONE. SHE FLEW OFF WITH THE SKULL.
HE DEAD?
DON'T LET ROGUE SEE ME LIKE THIS.

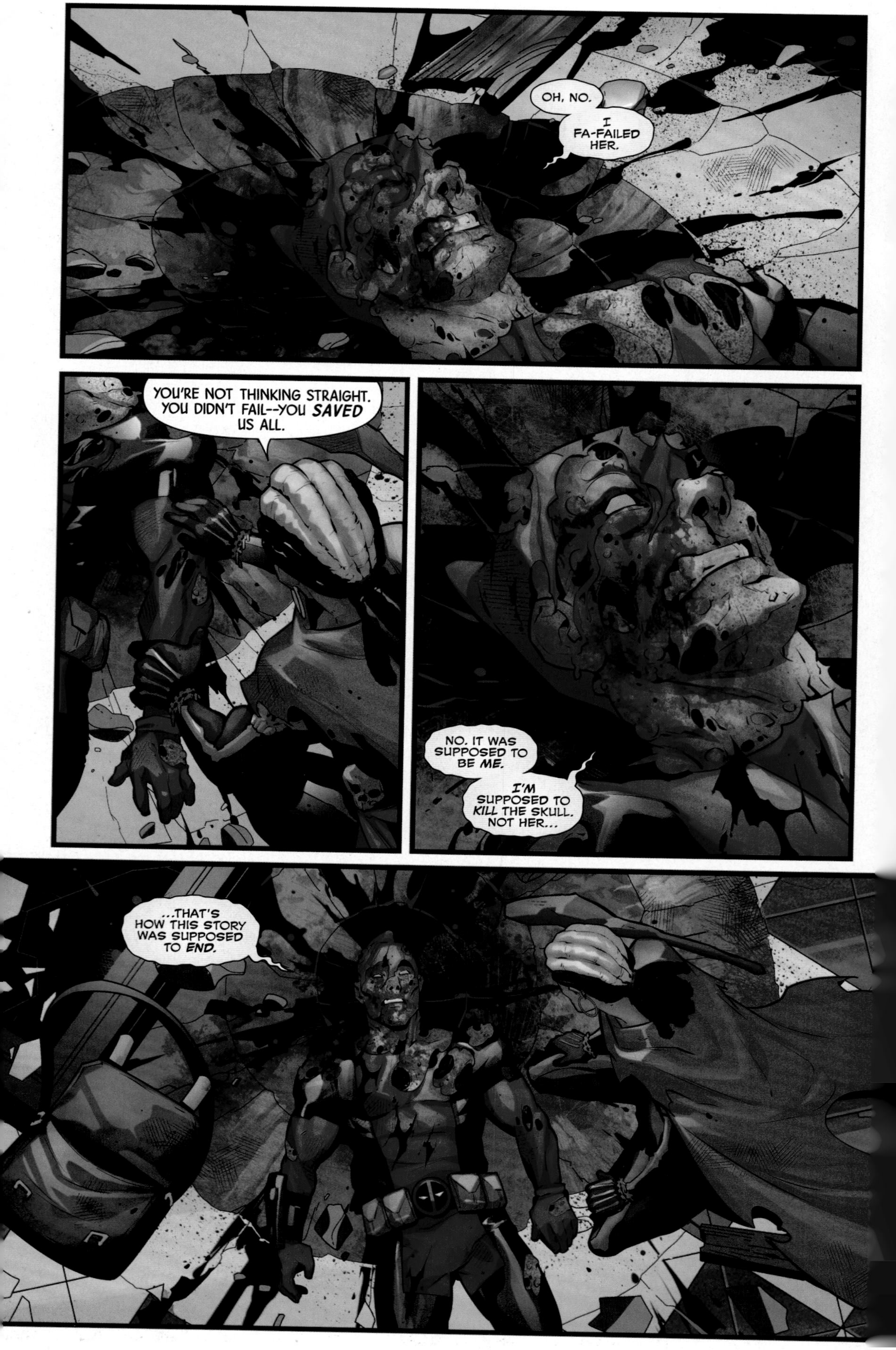
OH, NO.
I FA-FAILED HER.
YOU'RE NOT THINKING STRAIGHT. YOU DIDN'T FAIL--YOU **SAVED** US ALL.
NO. IT WAS SUPPOSED TO BE *ME.*
I'M SUPPOSED TO *KILL* THE SKULL, NOT HER...
...THAT'S HOW THIS STORY WAS SUPPOSED TO *END.*

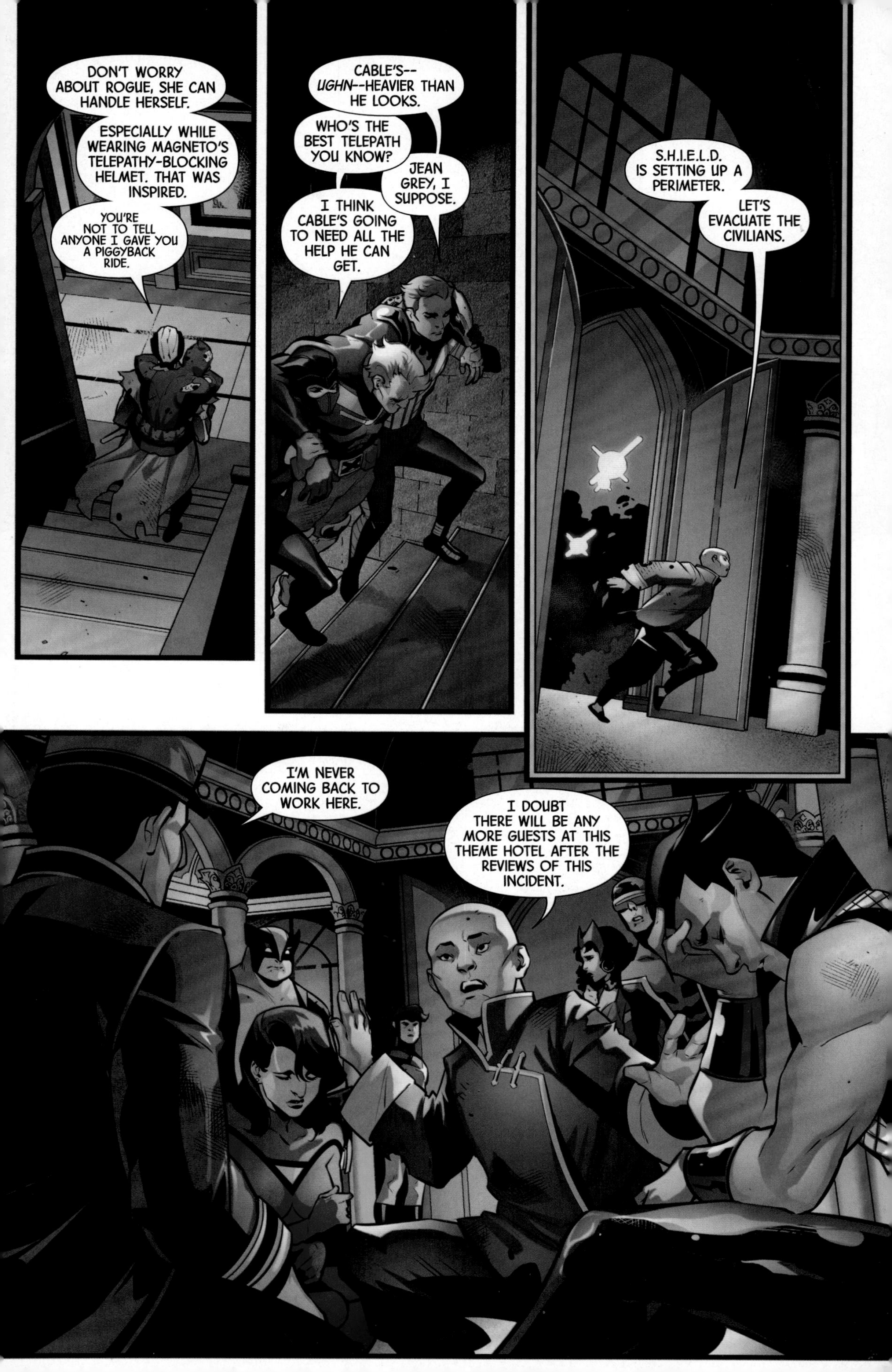

DON'T WORRY ABOUT ROGUE, SHE CAN HANDLE HERSELF.
ESPECIALLY WHILE WEARING MAGNETO'S TELEPATHY-BLOCKING HELMET. THAT WAS INSPIRED.
YOU'RE NOT TO TELL ANYONE I GAVE YOU A PIGGYBACK RIDE.
CABLE'S-- *UGHN*--HEAVIER THAN HE LOOKS.
WHO'S THE BEST TELEPATH YOU KNOW?
JEAN GREY, I SUPPOSE.
I THINK CABLE'S GOING TO NEED ALL THE HELP HE CAN GET.
S.H.I.E.L.D. IS SETTING UP A PERIMETER.
LET'S EVACUATE THE CIVILIANS.
I'M NEVER COMING BACK TO WORK HERE.
I DOUBT THERE WILL BE ANY MORE GUESTS AT THIS THEME HOTEL AFTER THE REVIEWS OF THIS INCIDENT.

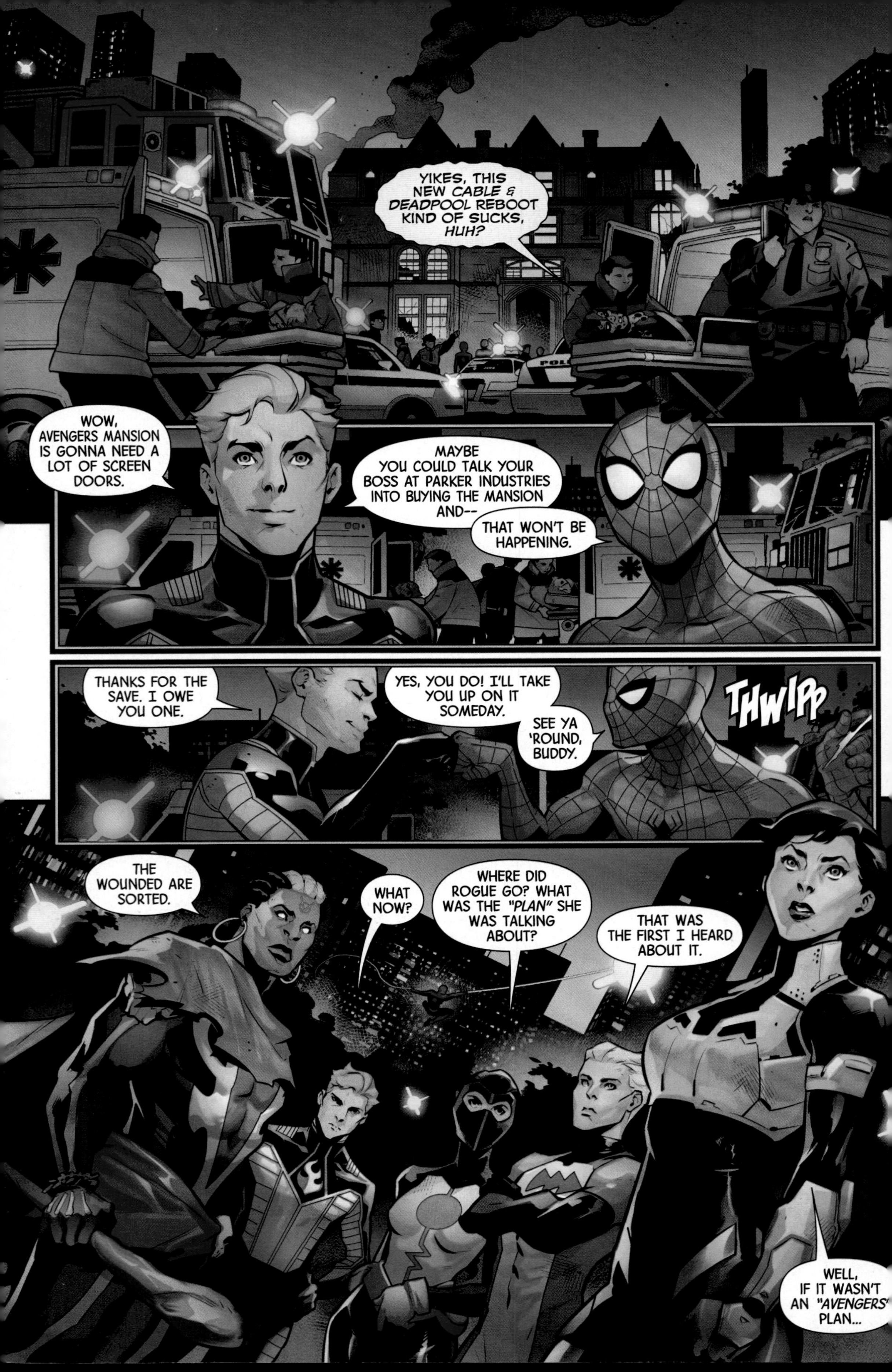
YIKES, THIS NEW CABLE & DEADPOOL REBOOT KIND OF SUCKS, HUH?
WOW, AVENGERS MANSION IS GONNA NEED A LOT OF SCREEN DOORS.
MAYBE YOU COULD TALK YOUR BOSS AT PARKER INDUSTRIES INTO BUYING THE MANSION AND--
THAT WON'T BE HAPPENING.
THANKS FOR THE SAVE. I OWE YOU ONE.
YES, YOU DO! I'LL TAKE YOU UP ON IT SOMEDAY.
SEE YA 'ROUND, BUDDY.
THWIPP
THE WOUNDED ARE SORTED.
WHAT NOW?
WHERE DID ROGUE GO? WHAT WAS THE "PLAN" SHE WAS TALKING ABOUT?
THAT WAS THE FIRST I HEARD ABOUT IT.
WELL, IF IT WASN'T AN "AVENGERS" PLAN...

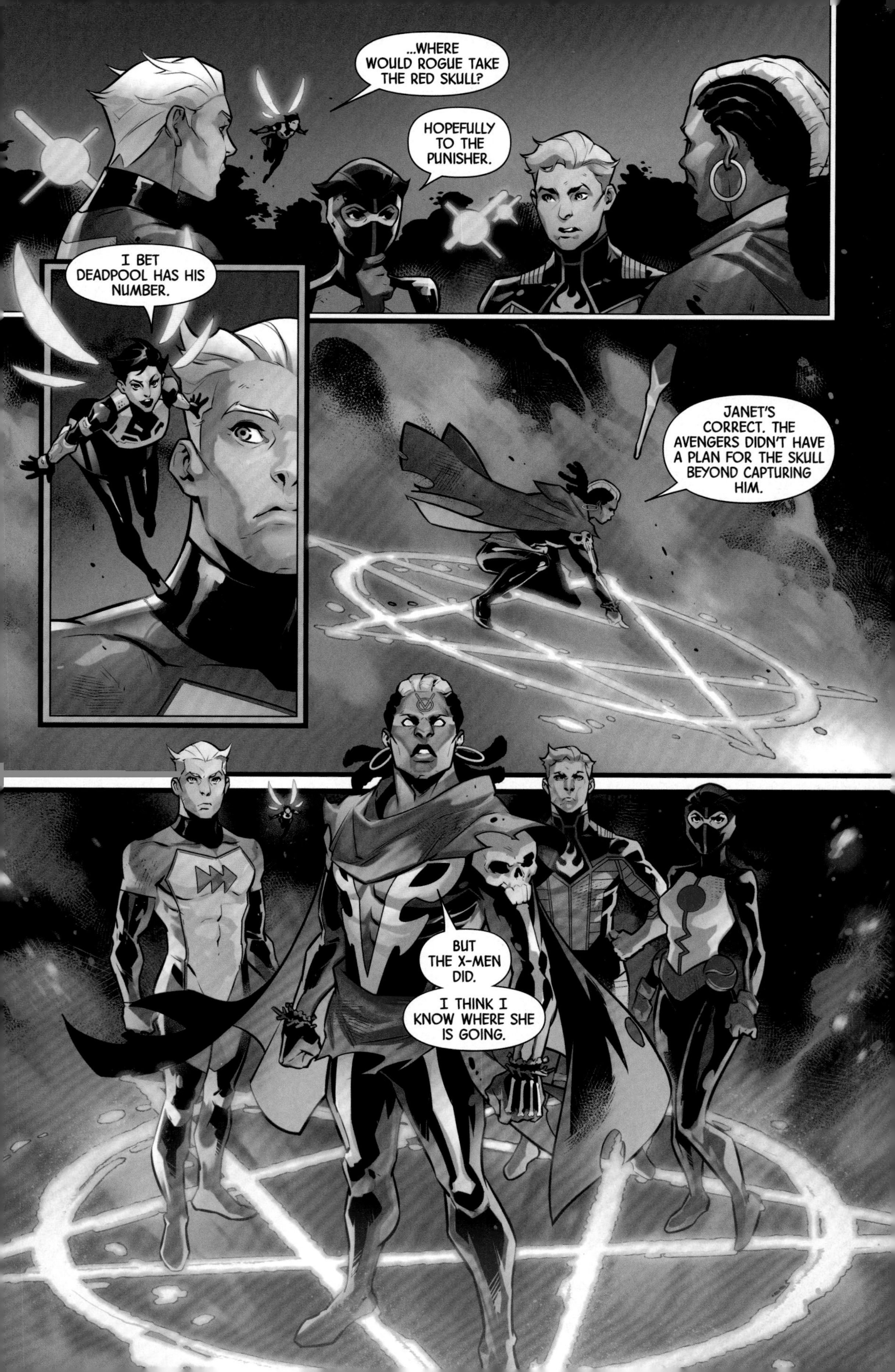
...WHERE WOULD ROGUE TAKE THE RED SKULL?
HOPEFULLY TO THE PUNISHER.
I BET DEADPOOL HAS HIS NUMBER.
JANET'S CORRECT. THE AVENGERS DIDN'T HAVE A PLAN FOR THE SKULL BEYOND CAPTURING HIM.
BUT THE X-MEN DID.
I THINK I KNOW WHERE SHE IS GOING.

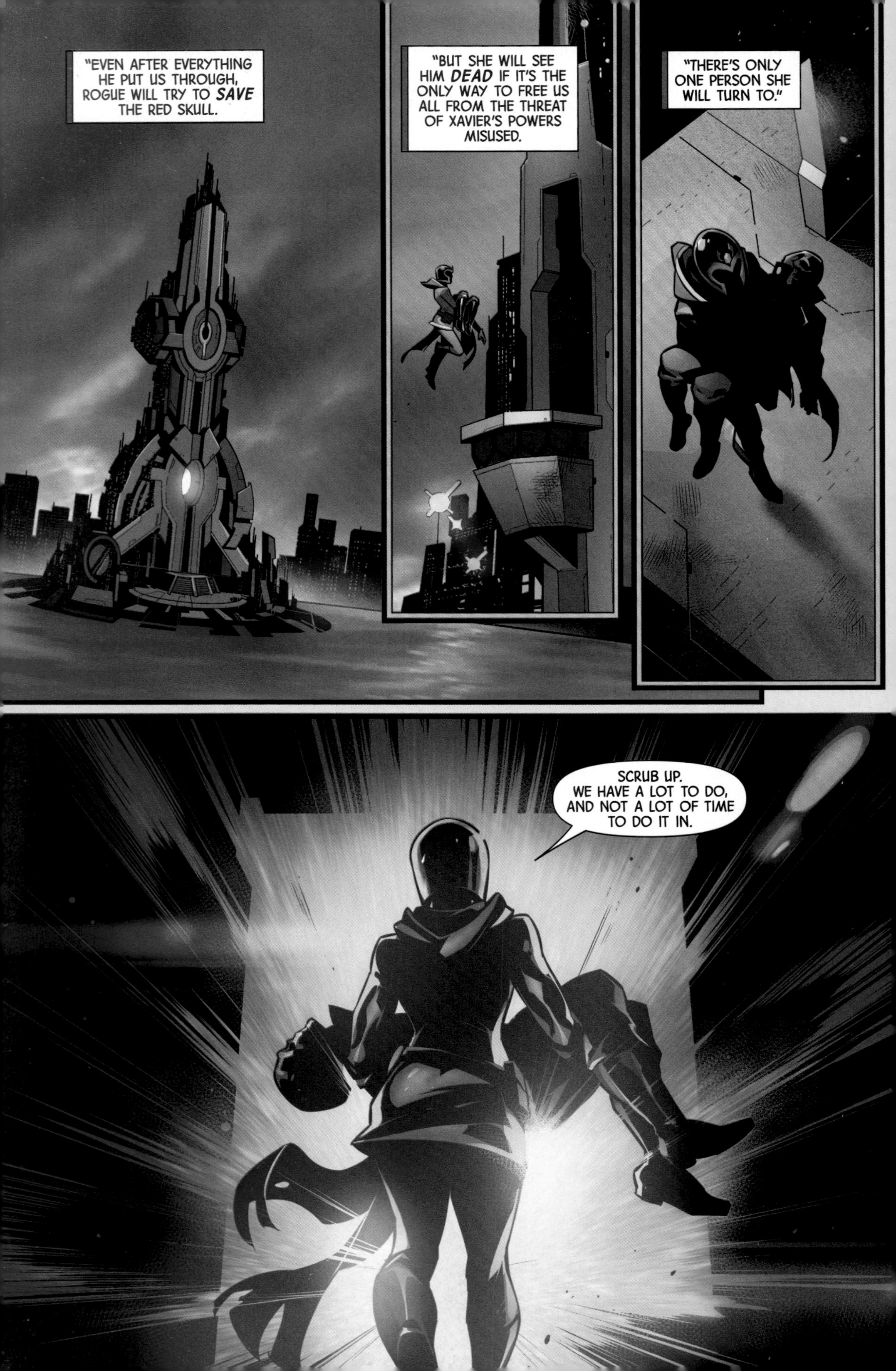
"EVEN AFTER EVERYTHING HE PUT US THROUGH, ROGUE WILL TRY TO SAVE THE RED SKULL.
"BUT SHE WILL SEE HIM DEAD IF IT'S THE ONLY WAY TO FREE US ALL FROM THE THREAT OF XAVIER'S POWERS MISUSED.
"THERE'S ONLY ONE PERSON SHE WILL TURN TO."
SCRUB UP. WE HAVE A LOT TO DO, AND NOT A LOT OF TIME TO DO IT IN.

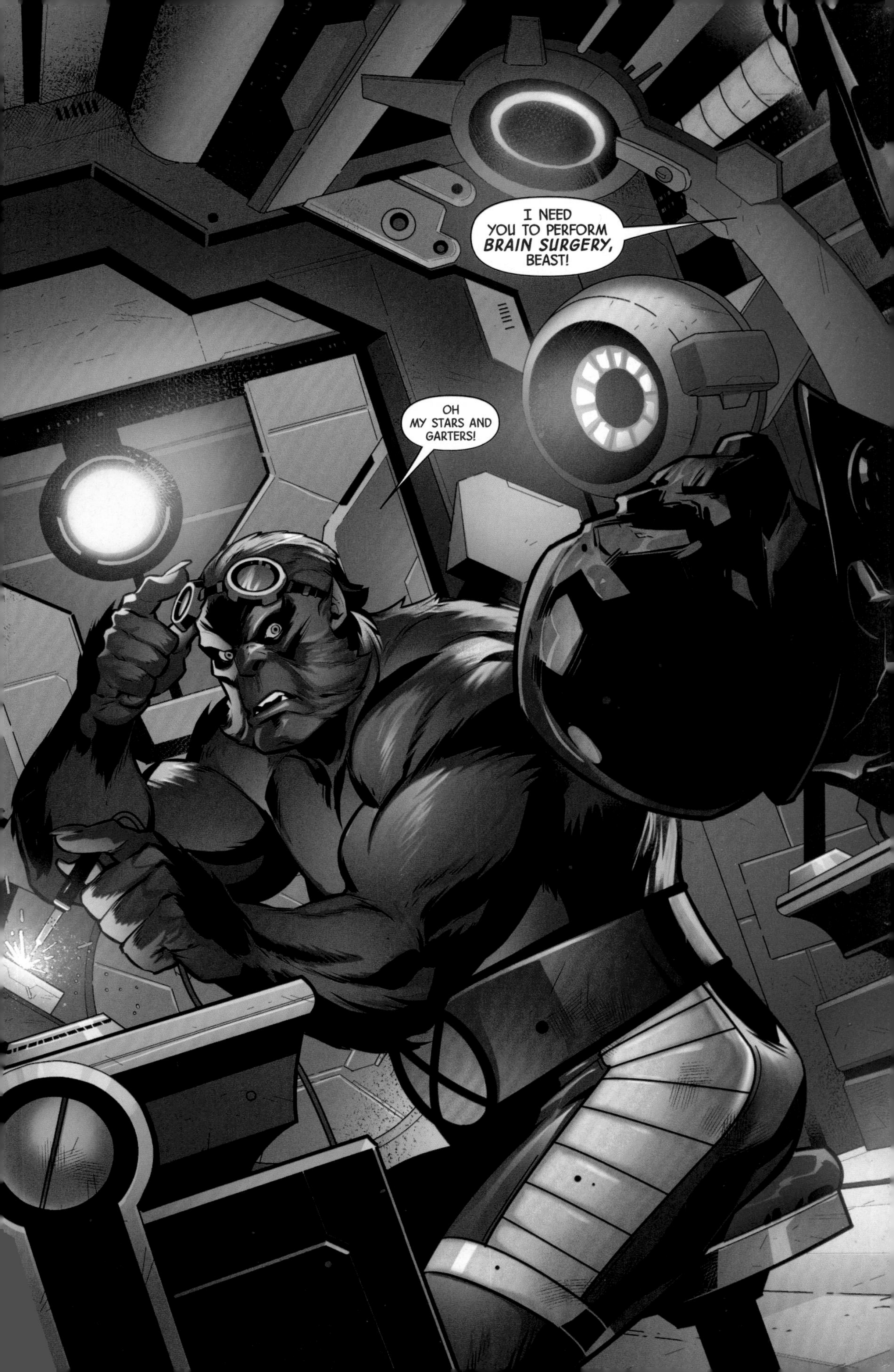
I NEED YOU TO PERFORM BRAIN SURGERY, BEAST!
OH MY STARS AND GARTERS!

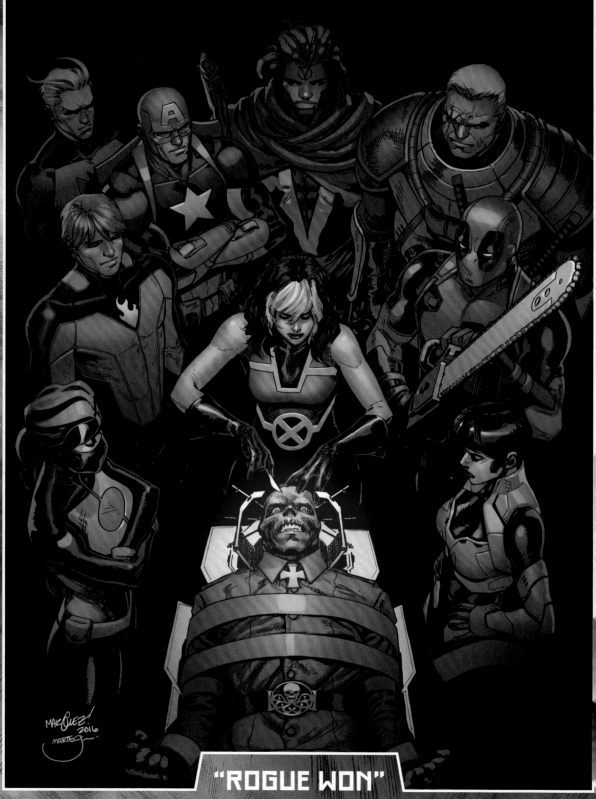

"ROGUE WON"

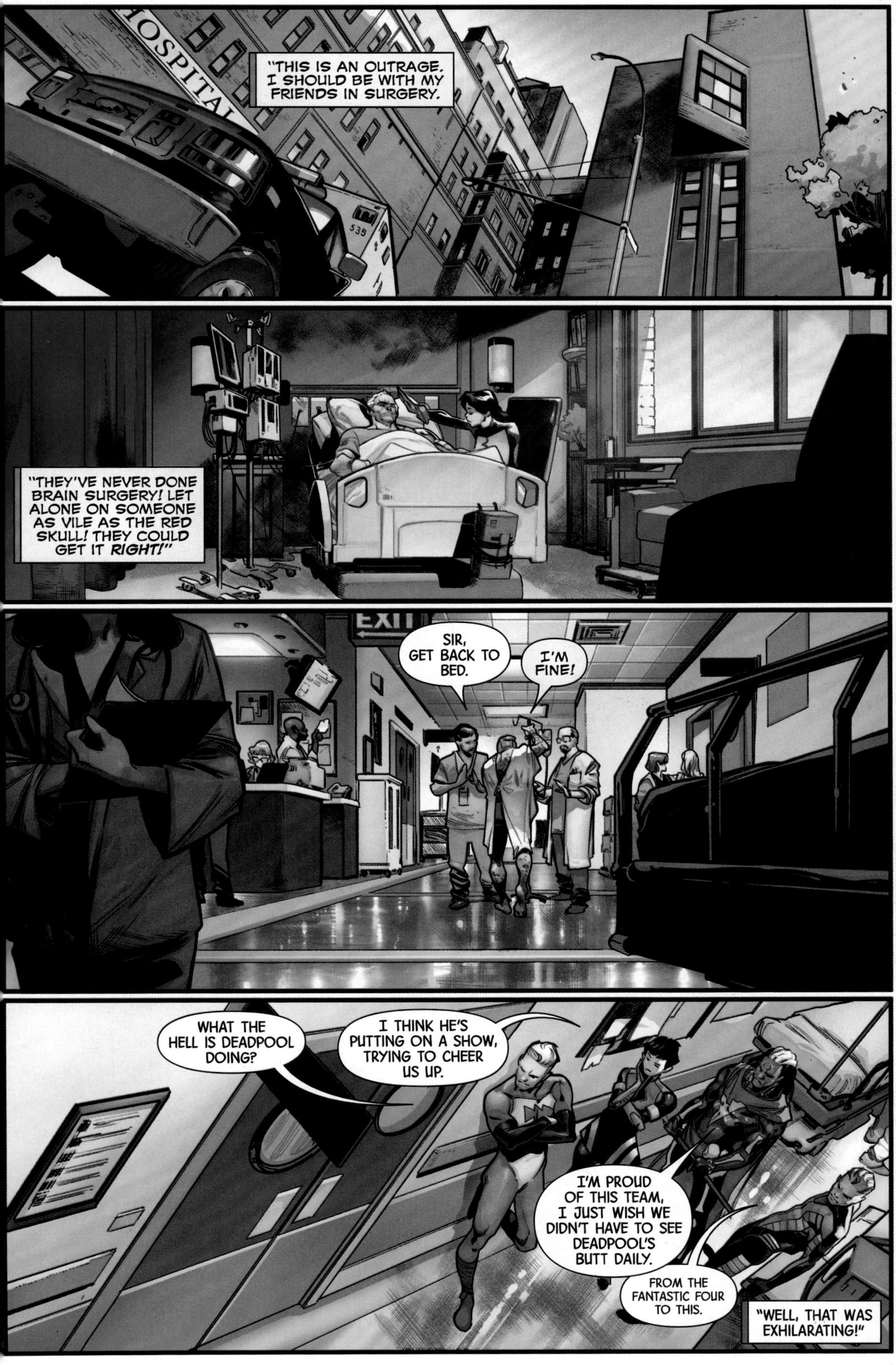
HOSPITAL
"THIS IS AN OUTRAGE. I SHOULD BE WITH MY FRIENDS IN SURGERY.
"THEY'VE NEVER DONE BRAIN SURGERY! LET ALONE ON SOMEONE AS VILE AS THE RED SKULL! THEY COULD GET IT RIGHT!"
EXIT
SIR, GET BACK TO BED.
I'M FINE!
WHAT THE HELL IS DEADPOOL DOING?
I THINK HE'S PUTTING ON A SHOW, TRYING TO CHEER US UP.
I'M PROUD OF THIS TEAM, I JUST WISH WE DIDN'T HAVE TO SEE DEADPOOL'S BUTT DAILY.
FROM THE FANTASTIC FOUR TO THIS.
"WELL, THAT WAS EXHILARATING!"

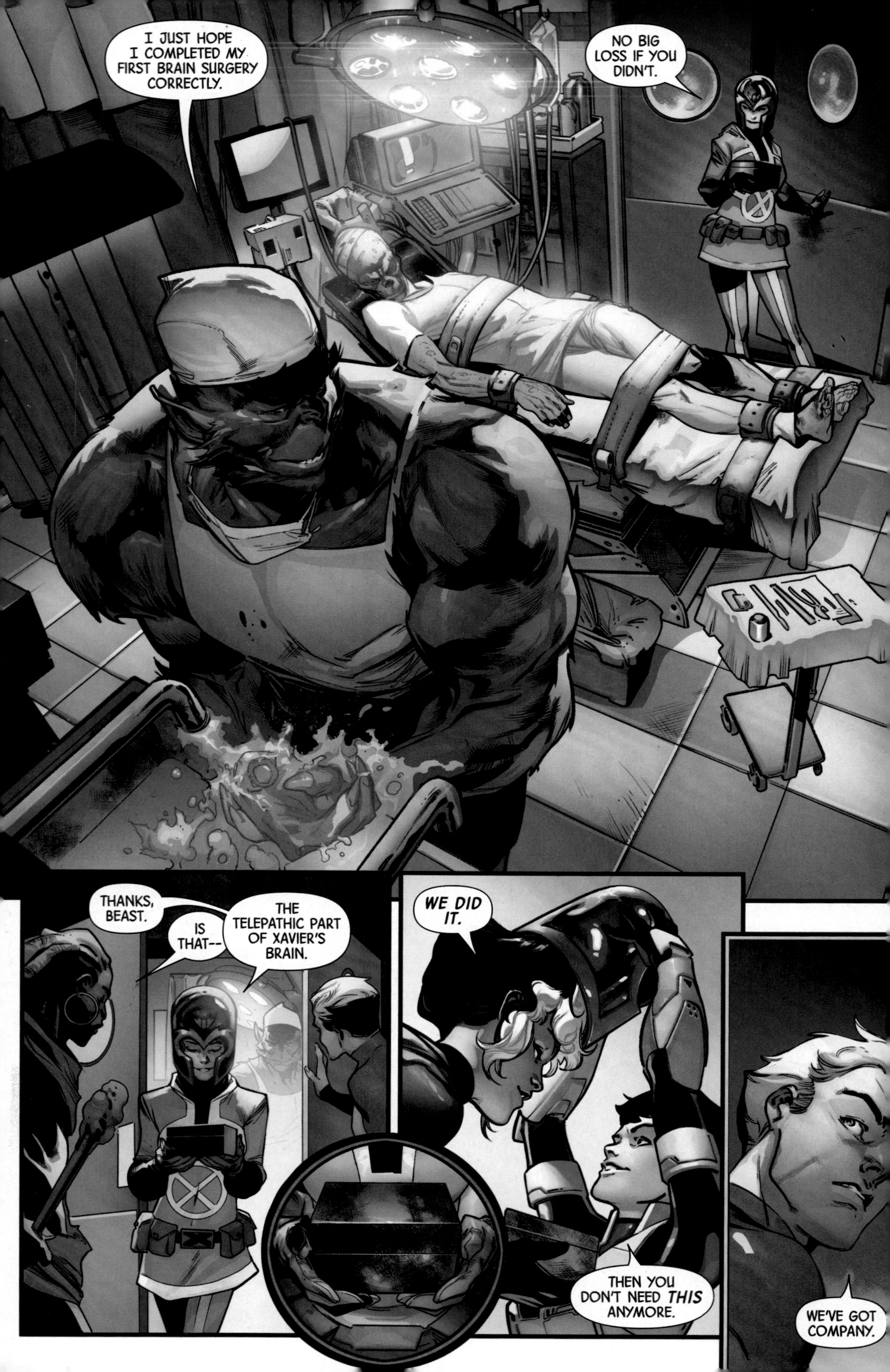
I JUST HOPE I COMPLETED MY FIRST BRAIN SURGERY CORRECTLY.
NO BIG LOSS IF YOU DIDN'T.
THANKS, BEAST.
IS THAT--
THE TELEPATHIC PART OF XAVIER'S BRAIN.
WE DID IT.
THEN YOU DON'T NEED THIS ANYMORE.
WE'VE GOT COMPANY.

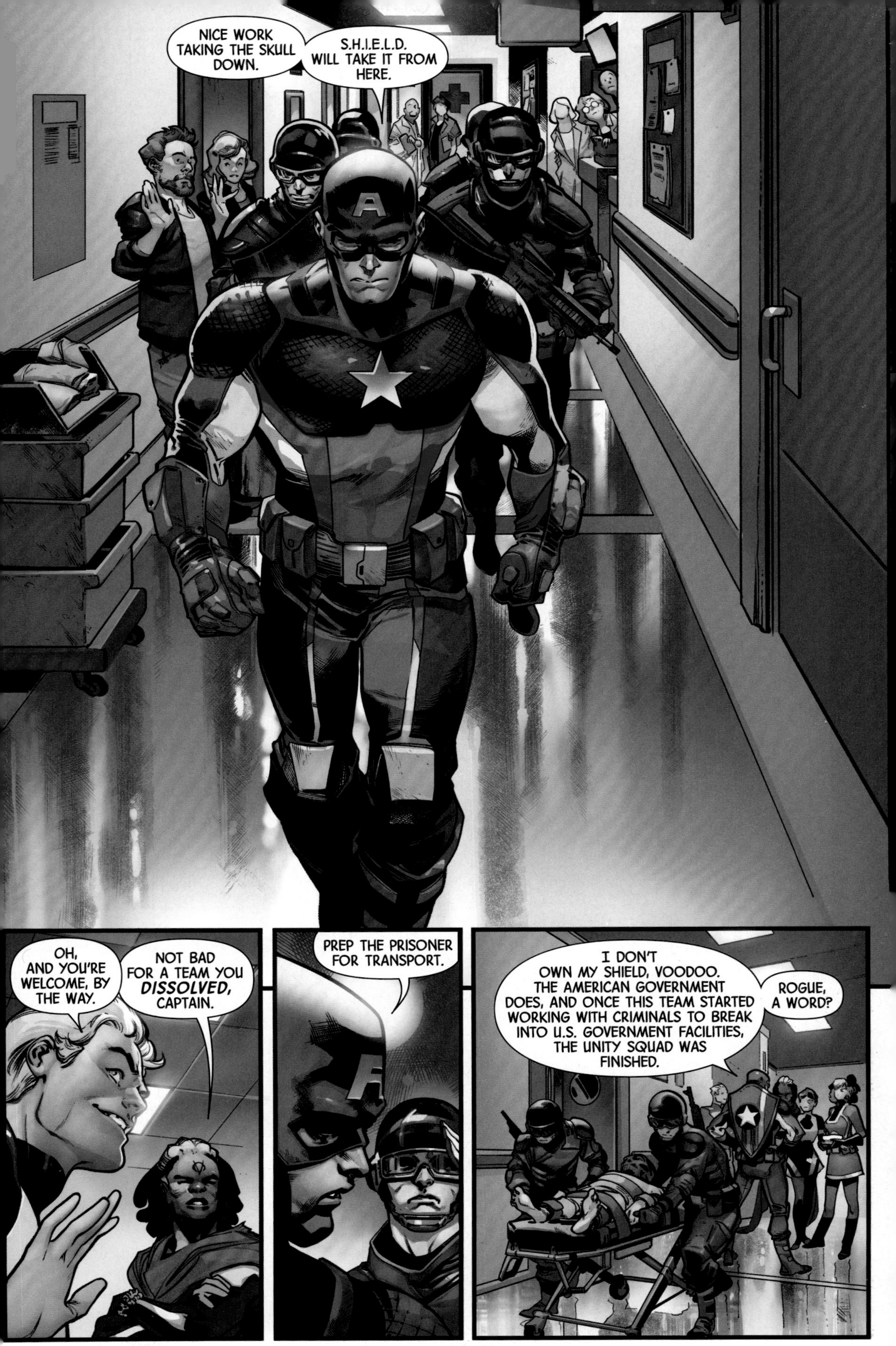
NICE WORK TAKING THE SKULL DOWN.
S.H.I.E.L.D. WILL TAKE IT FROM HERE.
OH, AND YOU'RE WELCOME, BY THE WAY.
NOT BAD FOR A TEAM YOU *DISSOLVED*, CAPTAIN.
PREP THE PRISONER FOR TRANSPORT.
I DON'T OWN MY SHIELD, VOODOO. THE AMERICAN GOVERNMENT DOES, AND ONCE THIS TEAM STARTED WORKING WITH CRIMINALS TO BREAK INTO U.S. GOVERNMENT FACILITIES, THE UNITY SQUAD WAS FINISHED.
ROGUE, A WORD?

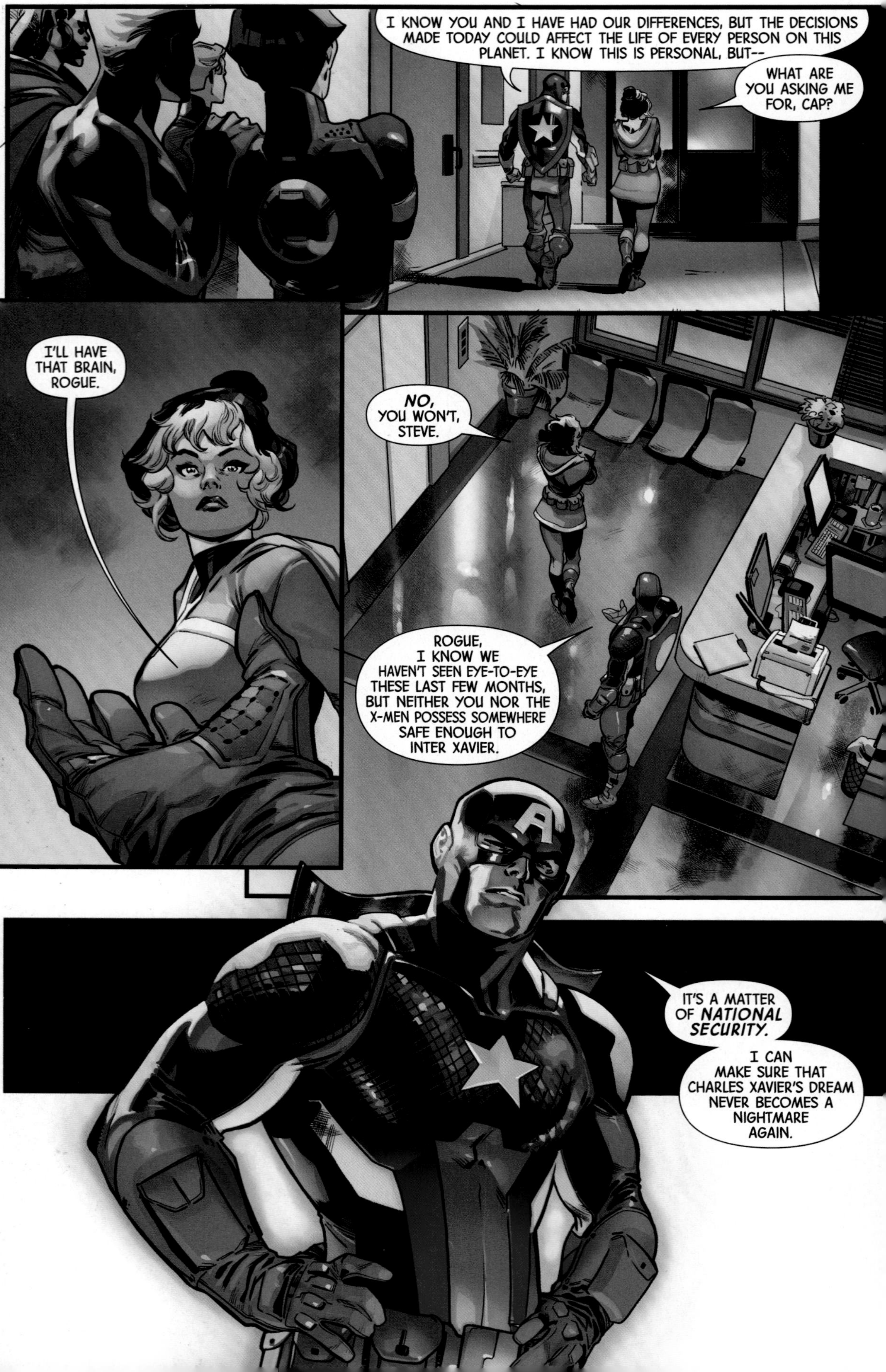
I KNOW YOU AND I HAVE HAD OUR DIFFERENCES, BUT THE DECISIONS MADE TODAY COULD AFFECT THE LIFE OF EVERY PERSON ON THIS PLANET. I KNOW THIS IS PERSONAL, BUT--
WHAT ARE YOU ASKING ME FOR, CAP?
I'LL HAVE THAT BRAIN, ROGUE.
NO, YOU WON'T, STEVE.
ROGUE, I KNOW WE HAVEN'T SEEN EYE-TO-EYE THESE LAST FEW MONTHS, BUT NEITHER YOU NOR THE X-MEN POSSESS SOMEWHERE SAFE ENOUGH TO INTER XAVIER.
IT'S A MATTER OF NATIONAL SECURITY.
I CAN MAKE SURE THAT CHARLES XAVIER'S DREAM NEVER BECOMES A NIGHTMARE AGAIN.

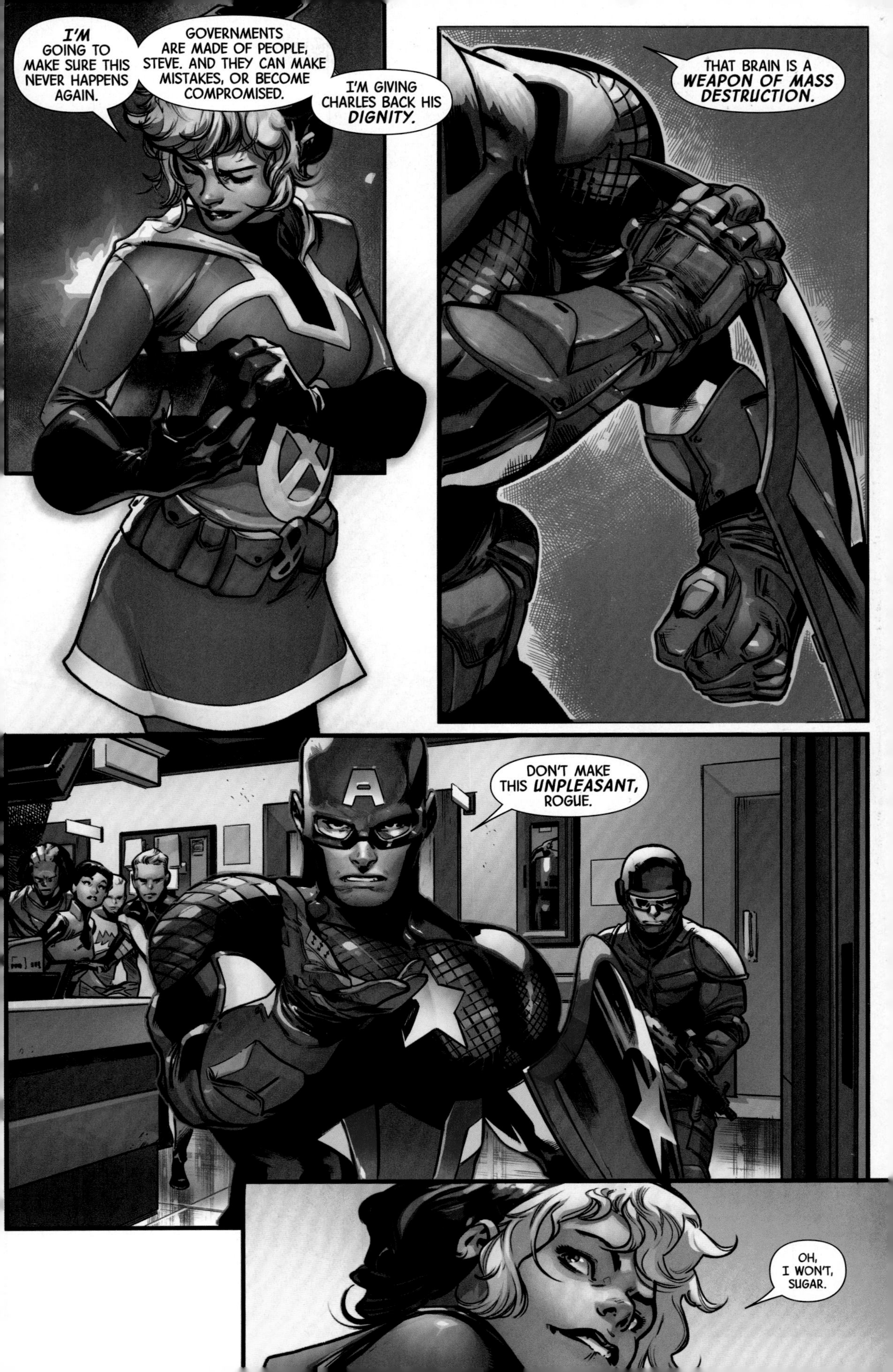
I'M GOING TO MAKE SURE THIS NEVER HAPPENS AGAIN.
GOVERNMENTS ARE MADE OF PEOPLE, STEVE. AND THEY CAN MAKE MISTAKES, OR BECOME COMPROMISED.
I'M GIVING CHARLES BACK HIS DIGNITY.
THAT BRAIN IS A WEAPON OF MASS DESTRUCTION.
DON'T MAKE THIS UNPLEASANT, ROGUE.
OH, I WON'T, SUGAR.

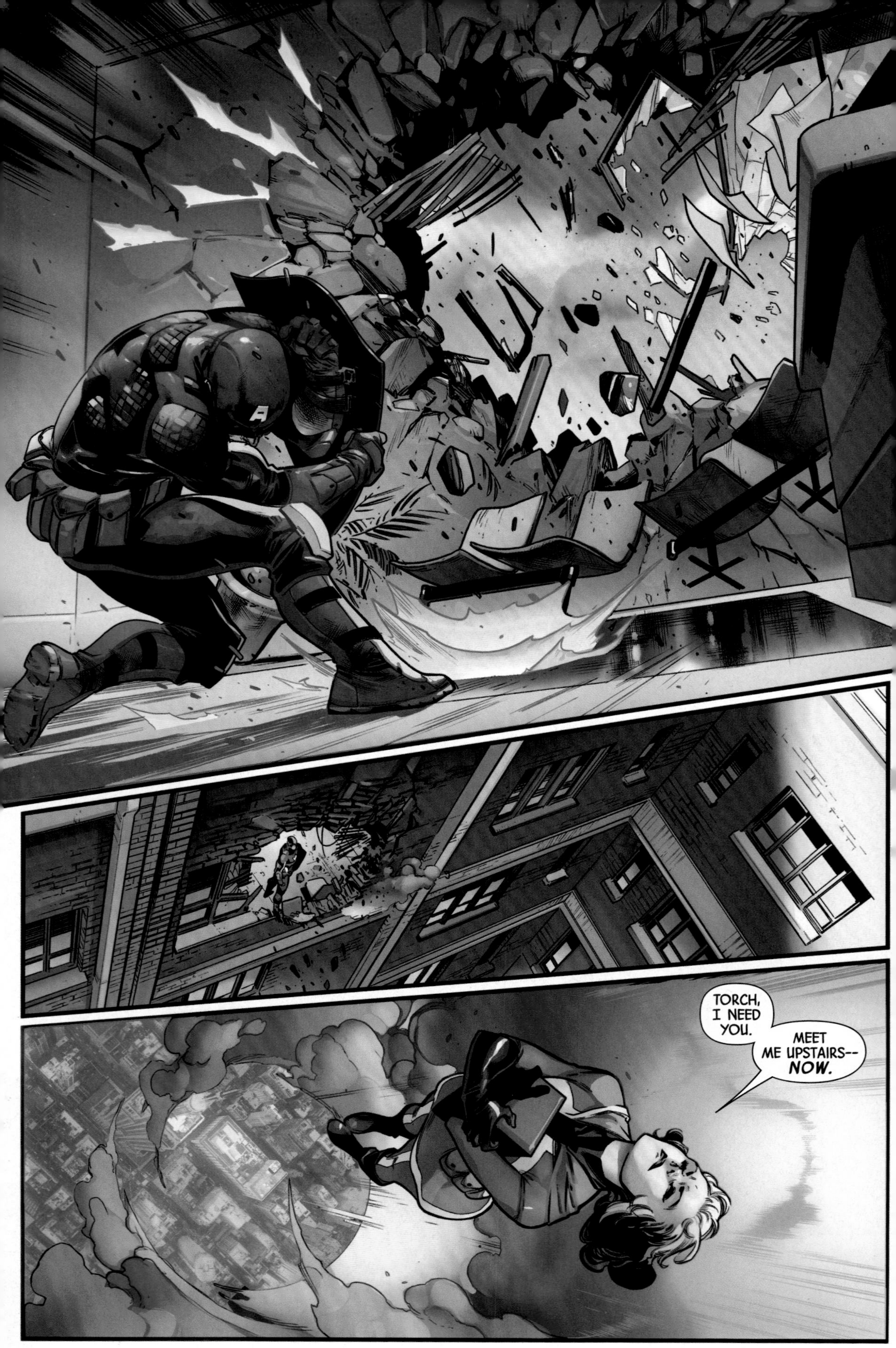
TORCH, I NEED YOU.
MEET ME UPSTAIRS-- NOW.

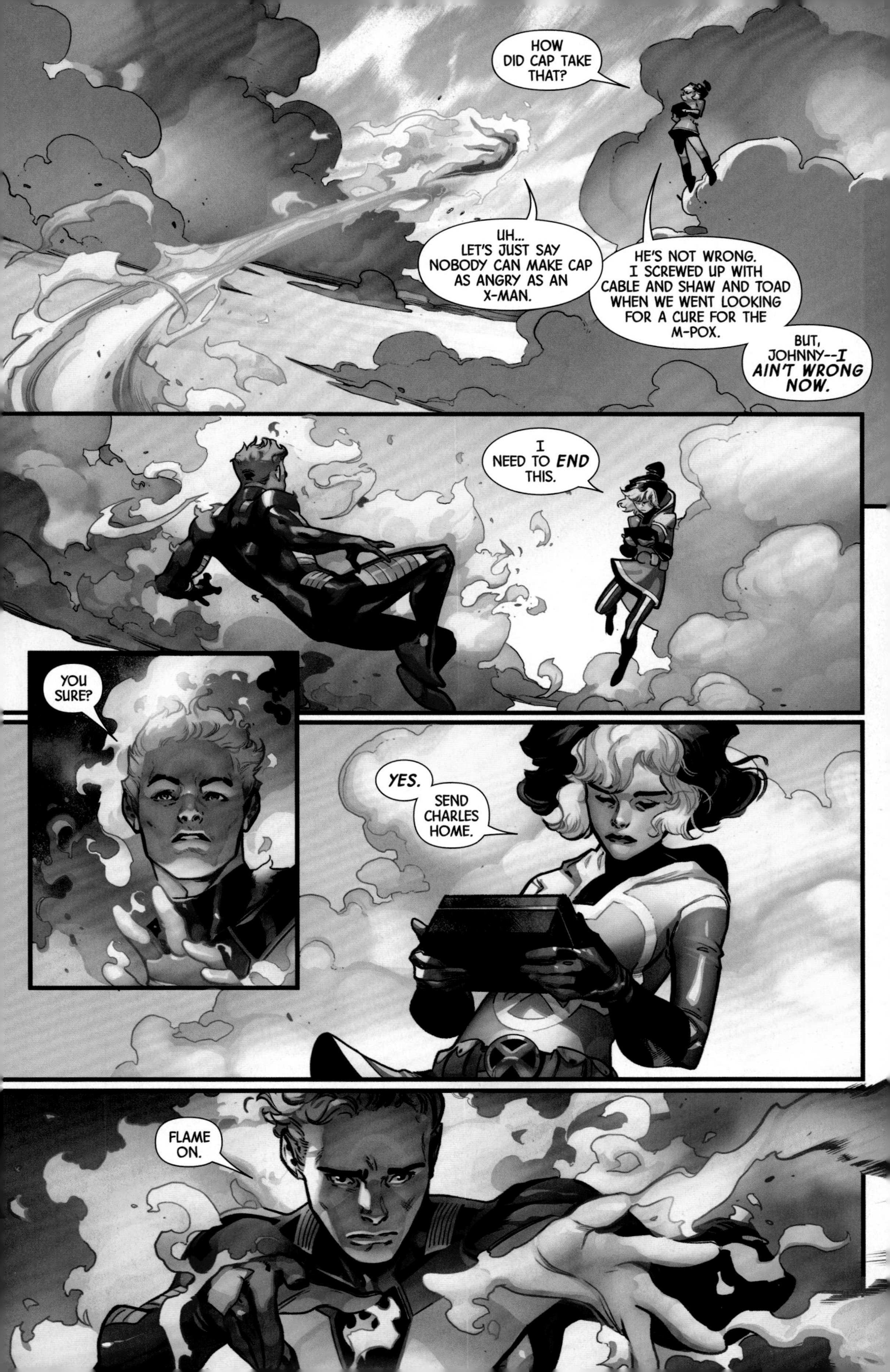
HOW DID CAP TAKE THAT?
UH... LET'S JUST SAY NOBODY CAN MAKE CAP AS ANGRY AS AN X-MAN.
HE'S NOT WRONG. I SCREWED UP WITH CABLE AND SHAW AND TOAD WHEN WE WENT LOOKING FOR A CURE FOR THE M-POX.
BUT, JOHNNY--I AIN'T WRONG NOW.
I NEED TO END THIS.
YOU SURE?
YES.
SEND CHARLES HOME.
FLAME ON.

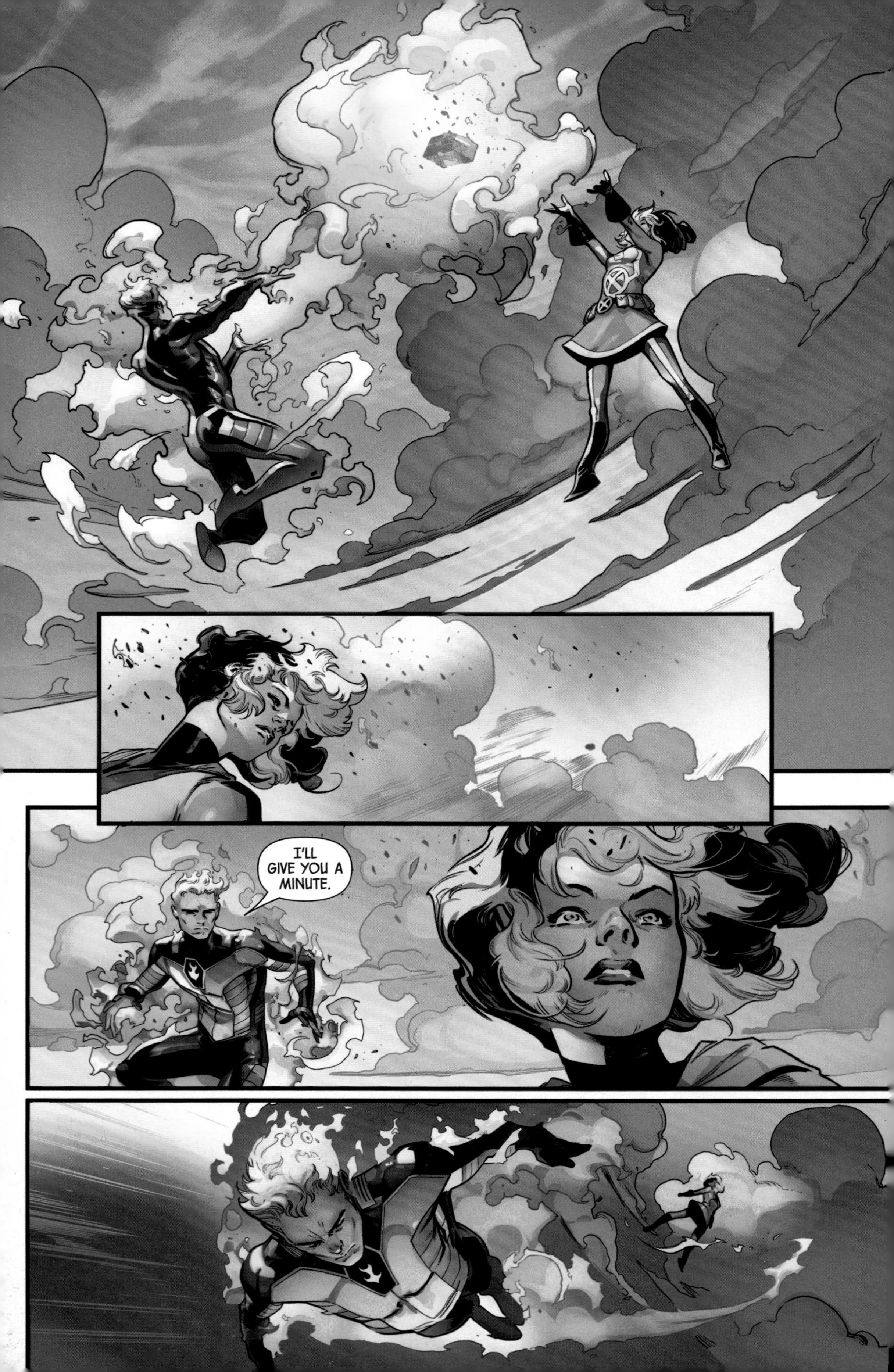
I'LL GIVE YOU A MINUTE.

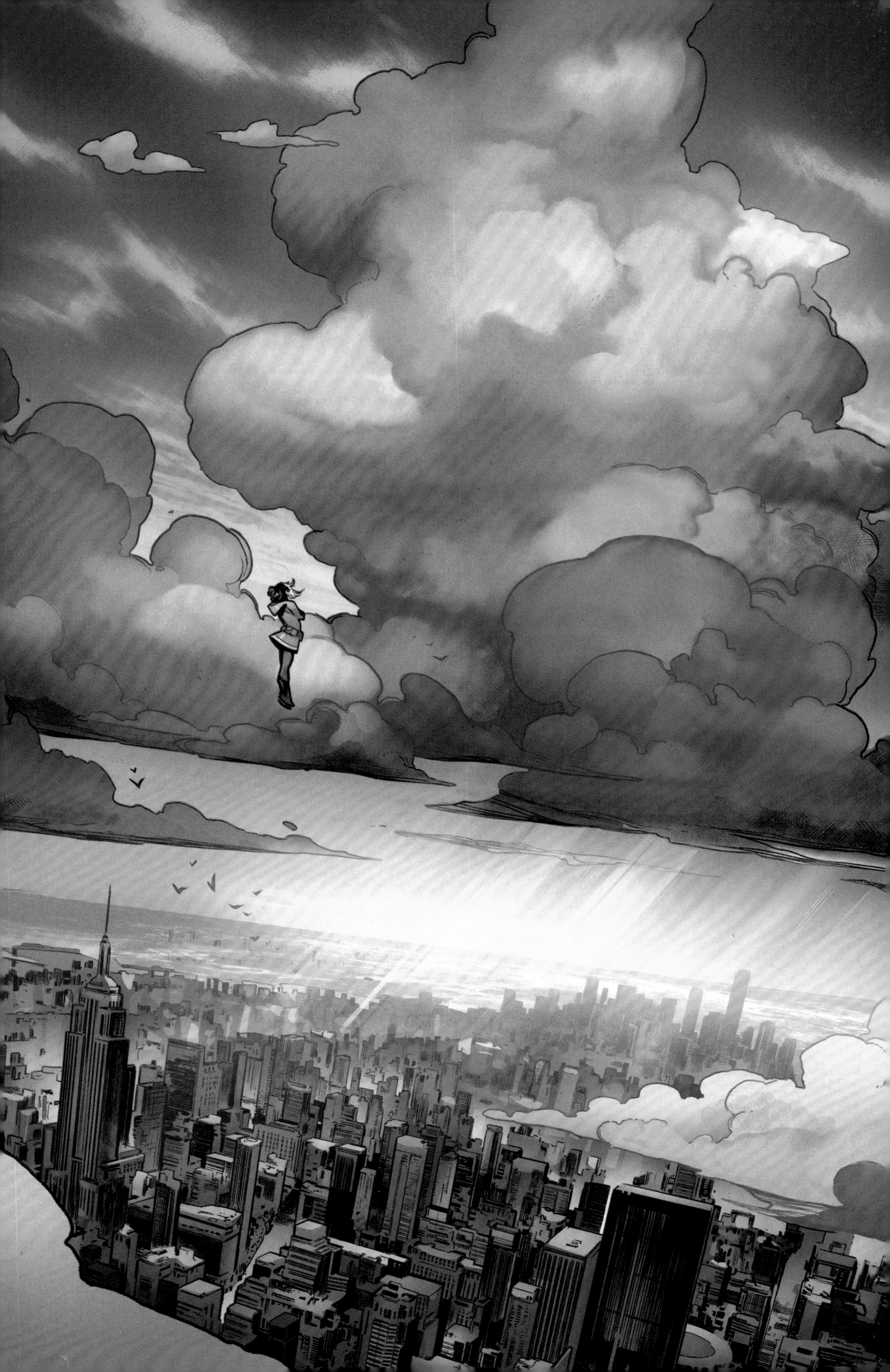

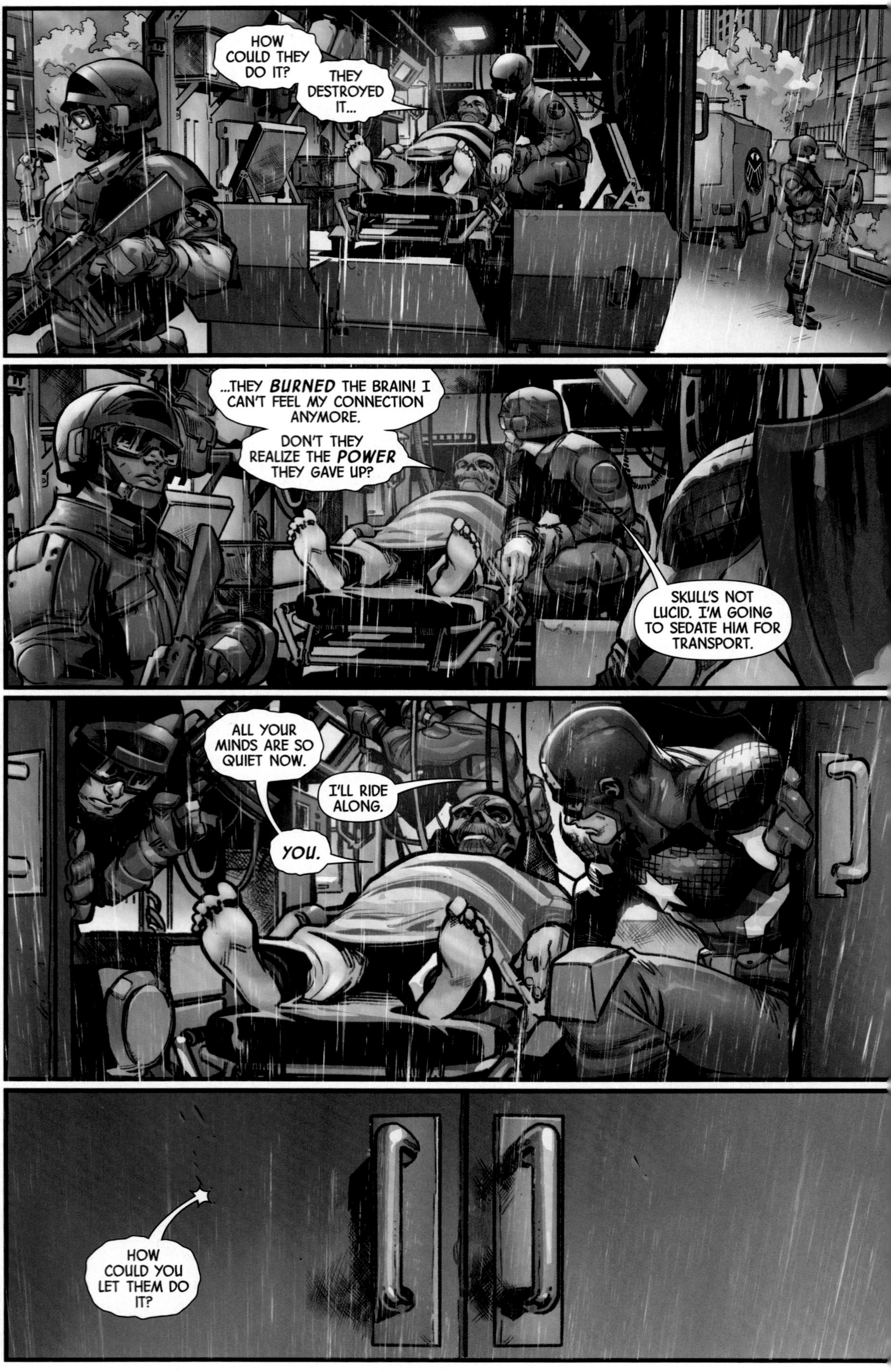
HOW COULD THEY DO IT?
THEY DESTROYED IT...
...THEY BURNED THE BRAIN! I CAN'T FEEL MY CONNECTION ANYMORE.
DON'T THEY REALIZE THE POWER THEY GAVE UP?
SKULL'S NOT LUCID. I'M GOING TO SEDATE HIM FOR TRANSPORT.
ALL YOUR MINDS ARE SO QUIET NOW.
I'LL RIDE ALONG.
YOU.
HOW COULD YOU LET THEM DO IT?

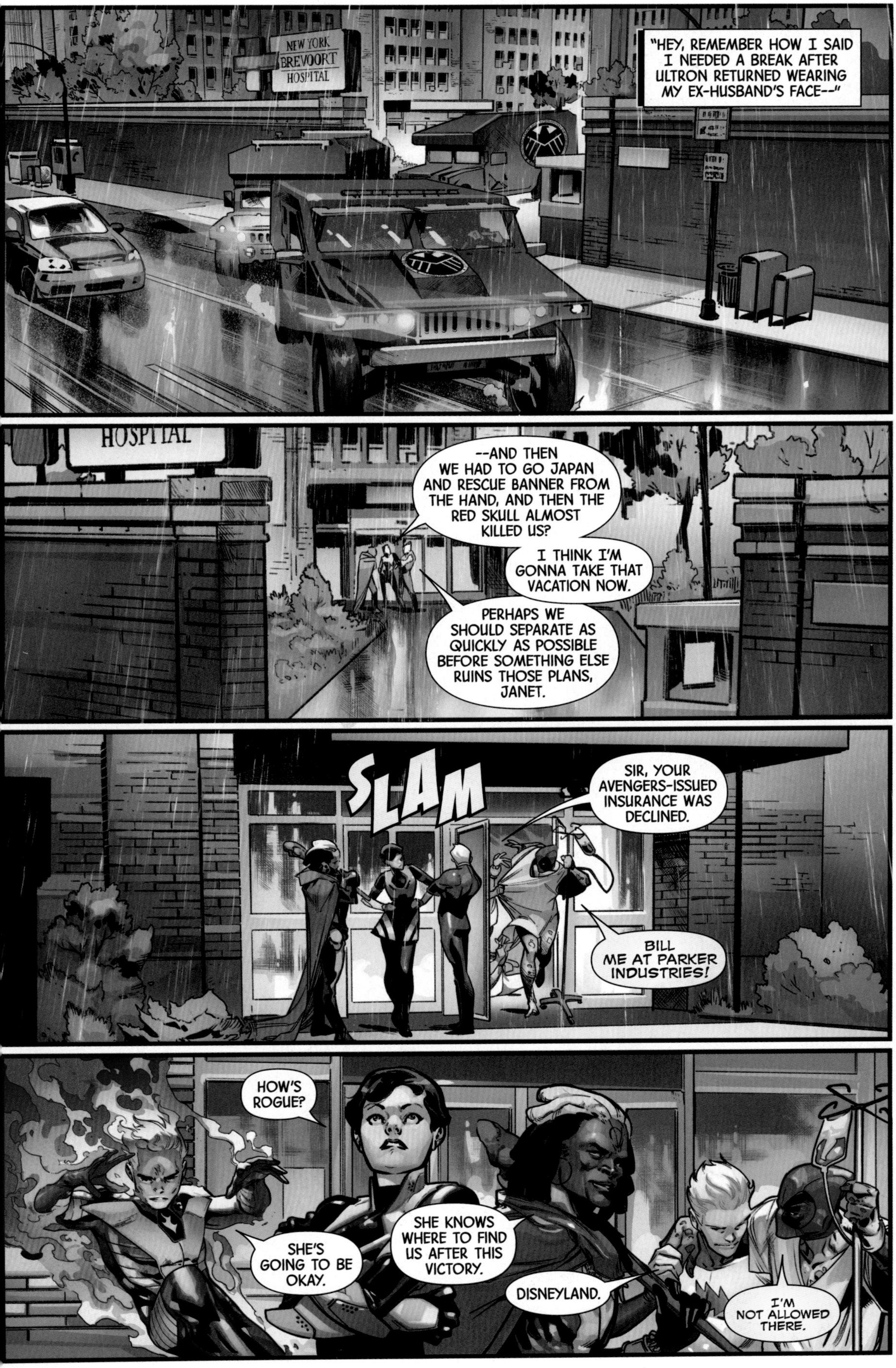
NEW YORK BREVOORT HOSPITAL
"HEY, REMEMBER HOW I SAID I NEEDED A BREAK AFTER ULTRON RETURNED WEARING MY EX-HUSBAND'S FACE--"
HOSPITAL
--AND THEN WE HAD TO GO JAPAN AND RESCUE BANNER FROM THE HAND, AND THEN THE RED SKULL ALMOST KILLED US?
I THINK I'M GONNA TAKE THAT VACATION NOW.
PERHAPS WE SHOULD SEPARATE AS QUICKLY AS POSSIBLE BEFORE SOMETHING ELSE RUINS THOSE PLANS, JANET.
SLAM
SIR, YOUR AVENGERS-ISSUED INSURANCE WAS DECLINED.
BILL ME AT PARKER INDUSTRIES!
HOW'S ROGUE?
SHE'S GOING TO BE OKAY.
SHE KNOWS WHERE TO FIND US AFTER THIS VICTORY.
DISNEYLAND.
I'M NOT ALLOWED THERE.

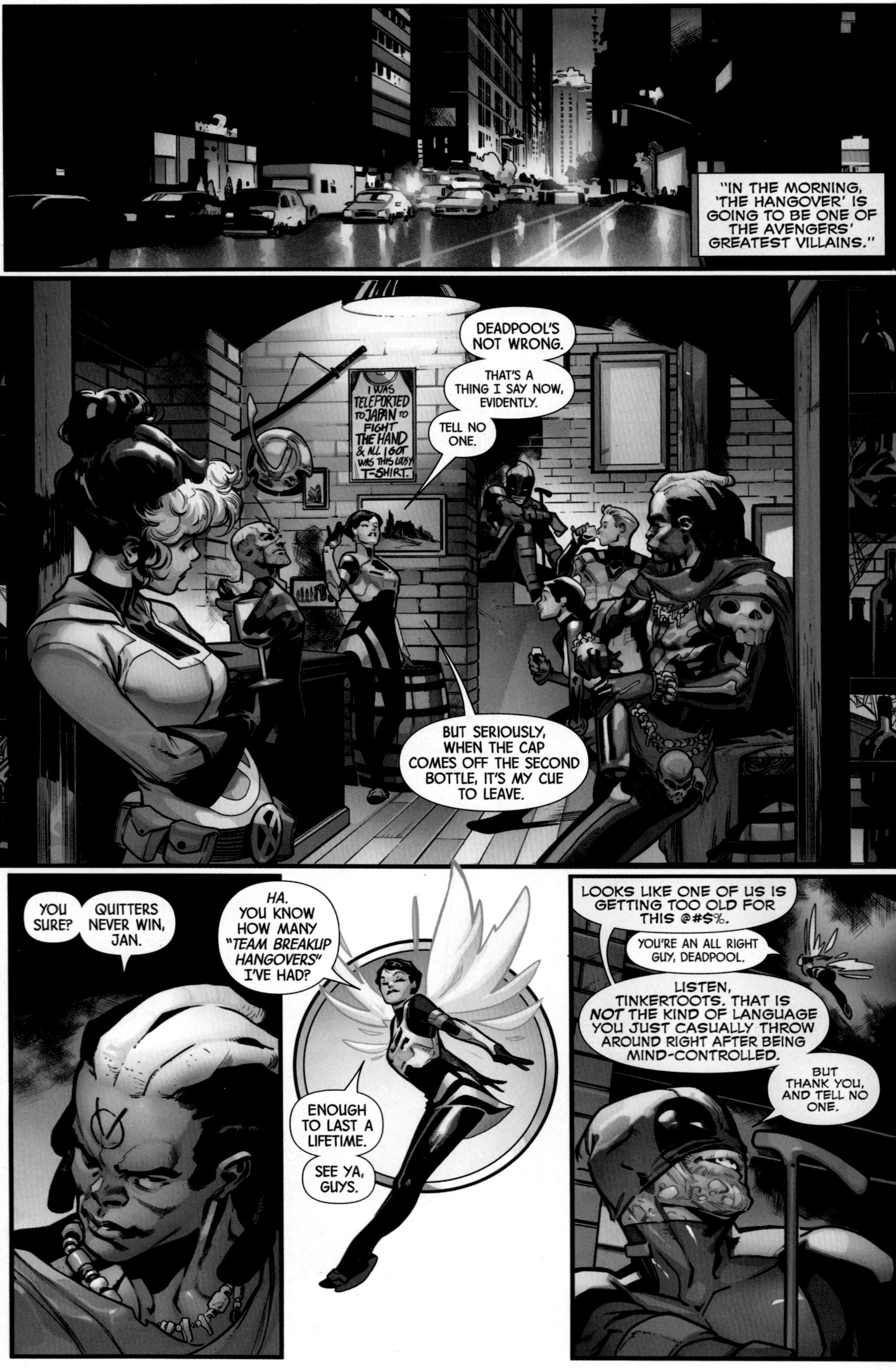
"IN THE MORNING, 'THE HANGOVER' IS GOING TO BE ONE OF THE AVENGERS' GREATEST VILLAINS."
DEADPOOL'S NOT WRONG.
THAT'S A THING I SAY NOW, EVIDENTLY.
TELL NO ONE.
I WAS TELEPORTED TO JAPAN TO FIGHT THE HAND & ALL I GOT WAS THIS LOUSY T-SHIRT.
BUT SERIOUSLY, WHEN THE CAP COMES OFF THE SECOND BOTTLE, IT'S MY CUE TO LEAVE.
YOU SURE?
QUITTERS NEVER WIN, JAN.
HA. YOU KNOW HOW MANY "TEAM BREAKUP HANGOVERS" I'VE HAD?
ENOUGH TO LAST A LIFETIME.
SEE YA, GUYS.
LOOKS LIKE ONE OF US IS GETTING TOO OLD FOR THIS @#$%.
YOU'RE AN ALL RIGHT GUY, DEADPOOL.
LISTEN, TINKERTOOTS. THAT IS NOT THE KIND OF LANGUAGE YOU JUST CASUALLY THROW AROUND RIGHT AFTER BEING MIND-CONTROLLED.
BUT THANK YOU, AND TELL NO ONE.

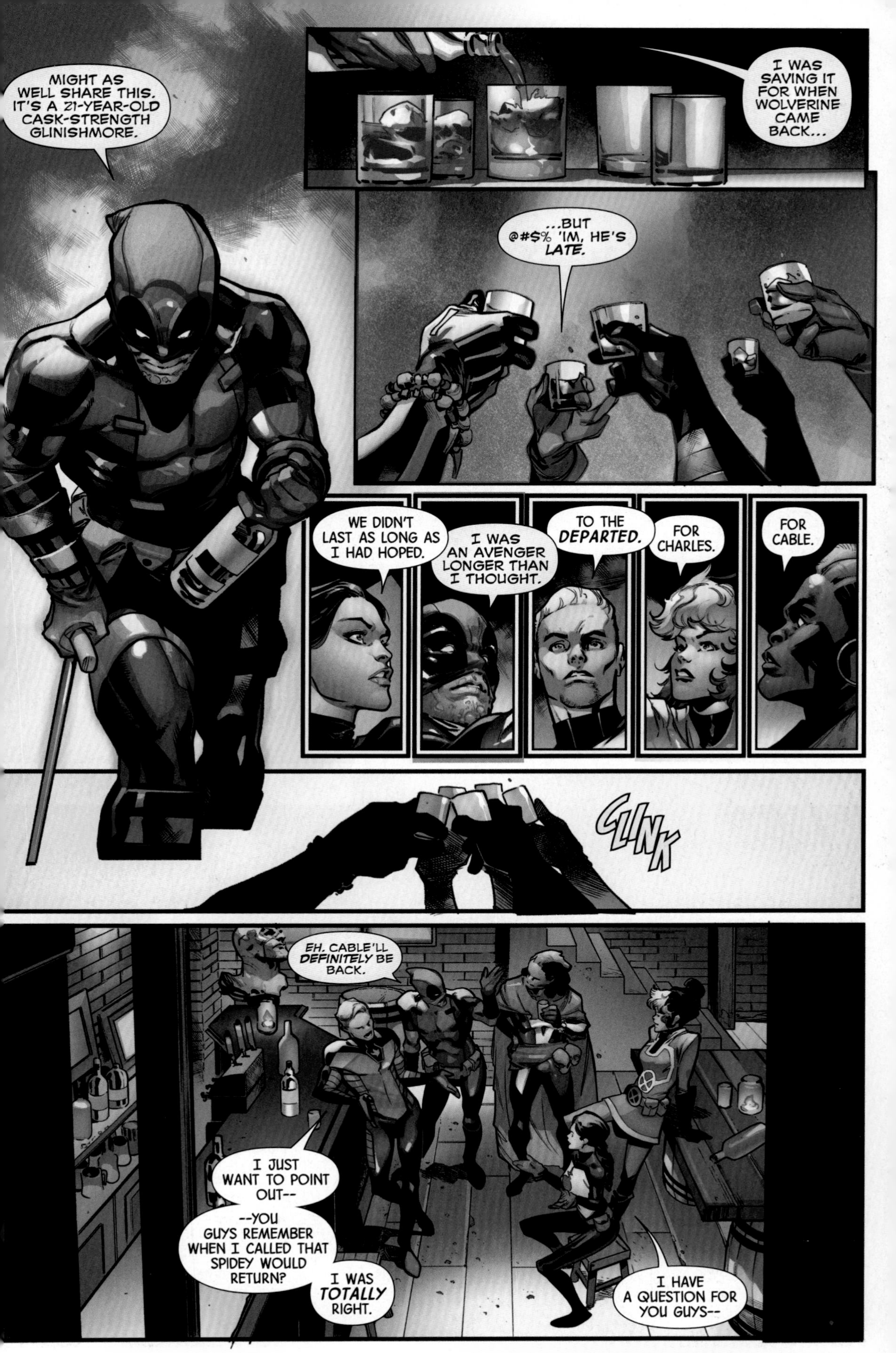
MIGHT AS WELL SHARE THIS. IT'S A 21-YEAR-OLD CASK-STRENGTH GLINISHMORE.
I WAS SAVING IT FOR WHEN WOLVERINE CAME BACK...
...BUT @#$% 'IM, HE'S LATE.
WE DIDN'T LAST AS LONG AS I HAD HOPED.
I WAS AN AVENGER LONGER THAN I THOUGHT.
TO THE DEPARTED.
FOR CHARLES.
FOR CABLE.
CLINK
EH. CABLE'LL DEFINITELY BE BACK.
I JUST WANT TO POINT OUT--
--YOU GUYS REMEMBER WHEN I CALLED THAT SPIDEY WOULD RETURN?
I WAS TOTALLY RIGHT.
I HAVE A QUESTION FOR YOU GUYS--

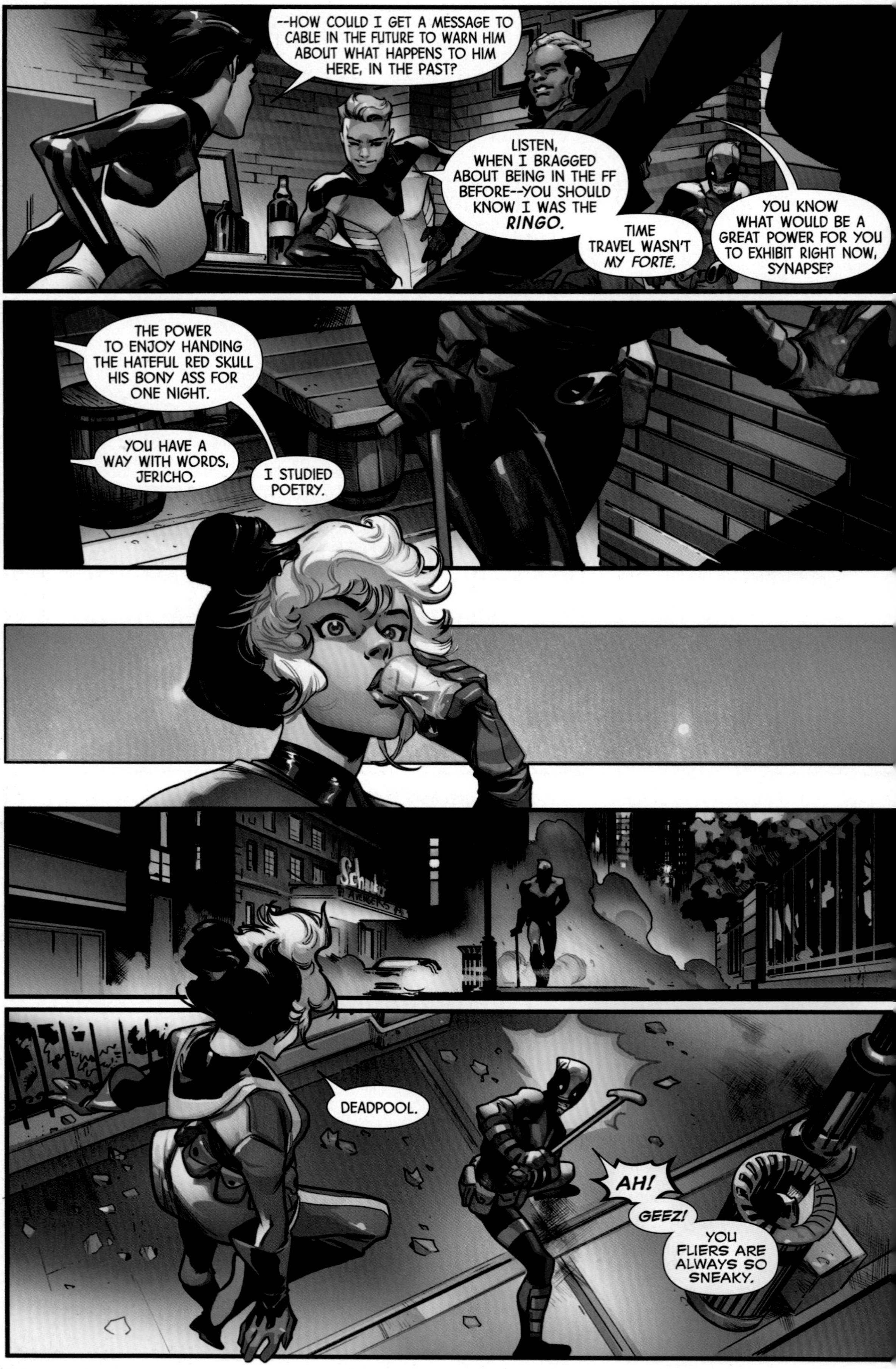
--HOW COULD I GET A MESSAGE TO CABLE IN THE FUTURE TO WARN HIM ABOUT WHAT HAPPENS TO HIM HERE, IN THE PAST?
LISTEN, WHEN I BRAGGED ABOUT BEING IN THE FF BEFORE--YOU SHOULD KNOW I WAS THE RINGO.
TIME TRAVEL WASN'T MY FORTE.
YOU KNOW WHAT WOULD BE A GREAT POWER FOR YOU TO EXHIBIT RIGHT NOW, SYNAPSE?
THE POWER TO ENJOY HANDING THE HATEFUL RED SKULL HIS BONY ASS FOR ONE NIGHT.
YOU HAVE A WAY WITH WORDS, JERICHO.
I STUDIED POETRY.
DEADPOOL.
AH!
GEEZ!
YOU FLIERS ARE ALWAYS SO SNEAKY.

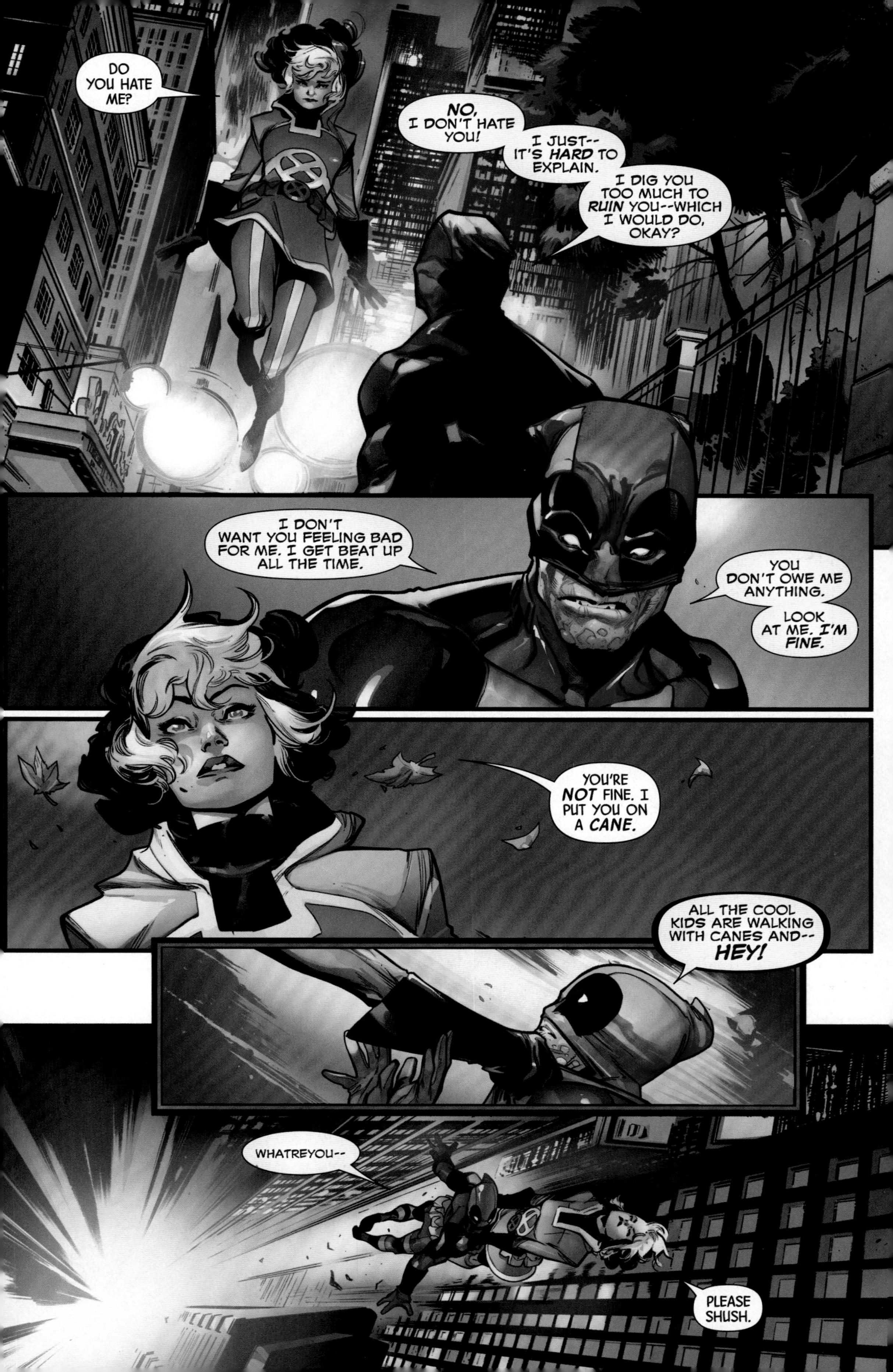

DO YOU HATE ME?
NO, I DON'T HATE YOU!
I JUST-- IT'S HARD TO EXPLAIN.
I DIG YOU TOO MUCH TO RUIN YOU--WHICH I WOULD DO, OKAY?
I DON'T WANT YOU FEELING BAD FOR ME. I GET BEAT UP ALL THE TIME.
YOU DON'T OWE ME ANYTHING.
LOOK AT ME. I'M FINE.
YOU'RE NOT FINE. I PUT YOU ON A CANE.
ALL THE COOL KIDS ARE WALKING WITH CANES AND-- HEY!
WHATREYOU--
PLEASE SHUSH.

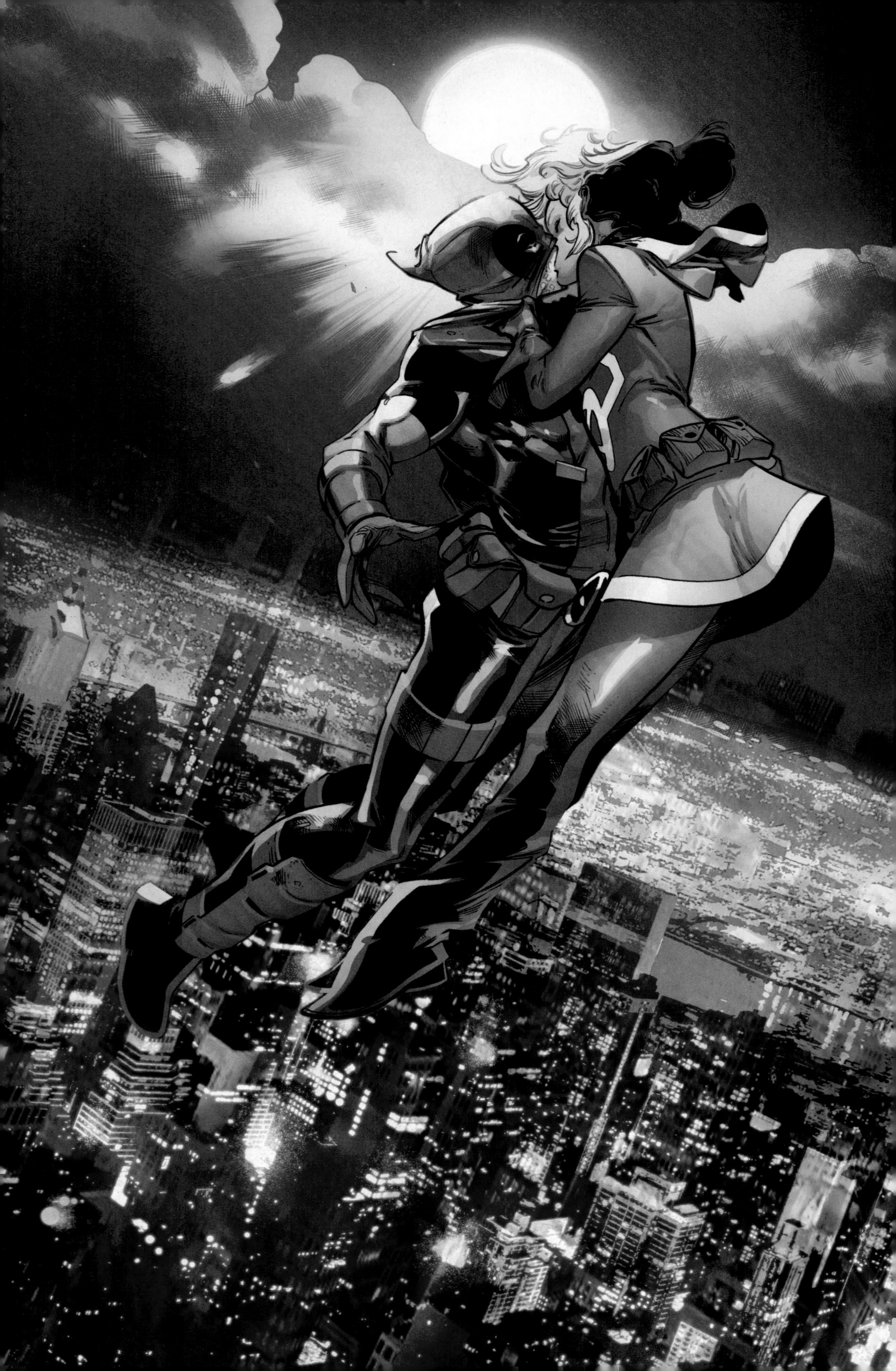

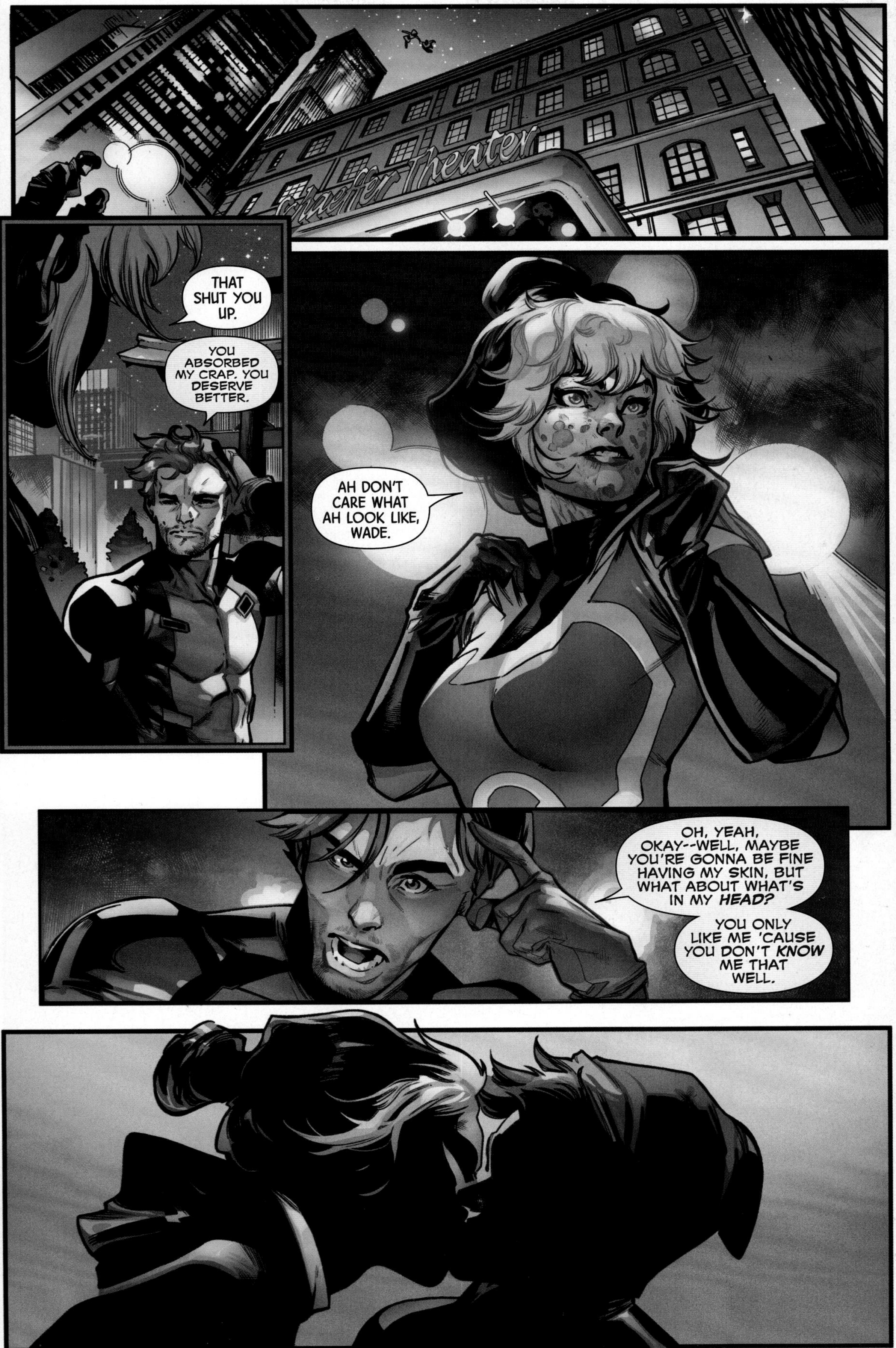
Schaeffer Theater
THAT SHUT YOU UP.
YOU ABSORBED MY CRAP. YOU DESERVE BETTER.
AH DON'T CARE WHAT AH LOOK LIKE, WADE.
OH, YEAH, OKAY--WELL, MAYBE YOU'RE GONNA BE FINE HAVING MY SKIN, BUT WHAT ABOUT WHAT'S IN MY HEAD?
YOU ONLY LIKE ME 'CAUSE YOU DON'T KNOW ME THAT WELL.

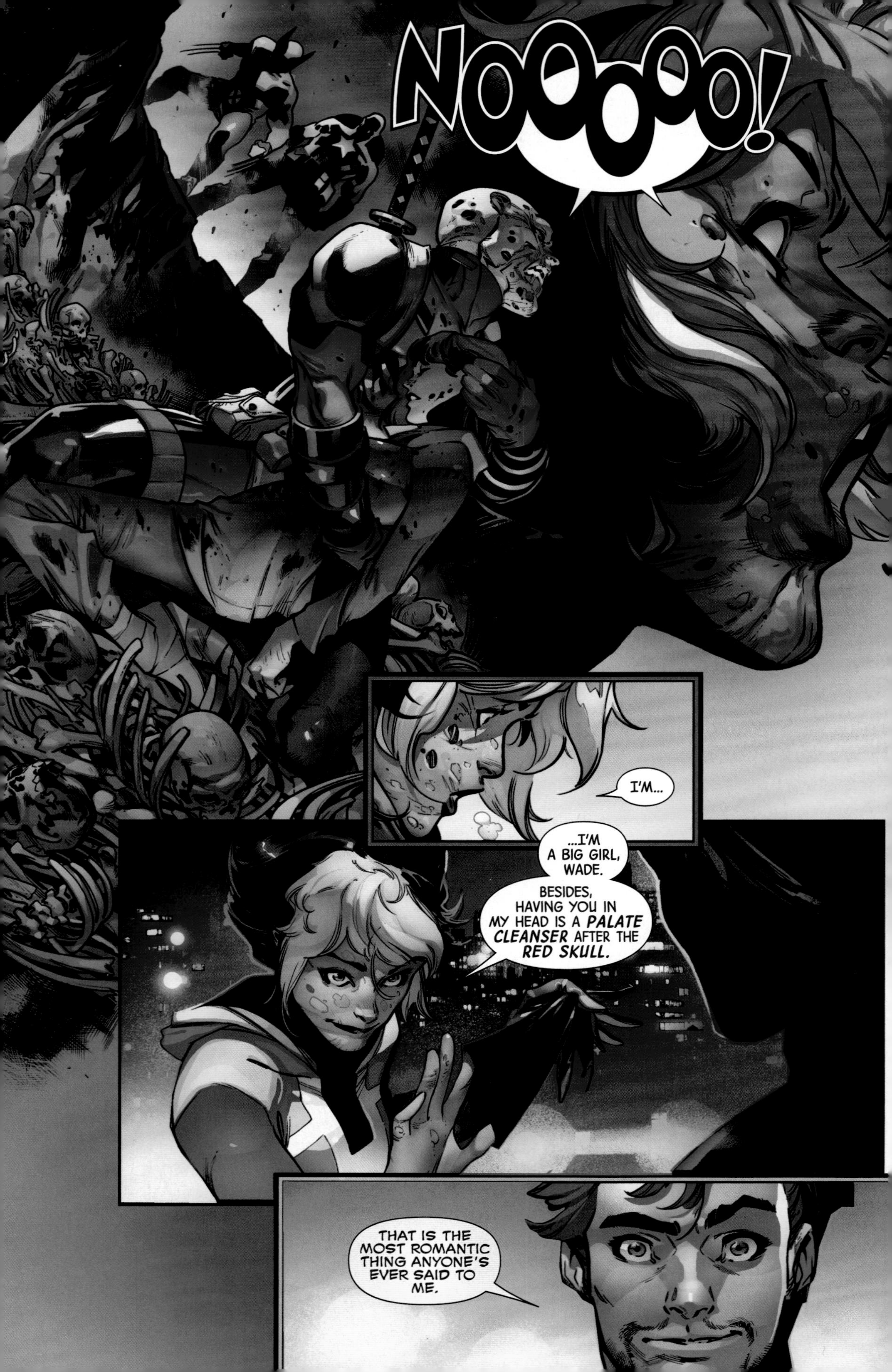
NOOOOO!
I'M...
...I'M A BIG GIRL, WADE.
BESIDES, HAVING YOU IN MY HEAD IS A *PALATE CLEANSER* AFTER THE *RED SKULL.*
THAT IS THE MOST ROMANTIC THING ANYONE'S EVER SAID TO ME.

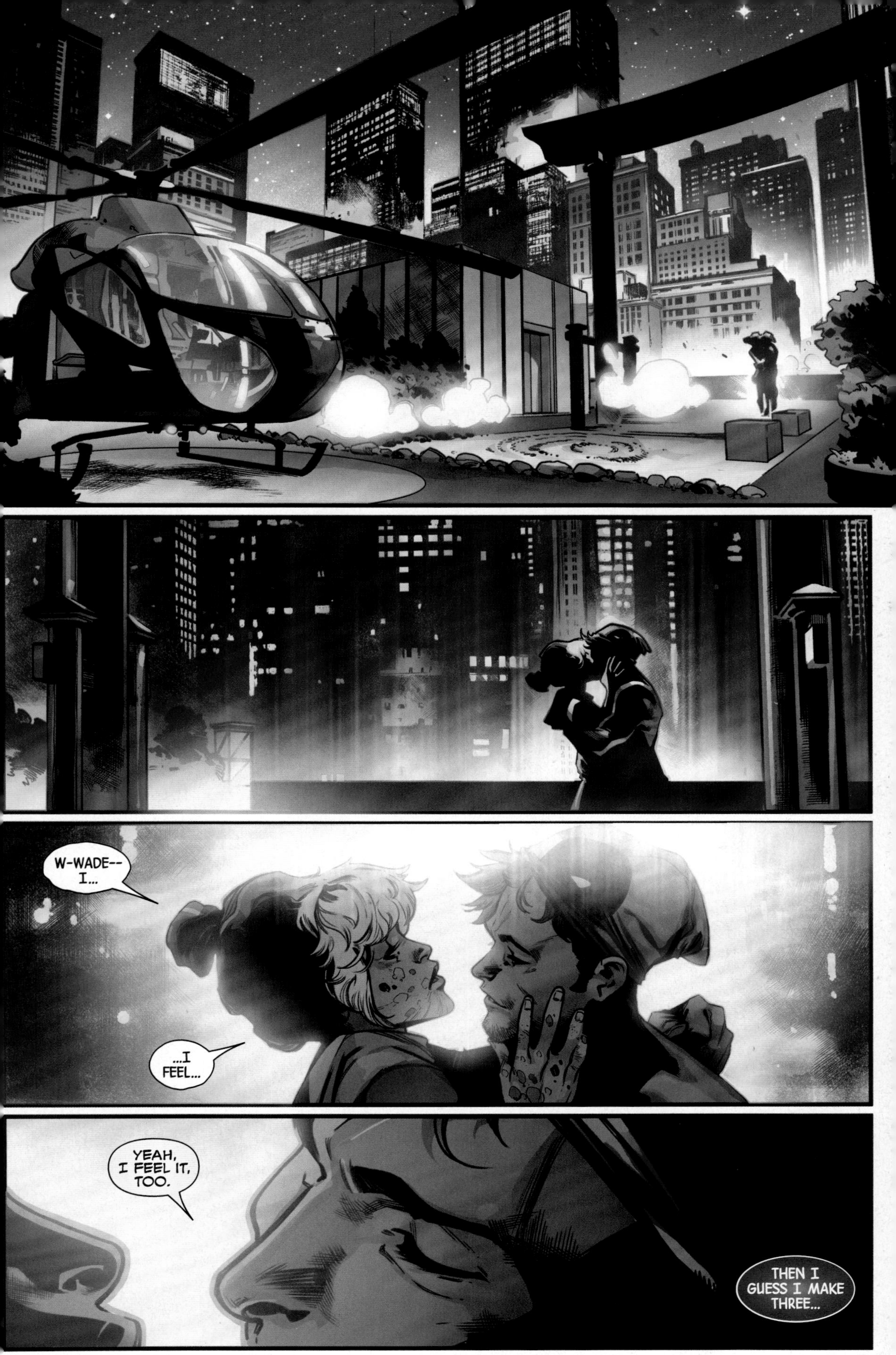
W-WADE--
I...
...I
FEEL...
YEAH,
I FEEL IT,
TOO.
THEN I
GUESS I MAKE
THREE...

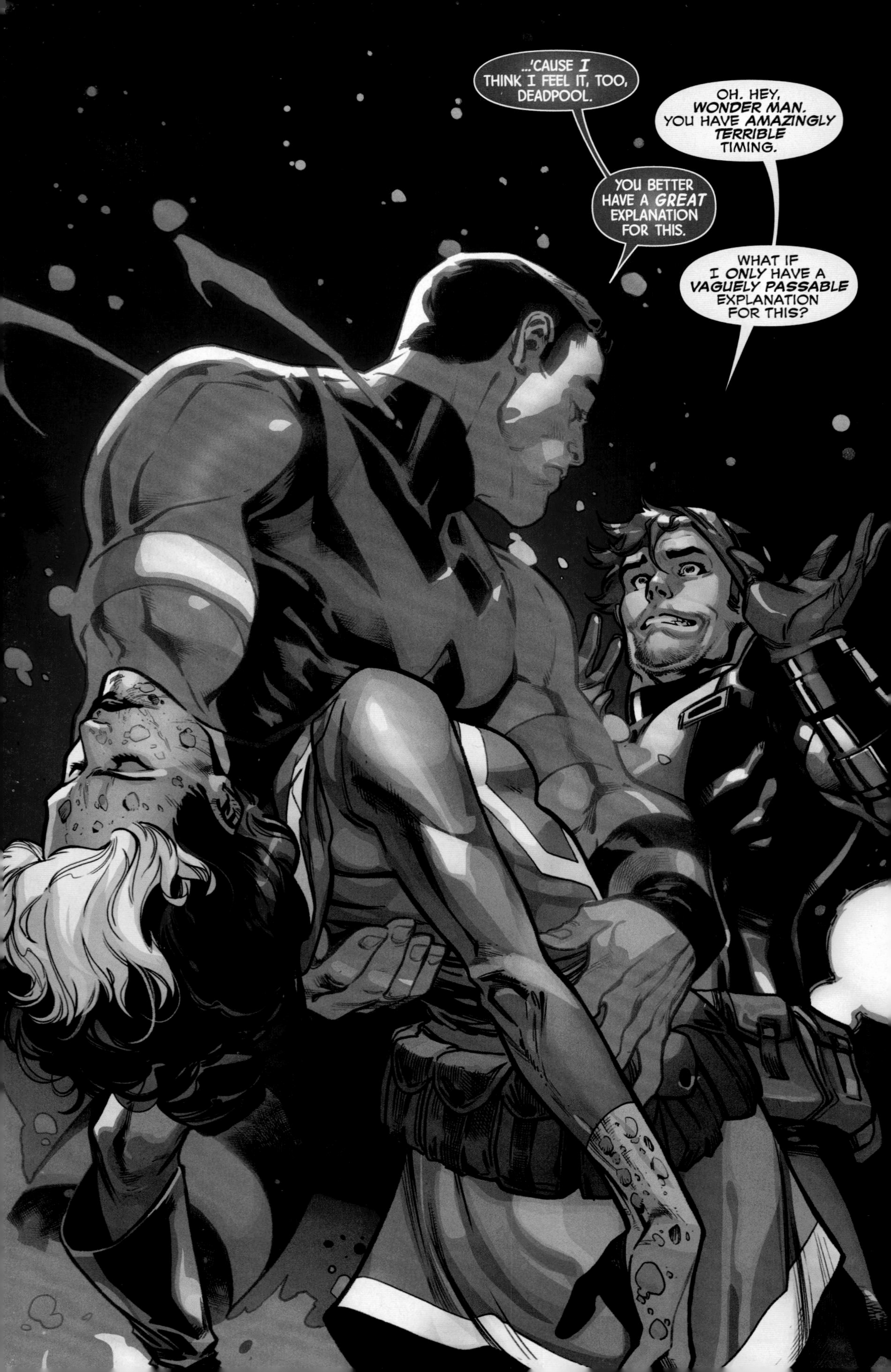
...'CAUSE *I* THINK I FEEL IT, TOO, DEADPOOL.
YOU BETTER HAVE A *GREAT* EXPLANATION FOR THIS.
OH. HEY, *WONDER MAN.* YOU HAVE *AMAZINGLY TERRIBLE* TIMING.
WHAT IF I *ONLY* HAVE A *VAGUELY PASSABLE* EXPLANATION FOR THIS?

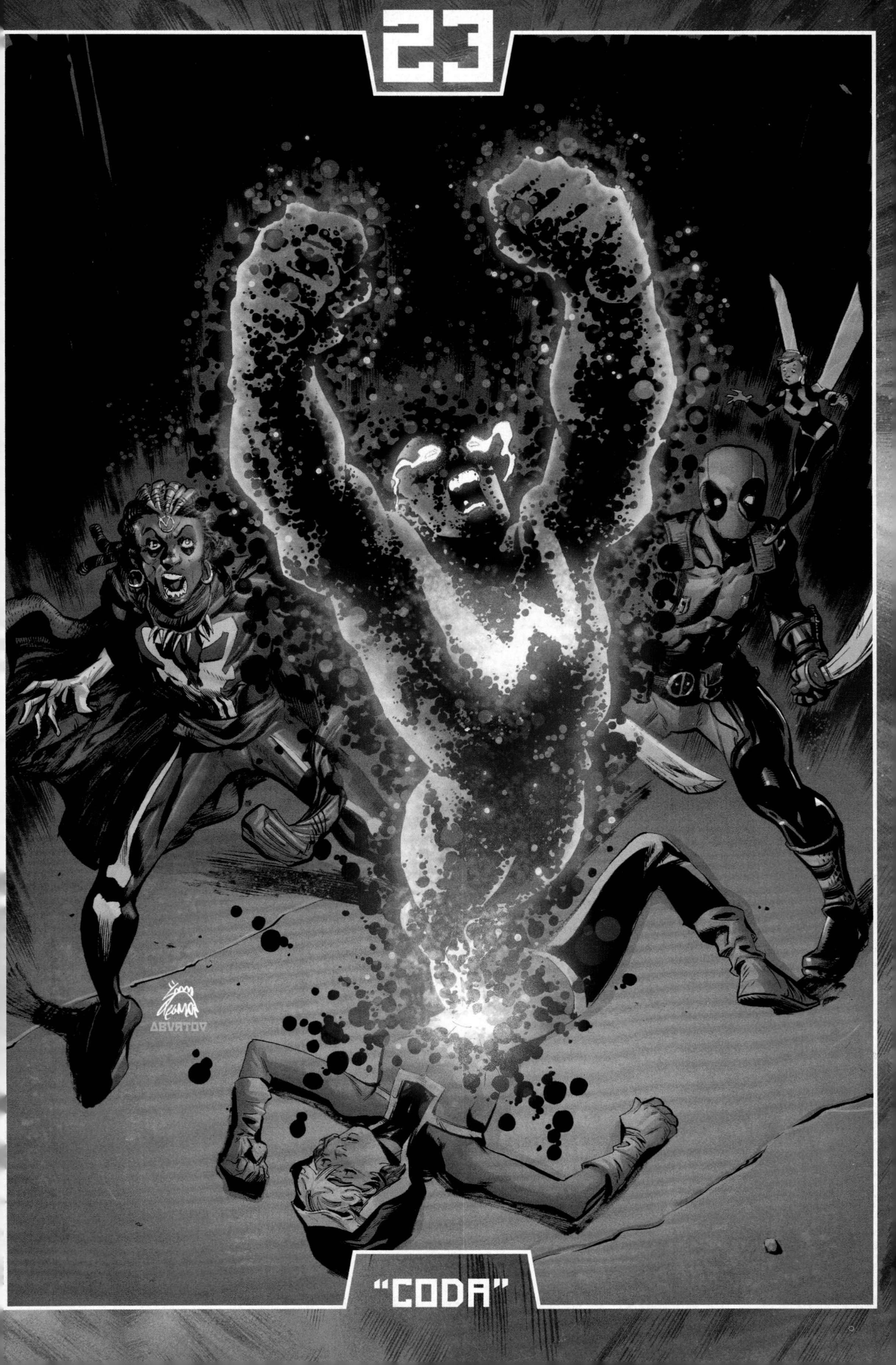
23
"CODA"

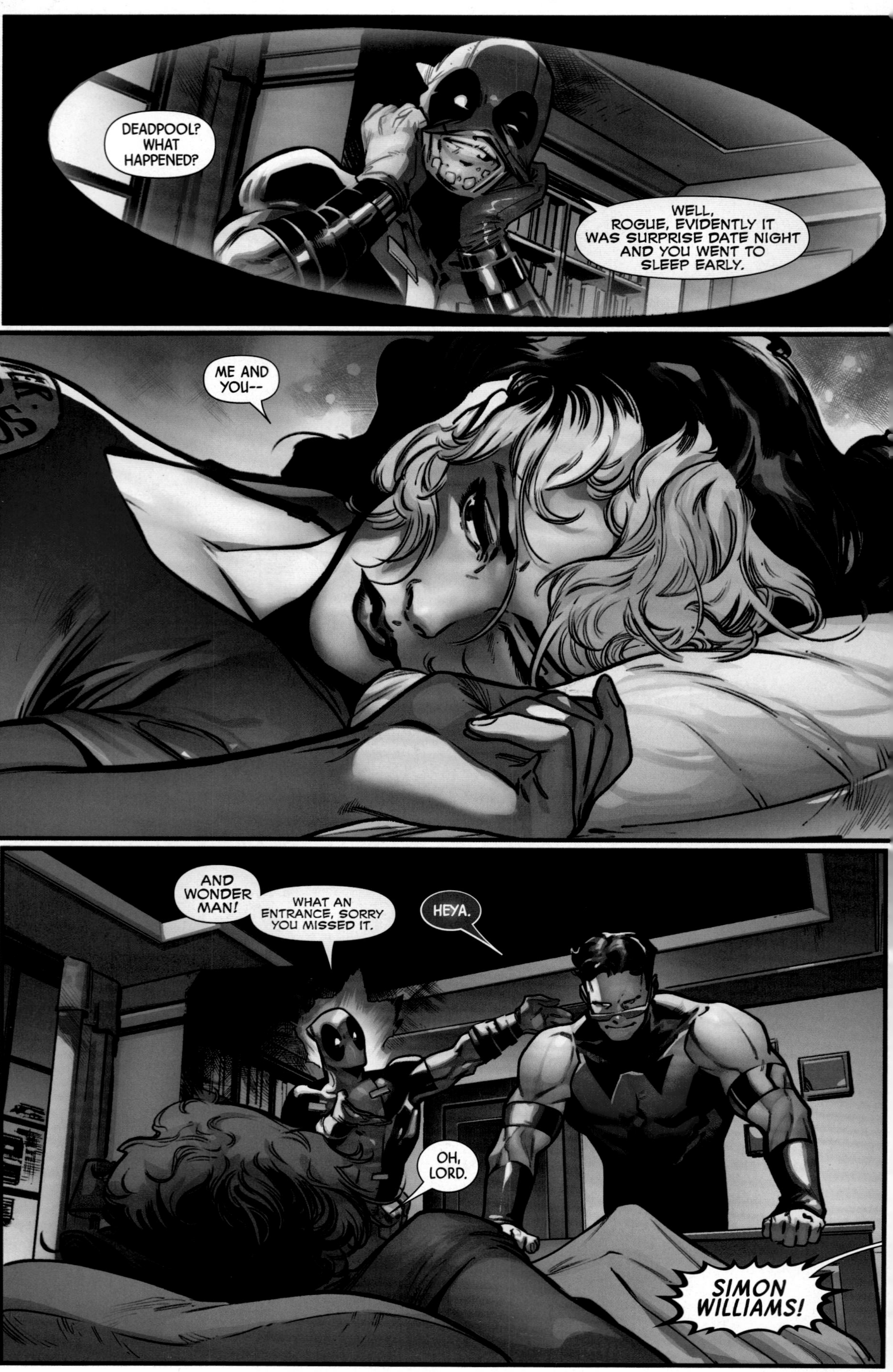
DEADPOOL? WHAT HAPPENED?
WELL, ROGUE, EVIDENTLY IT WAS SURPRISE DATE NIGHT AND YOU WENT TO SLEEP EARLY.
ME AND YOU--
AND WONDER MAN!
WHAT AN ENTRANCE, SORRY YOU MISSED IT.
HEYA.
OH, LORD.
SIMON WILLIAMS!

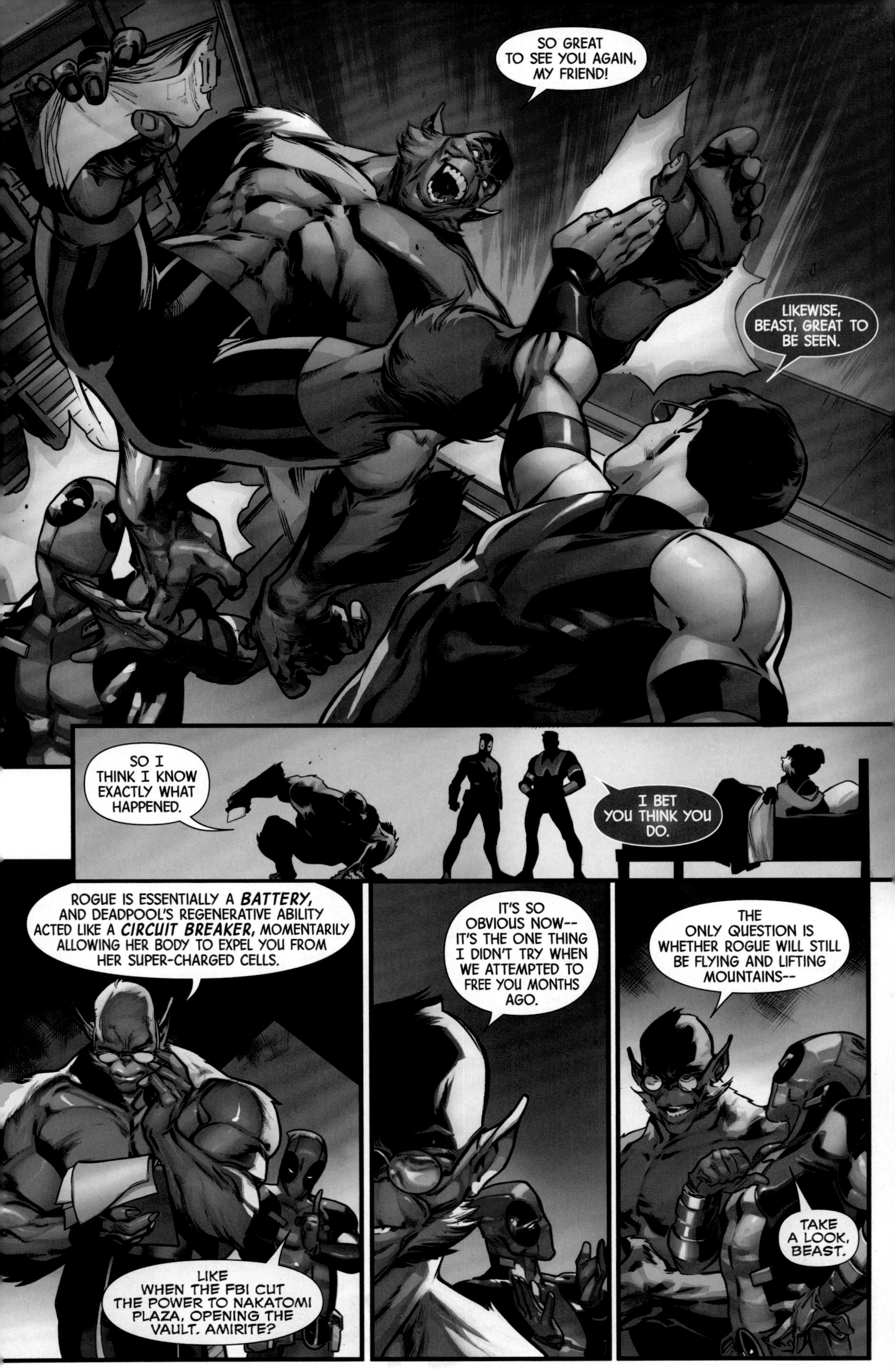
SO GREAT TO SEE YOU AGAIN, MY FRIEND!
LIKEWISE, BEAST, GREAT TO BE SEEN.
SO I THINK I KNOW EXACTLY WHAT HAPPENED.
I BET YOU THINK YOU DO.
ROGUE IS ESSENTIALLY A BATTERY, AND DEADPOOL'S REGENERATIVE ABILITY ACTED LIKE A CIRCUIT BREAKER, MOMENTARILY ALLOWING HER BODY TO EXPEL YOU FROM HER SUPER-CHARGED CELLS.
LIKE WHEN THE FBI CUT THE POWER TO NAKATOMI PLAZA, OPENING THE VAULT. AMIRITE?
IT'S SO OBVIOUS NOW-- IT'S THE ONE THING I DIDN'T TRY WHEN WE ATTEMPTED TO FREE YOU MONTHS AGO.
THE ONLY QUESTION IS WHETHER ROGUE WILL STILL BE FLYING AND LIFTING MOUNTAINS--
TAKE A LOOK, BEAST.

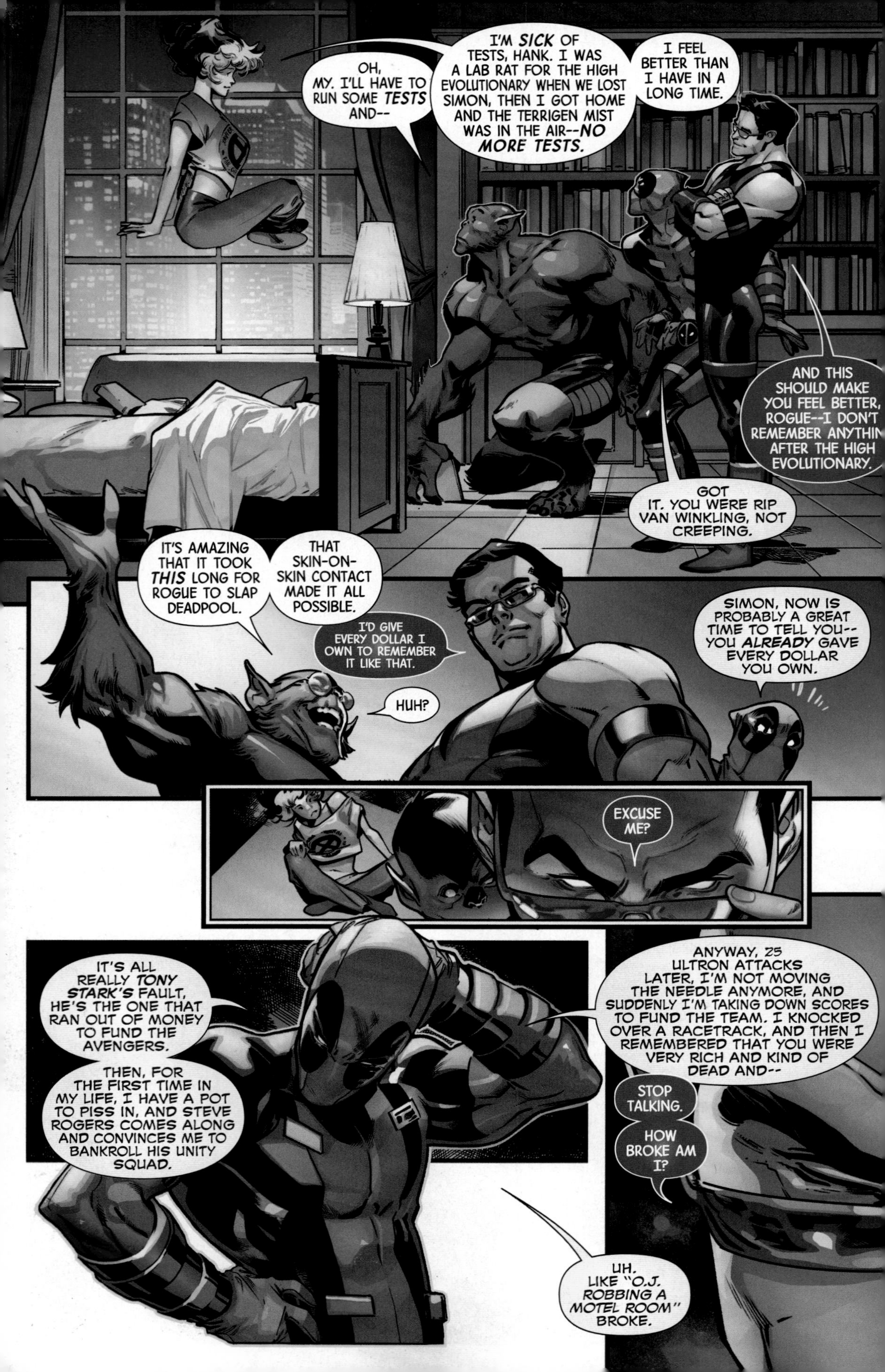
OH, MY. I'LL HAVE TO RUN SOME TESTS AND--
I'M SICK OF TESTS, HANK. I WAS A LAB RAT FOR THE HIGH EVOLUTIONARY WHEN WE LOST SIMON, THEN I GOT HOME AND THE TERRIGEN MIST WAS IN THE AIR--NO MORE TESTS.
I FEEL BETTER THAN I HAVE IN A LONG TIME.
AND THIS SHOULD MAKE YOU FEEL BETTER, ROGUE--I DON'T REMEMBER ANYTHIN AFTER THE HIGH EVOLUTIONARY.
GOT IT. YOU WERE RIP VAN WINKLING, NOT CREEPING.
IT'S AMAZING THAT IT TOOK THIS LONG FOR ROGUE TO SLAP DEADPOOL.
THAT SKIN-ON-SKIN CONTACT MADE IT ALL POSSIBLE.
I'D GIVE EVERY DOLLAR I OWN TO REMEMBER IT LIKE THAT.
SIMON, NOW IS PROBABLY A GREAT TIME TO TELL YOU--YOU ALREADY GAVE EVERY DOLLAR YOU OWN.
HUH?
EXCUSE ME?
IT'S ALL REALLY TONY STARK'S FAULT, HE'S THE ONE THAT RAN OUT OF MONEY TO FUND THE AVENGERS.
THEN, FOR THE FIRST TIME IN MY LIFE, I HAVE A POT TO PISS IN, AND STEVE ROGERS COMES ALONG AND CONVINCES ME TO BANKROLL HIS UNITY SQUAD.
ANYWAY, 25 ULTRON ATTACKS LATER, I'M NOT MOVING THE NEEDLE ANYMORE, AND SUDDENLY I'M TAKING DOWN SCORES TO FUND THE TEAM. I KNOCKED OVER A RACETRACK, AND THEN I REMEMBERED THAT YOU WERE VERY RICH AND KIND OF DEAD AND--
STOP TALKING.
HOW BROKE AM I?
UH. LIKE "O.J. ROBBING A MOTEL ROOM" BROKE.

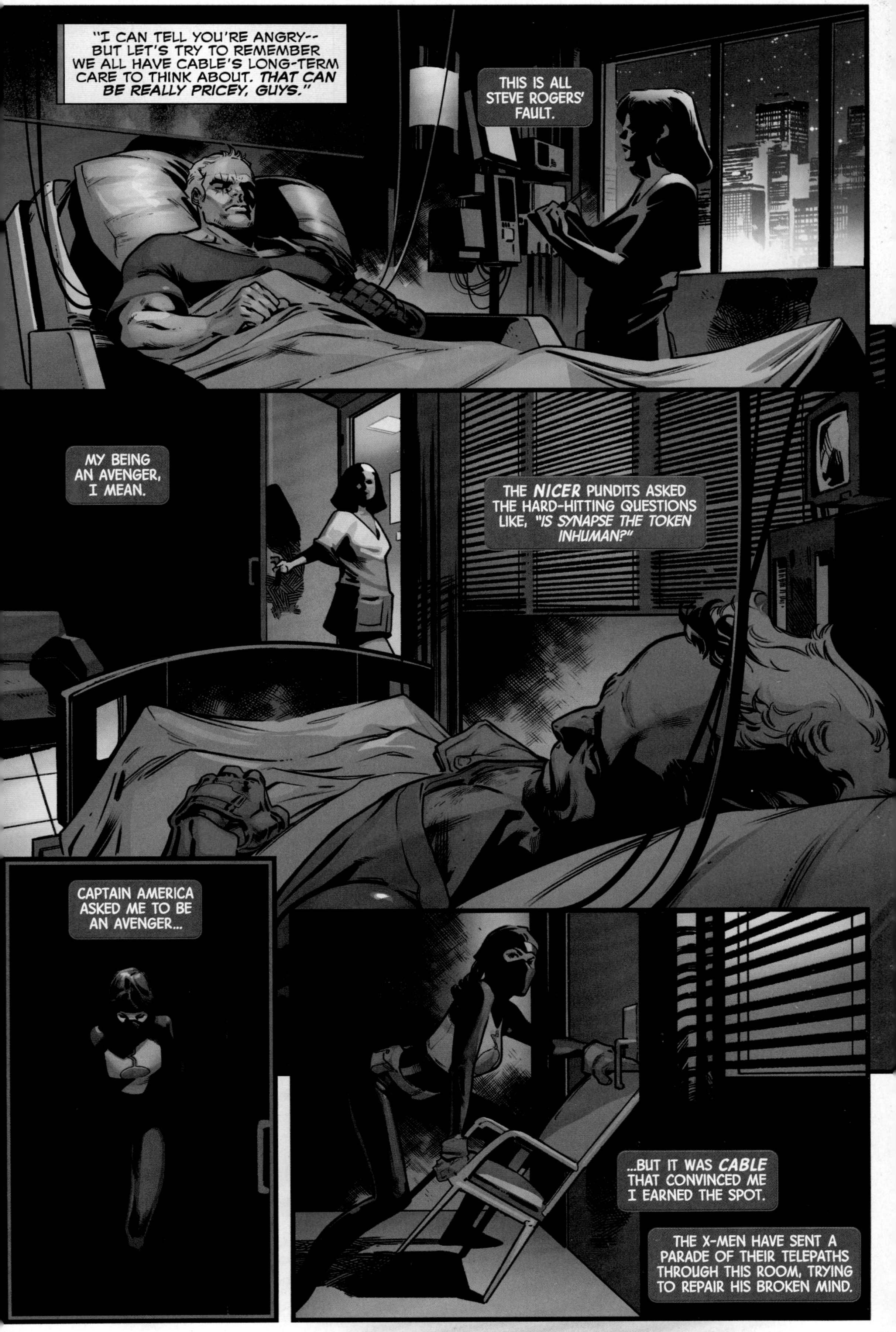
"I CAN TELL YOU'RE ANGRY-- BUT LET'S TRY TO REMEMBER WE ALL HAVE CABLE'S LONG-TERM CARE TO THINK ABOUT. *THAT CAN BE REALLY PRICEY, GUYS.*"
THIS IS ALL STEVE ROGERS' FAULT.
MY BEING AN AVENGER, I MEAN.
THE ***NICER*** PUNDITS ASKED THE HARD-HITTING QUESTIONS LIKE, *"IS SYNAPSE THE TOKEN INHUMAN?"*
CAPTAIN AMERICA ASKED ME TO BE AN AVENGER...
...BUT IT WAS ***CABLE*** THAT CONVINCED ME I EARNED THE SPOT.
THE X-MEN HAVE SENT A PARADE OF THEIR TELEPATHS THROUGH THIS ROOM, TRYING TO REPAIR HIS BROKEN MIND.

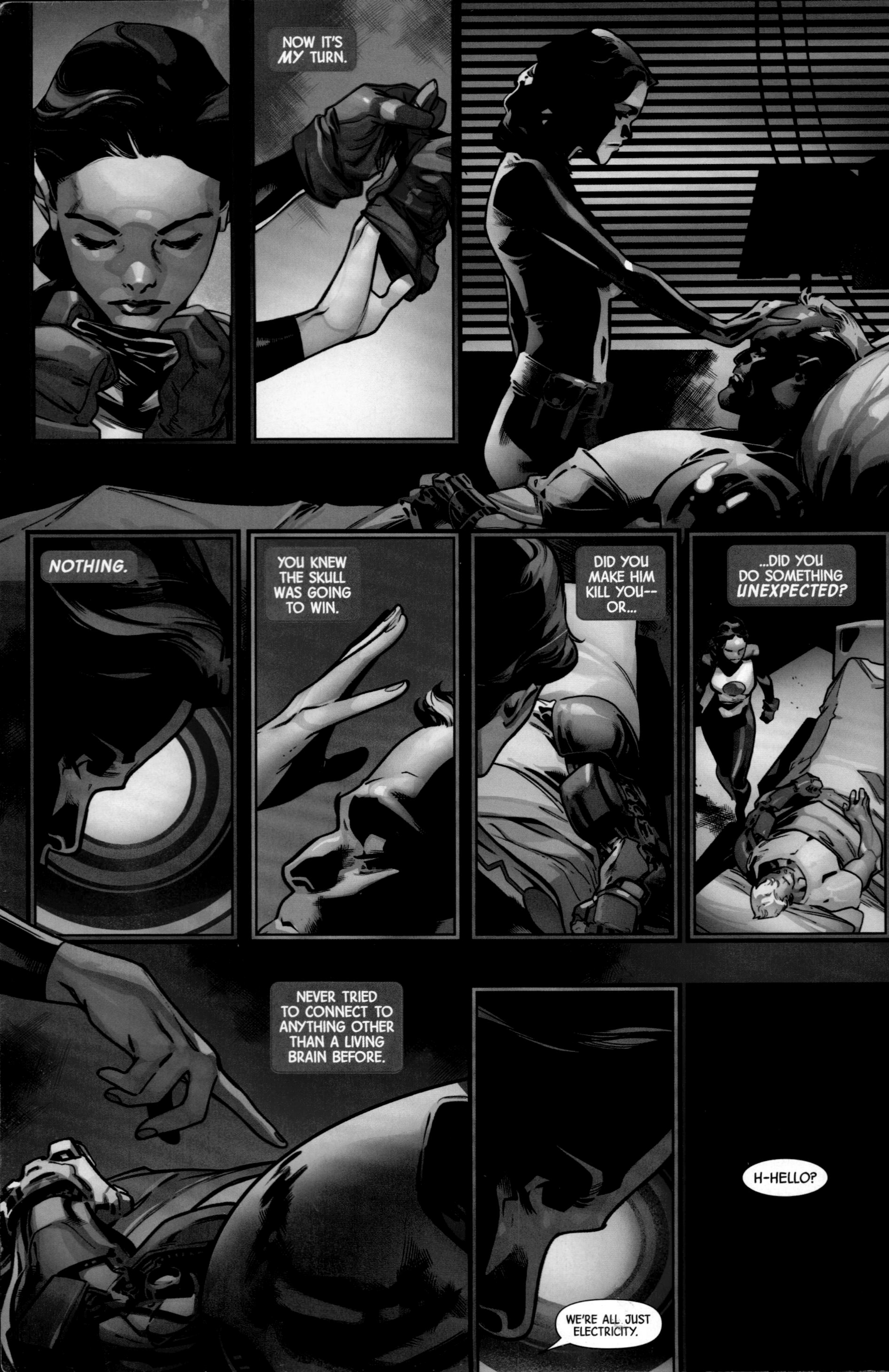
NOW IT'S MY TURN.
NOTHING.
YOU KNEW THE SKULL WAS GOING TO WIN.
DID YOU MAKE HIM KILL YOU-- OR...
...DID YOU DO SOMETHING UNEXPECTED?
NEVER TRIED TO CONNECT TO ANYTHING OTHER THAN A LIVING BRAIN BEFORE.
WE'RE ALL JUST ELECTRICITY.
H-HELLO?

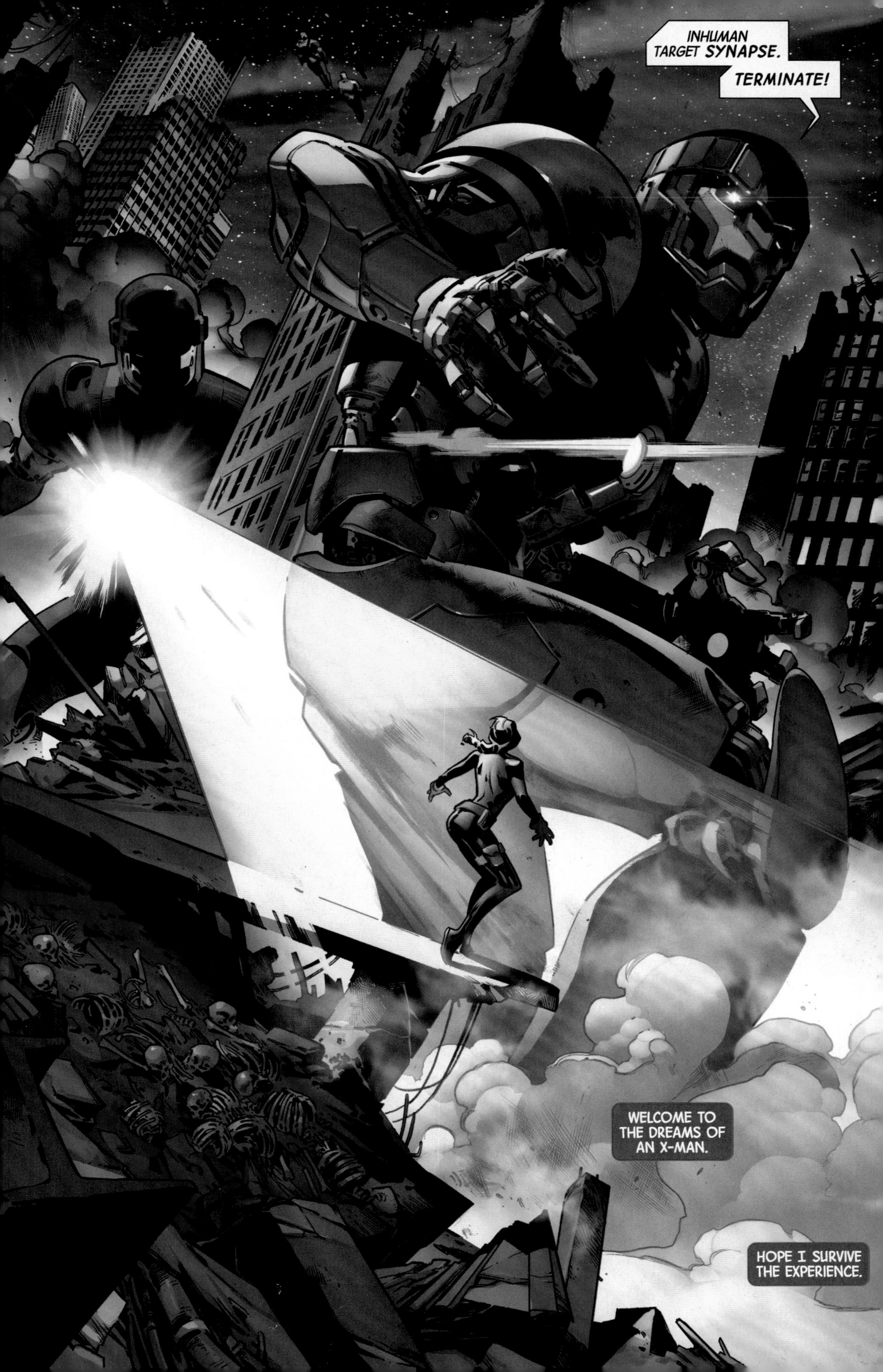
INHUMAN TARGET SYNAPSE.
TERMINATE!
WELCOME TO THE DREAMS OF AN X-MAN.
HOPE I SURVIVE THE EXPERIENCE.

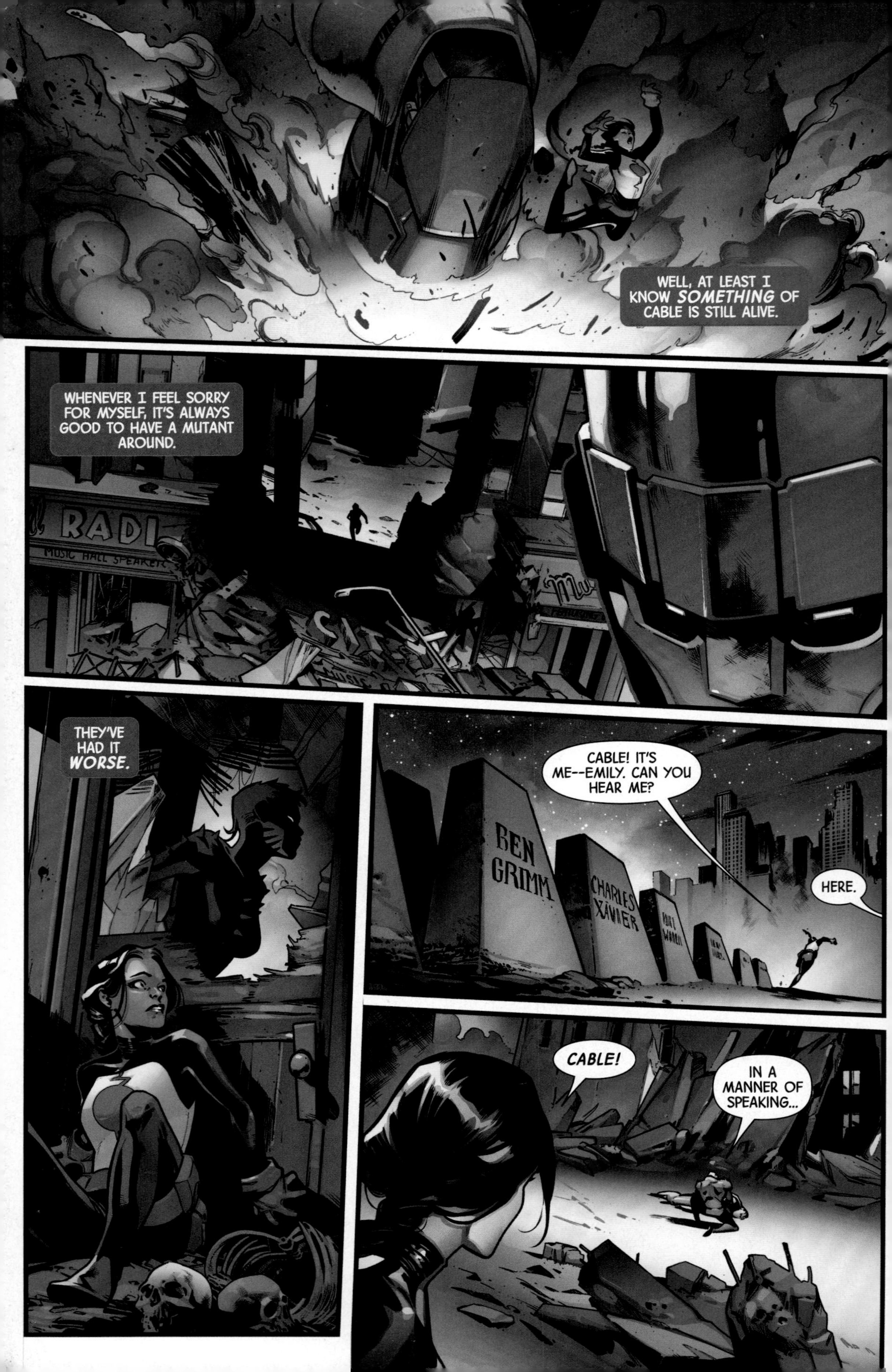

WELL, AT LEAST I KNOW SOMETHING OF CABLE IS STILL ALIVE.
WHENEVER I FEEL SORRY FOR MYSELF, IT'S ALWAYS GOOD TO HAVE A MUTANT AROUND.
RADI
MUSIC HALL SPEAKER
THEY'VE HAD IT WORSE.
CABLE! IT'S ME--EMILY. CAN YOU HEAR ME?
HERE.
BEN GRIMM
CHARLES XAVIER
CABLE!
IN A MANNER OF SPEAKING...

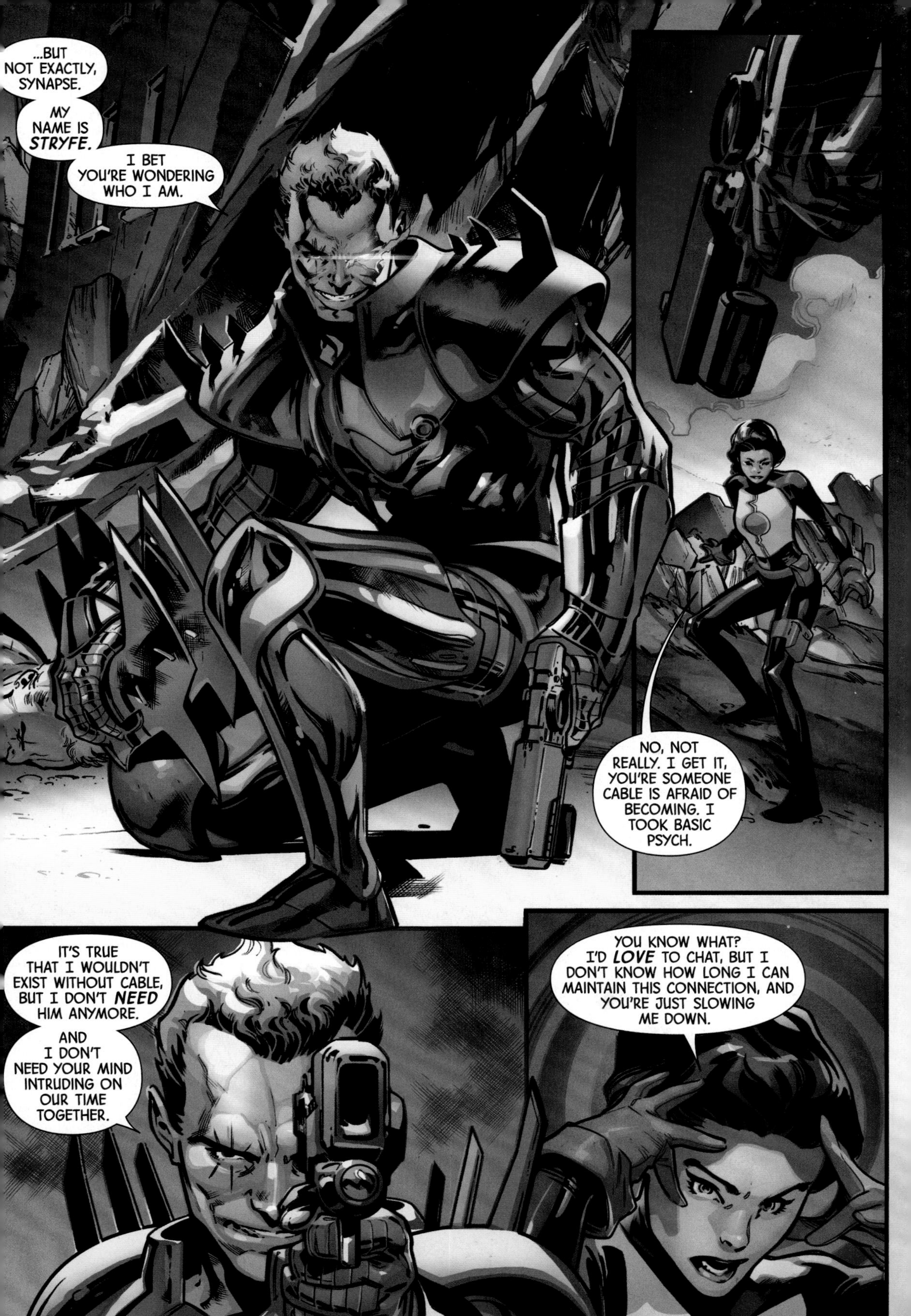
...BUT NOT EXACTLY, SYNAPSE.
MY NAME IS STRYFE.
I BET YOU'RE WONDERING WHO I AM.
NO, NOT REALLY. I GET IT, YOU'RE SOMEONE CABLE IS AFRAID OF BECOMING. I TOOK BASIC PSYCH.
IT'S TRUE THAT I WOULDN'T EXIST WITHOUT CABLE, BUT I DON'T NEED HIM ANYMORE.
AND I DON'T NEED YOUR MIND INTRUDING ON OUR TIME TOGETHER.
YOU KNOW WHAT? I'D LOVE TO CHAT, BUT I DON'T KNOW HOW LONG I CAN MAINTAIN THIS CONNECTION, AND YOU'RE JUST SLOWING ME DOWN.

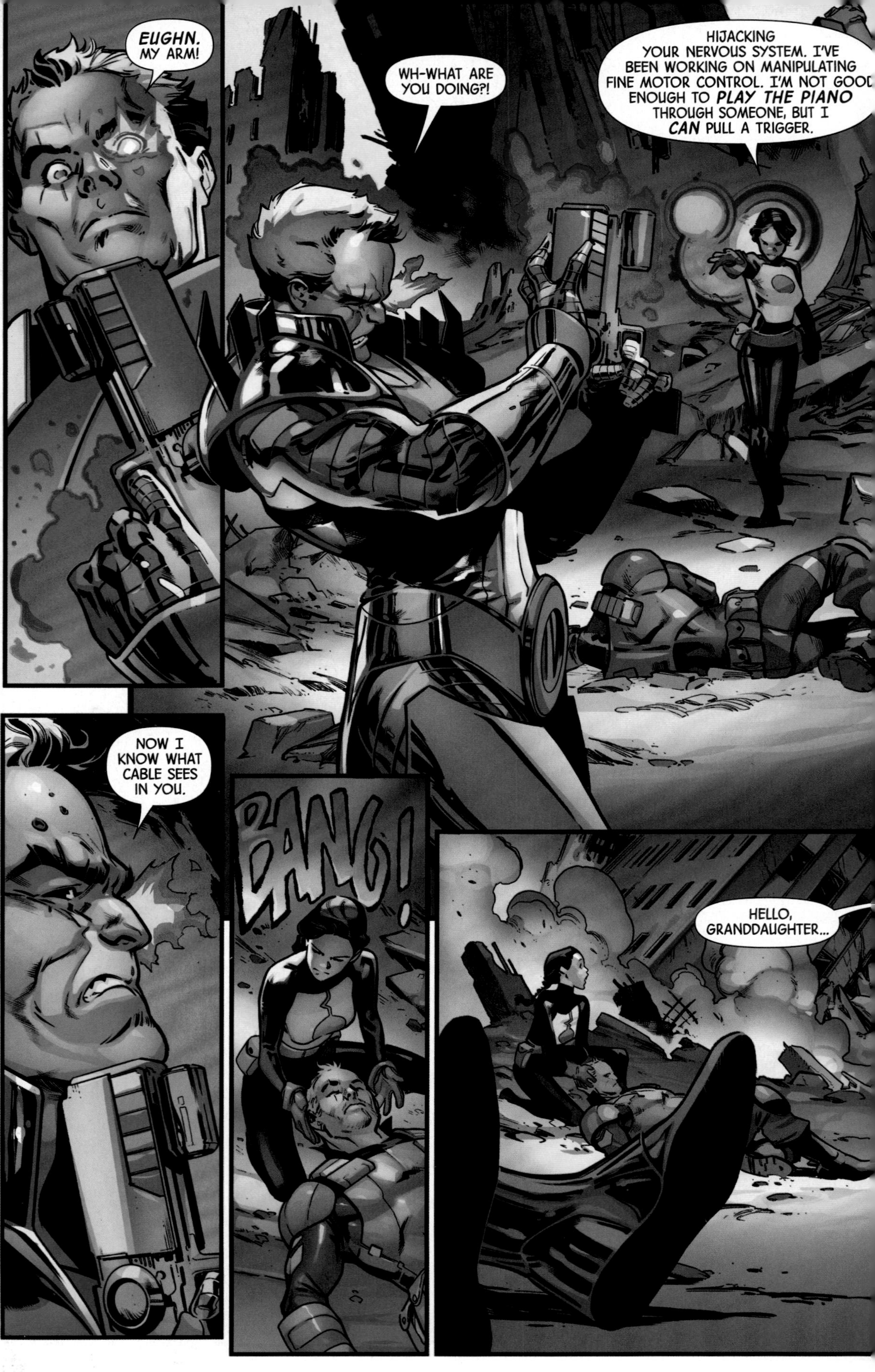

EUGHN. MY ARM!
WH-WHAT ARE YOU DOING?!
HIJACKING YOUR NERVOUS SYSTEM. I'VE BEEN WORKING ON MANIPULATING FINE MOTOR CONTROL. I'M NOT GOOD ENOUGH TO PLAY THE PIANO THROUGH SOMEONE, BUT I CAN PULL A TRIGGER.
NOW I KNOW WHAT CABLE SEES IN YOU.
BANG!
HELLO, GRANDDAUGHTER...

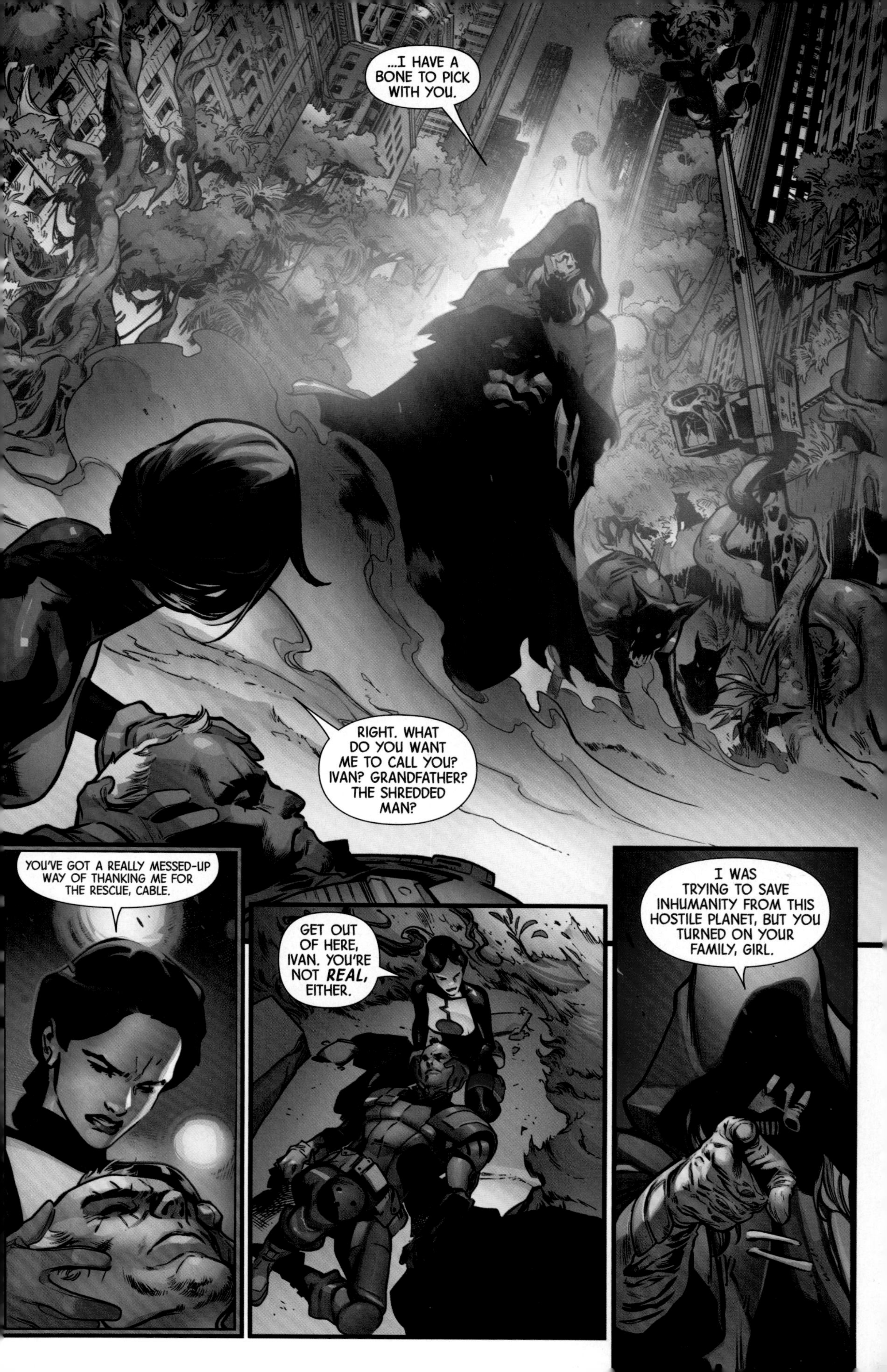
...I HAVE A BONE TO PICK WITH YOU.
RIGHT. WHAT DO YOU WANT ME TO CALL YOU? IVAN? GRANDFATHER? THE SHREDDED MAN?
YOU'VE GOT A REALLY MESSED-UP WAY OF THANKING ME FOR THE RESCUE, CABLE.
GET OUT OF HERE, IVAN. YOU'RE NOT REAL, EITHER.
I WAS TRYING TO SAVE INHUMANITY FROM THIS HOSTILE PLANET, BUT YOU TURNED ON YOUR FAMILY, GIRL.

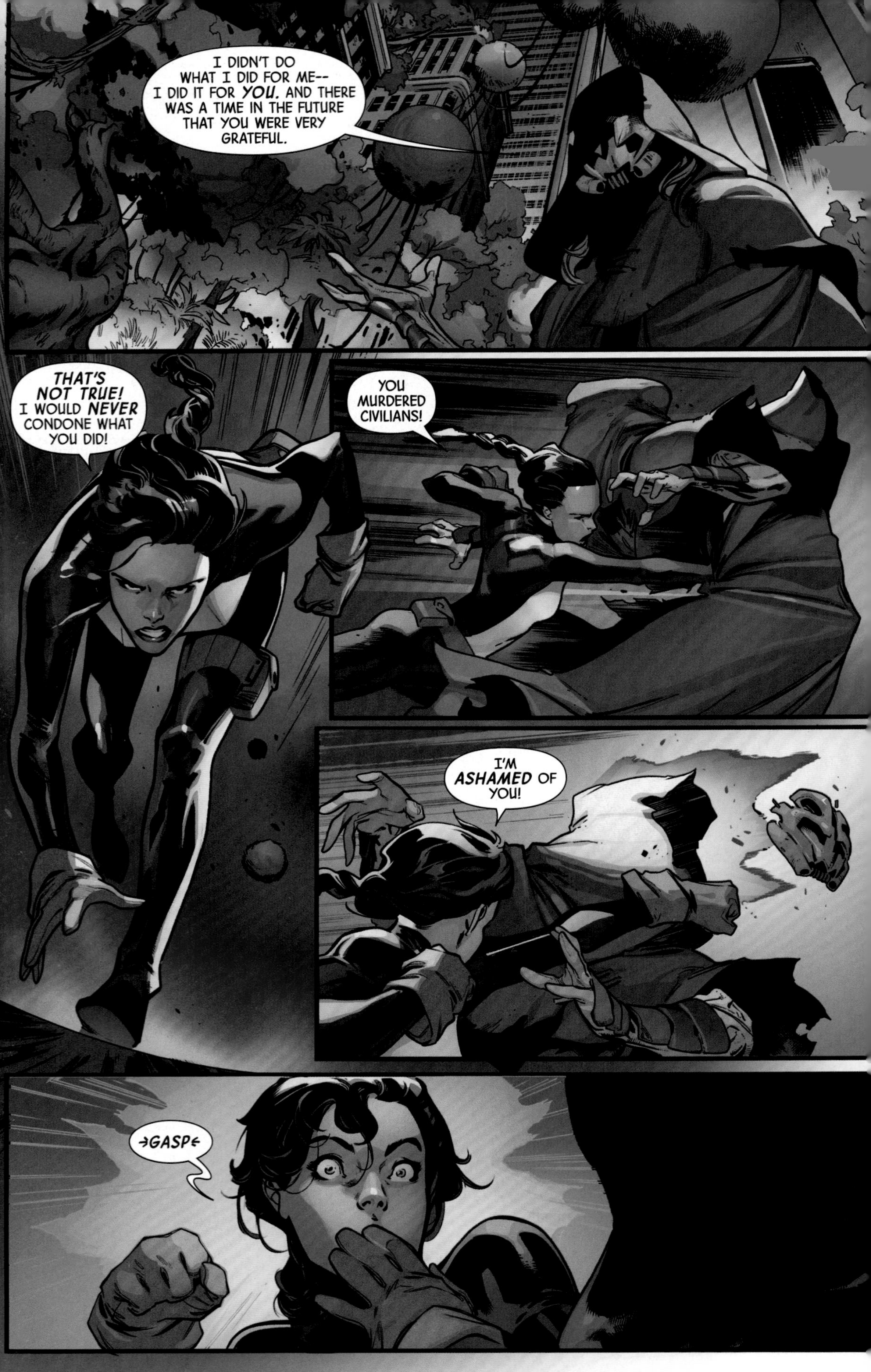
I DIDN'T DO WHAT I DID FOR ME-- I DID IT FOR YOU. AND THERE WAS A TIME IN THE FUTURE THAT YOU WERE VERY GRATEFUL.
THAT'S NOT TRUE! I WOULD NEVER CONDONE WHAT YOU DID!
YOU MURDERED CIVILIANS!
I'M ASHAMED OF YOU!
GASP

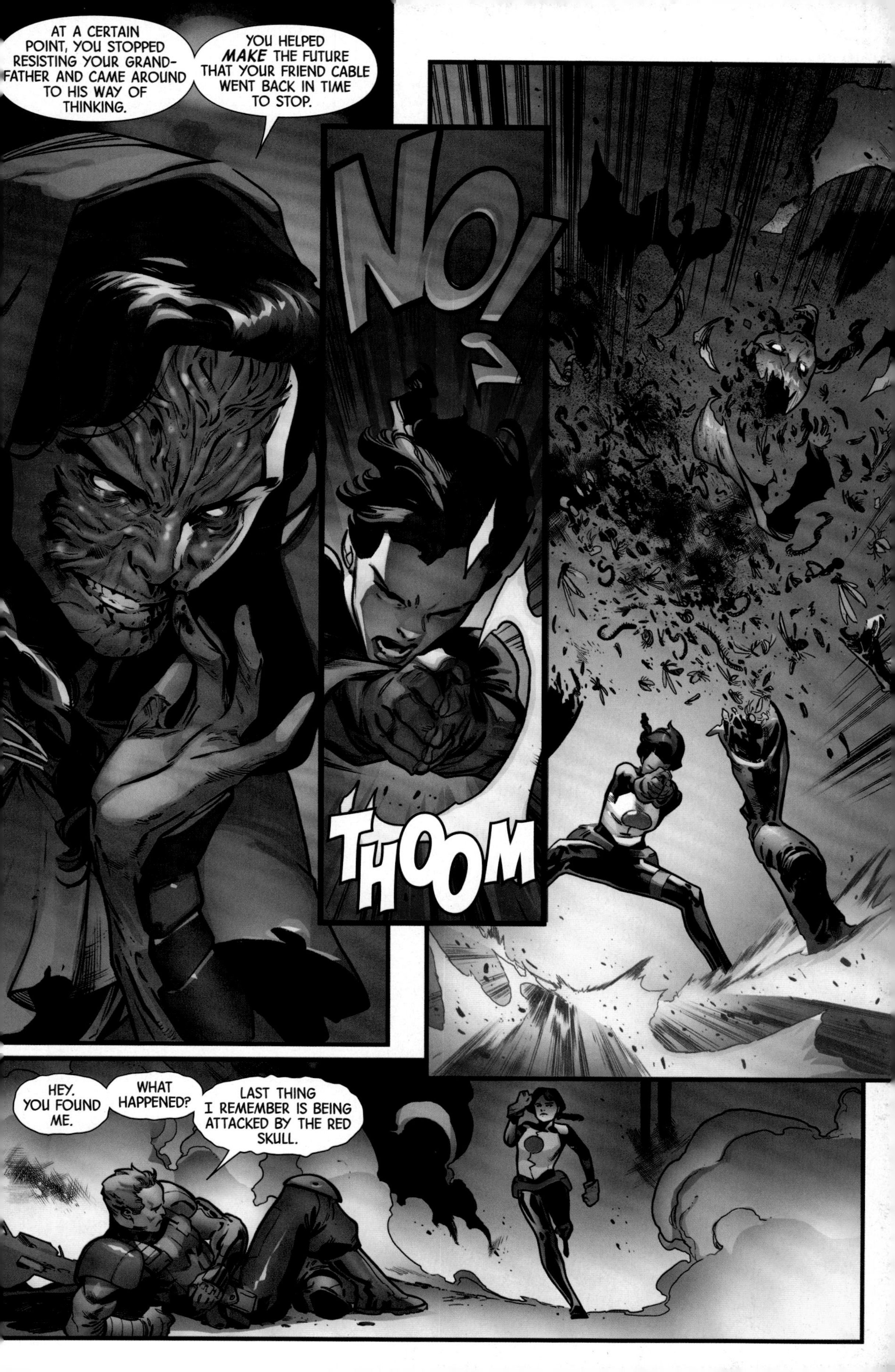
AT A CERTAIN POINT, YOU STOPPED RESISTING YOUR GRAND-FATHER AND CAME AROUND TO HIS WAY OF THINKING.
YOU HELPED *MAKE* THE FUTURE THAT YOUR FRIEND CABLE WENT BACK IN TIME TO STOP.
NO!
THOOM
HEY. YOU FOUND ME.
WHAT HAPPENED?
LAST THING I REMEMBER IS BEING ATTACKED BY THE RED SKULL.

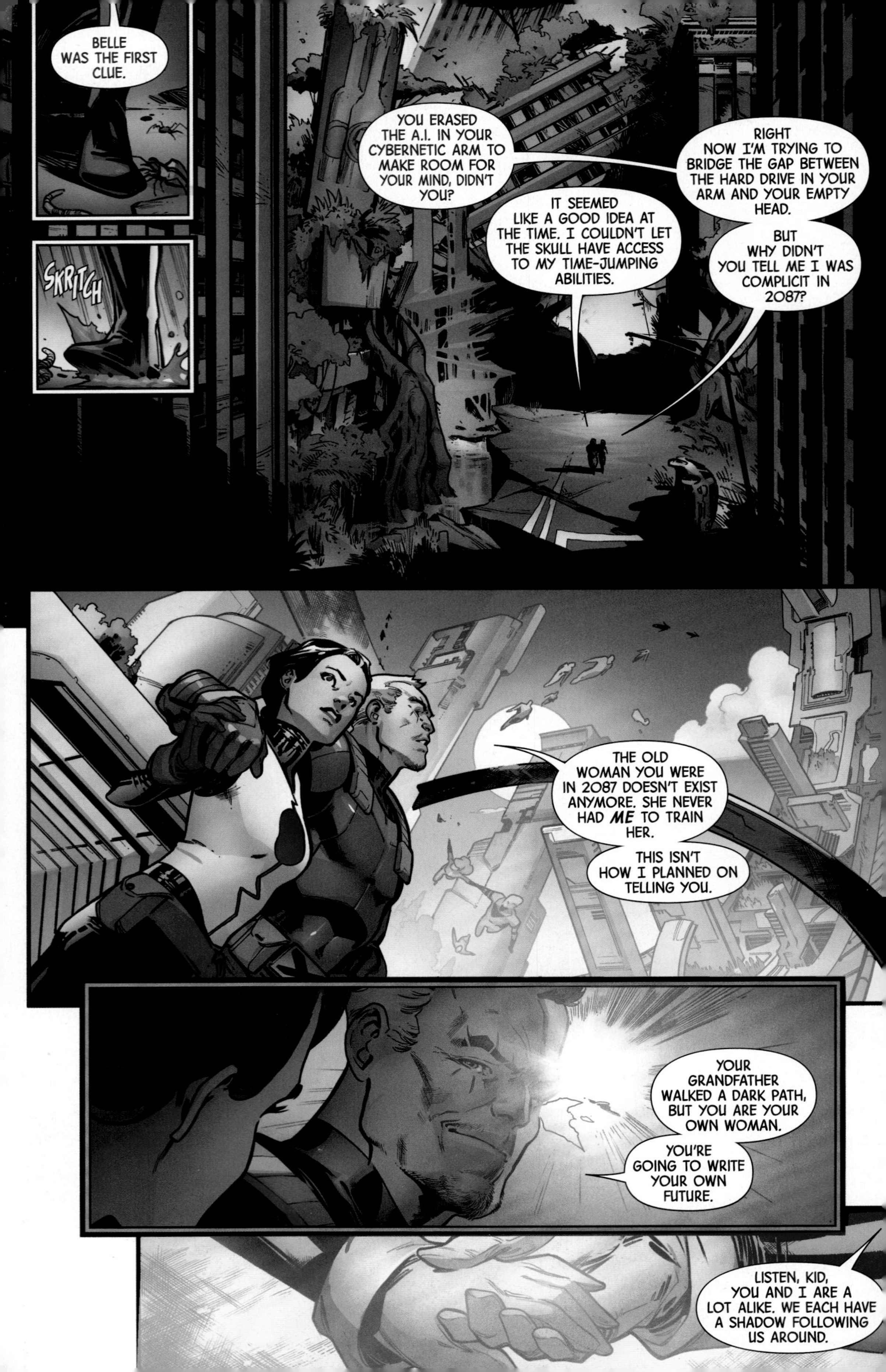
BELLE WAS THE FIRST CLUE.
SKRITCH
YOU ERASED THE A.I. IN YOUR CYBERNETIC ARM TO MAKE ROOM FOR YOUR MIND, DIDN'T YOU?
IT SEEMED LIKE A GOOD IDEA AT THE TIME. I COULDN'T LET THE SKULL HAVE ACCESS TO MY TIME-JUMPING ABILITIES.
RIGHT NOW I'M TRYING TO BRIDGE THE GAP BETWEEN THE HARD DRIVE IN YOUR ARM AND YOUR EMPTY HEAD.
BUT WHY DIDN'T YOU TELL ME I WAS COMPLICIT IN 2087?
THE OLD WOMAN YOU WERE IN 2087 DOESN'T EXIST ANYMORE. SHE NEVER HAD *ME* TO TRAIN HER.
THIS ISN'T HOW I PLANNED ON TELLING YOU.
YOUR GRANDFATHER WALKED A DARK PATH, BUT YOU ARE YOUR OWN WOMAN.
YOU'RE GOING TO WRITE YOUR OWN FUTURE.
LISTEN, KID, YOU AND I ARE A LOT ALIKE. WE EACH HAVE A SHADOW FOLLOWING US AROUND.

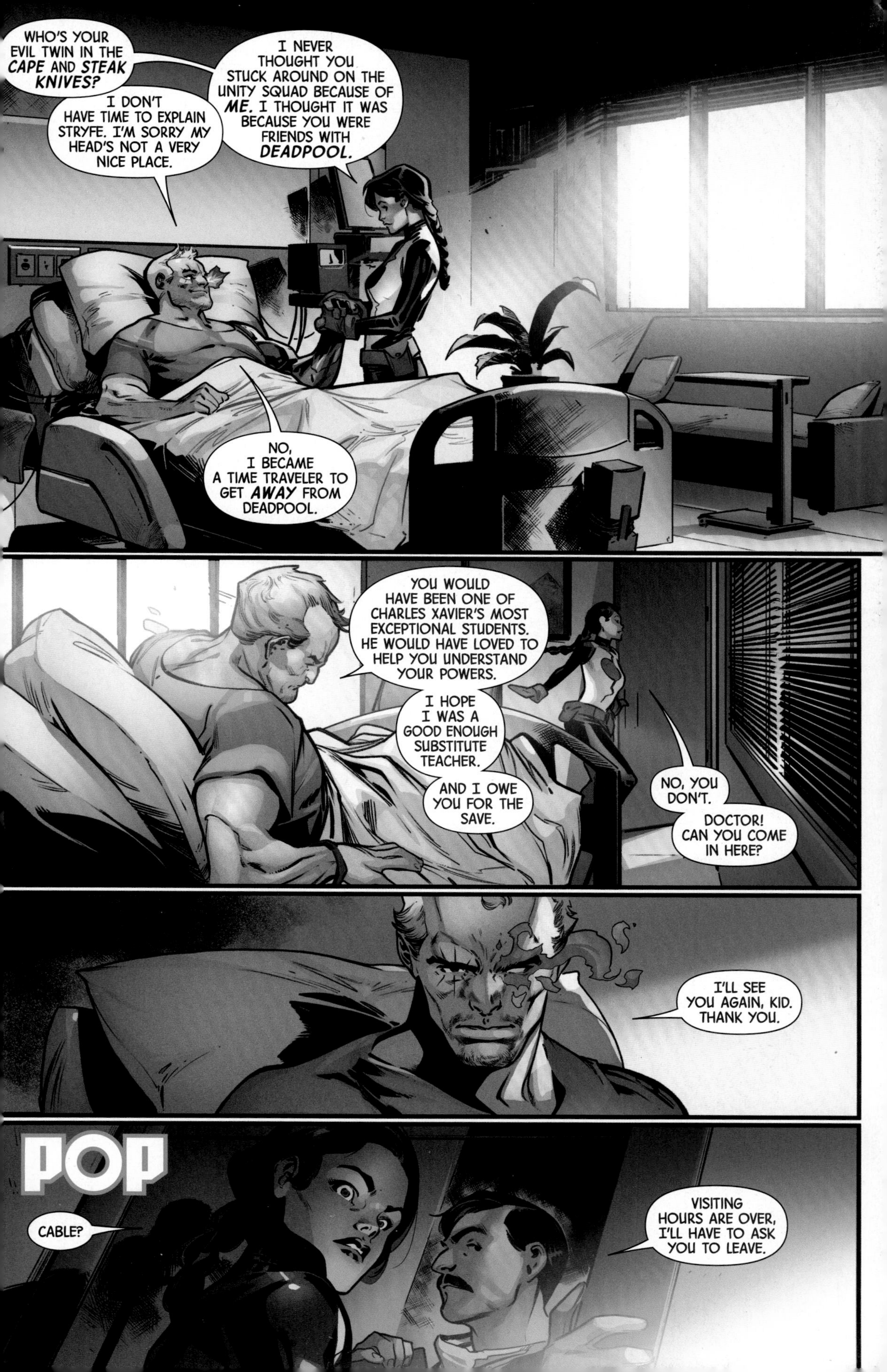
WHO'S YOUR EVIL TWIN IN THE CAPE AND STEAK KNIVES?
I DON'T HAVE TIME TO EXPLAIN STRYFE. I'M SORRY MY HEAD'S NOT A VERY NICE PLACE.
I NEVER THOUGHT YOU STUCK AROUND ON THE UNITY SQUAD BECAUSE OF ME. I THOUGHT IT WAS BECAUSE YOU WERE FRIENDS WITH DEADPOOL.
NO, I BECAME A TIME TRAVELER TO GET AWAY FROM DEADPOOL.
YOU WOULD HAVE BEEN ONE OF CHARLES XAVIER'S MOST EXCEPTIONAL STUDENTS. HE WOULD HAVE LOVED TO HELP YOU UNDERSTAND YOUR POWERS.
I HOPE I WAS A GOOD ENOUGH SUBSTITUTE TEACHER.
AND I OWE YOU FOR THE SAVE.
NO, YOU DON'T.
DOCTOR! CAN YOU COME IN HERE?
I'LL SEE YOU AGAIN, KID. THANK YOU.
POP
CABLE?
VISITING HOURS ARE OVER, I'LL HAVE TO ASK YOU TO LEAVE.

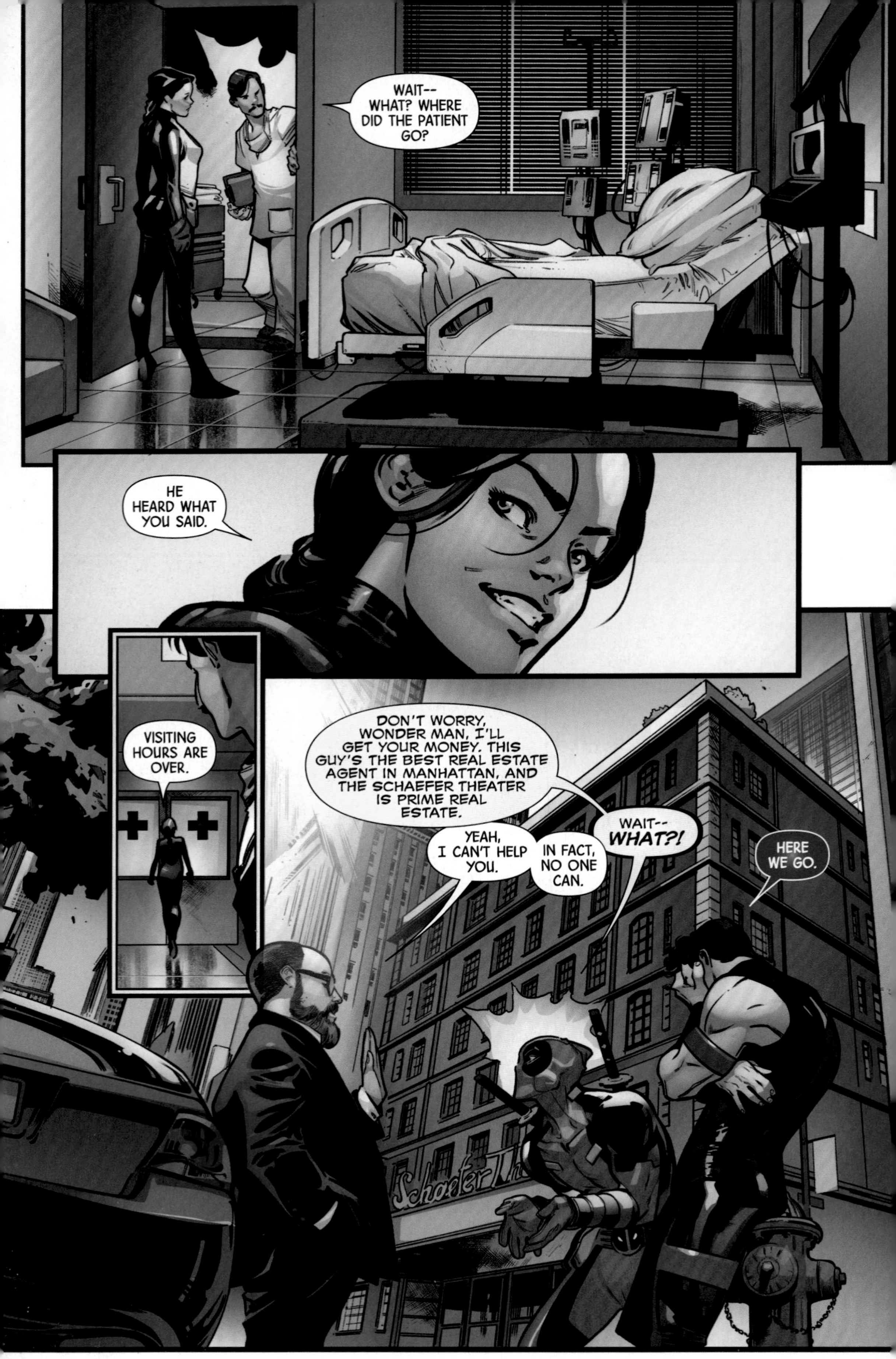
WAIT-- WHAT? WHERE DID THE PATIENT GO?
HE HEARD WHAT YOU SAID.
VISITING HOURS ARE OVER.
DON'T WORRY, WONDER MAN, I'LL GET YOUR MONEY. THIS GUY'S THE BEST REAL ESTATE AGENT IN MANHATTAN, AND THE SCHAEFER THEATER IS PRIME REAL ESTATE.
YEAH, I CAN'T HELP YOU.
IN FACT, NO ONE CAN.
WAIT-- WHAT?!
HERE WE GO.

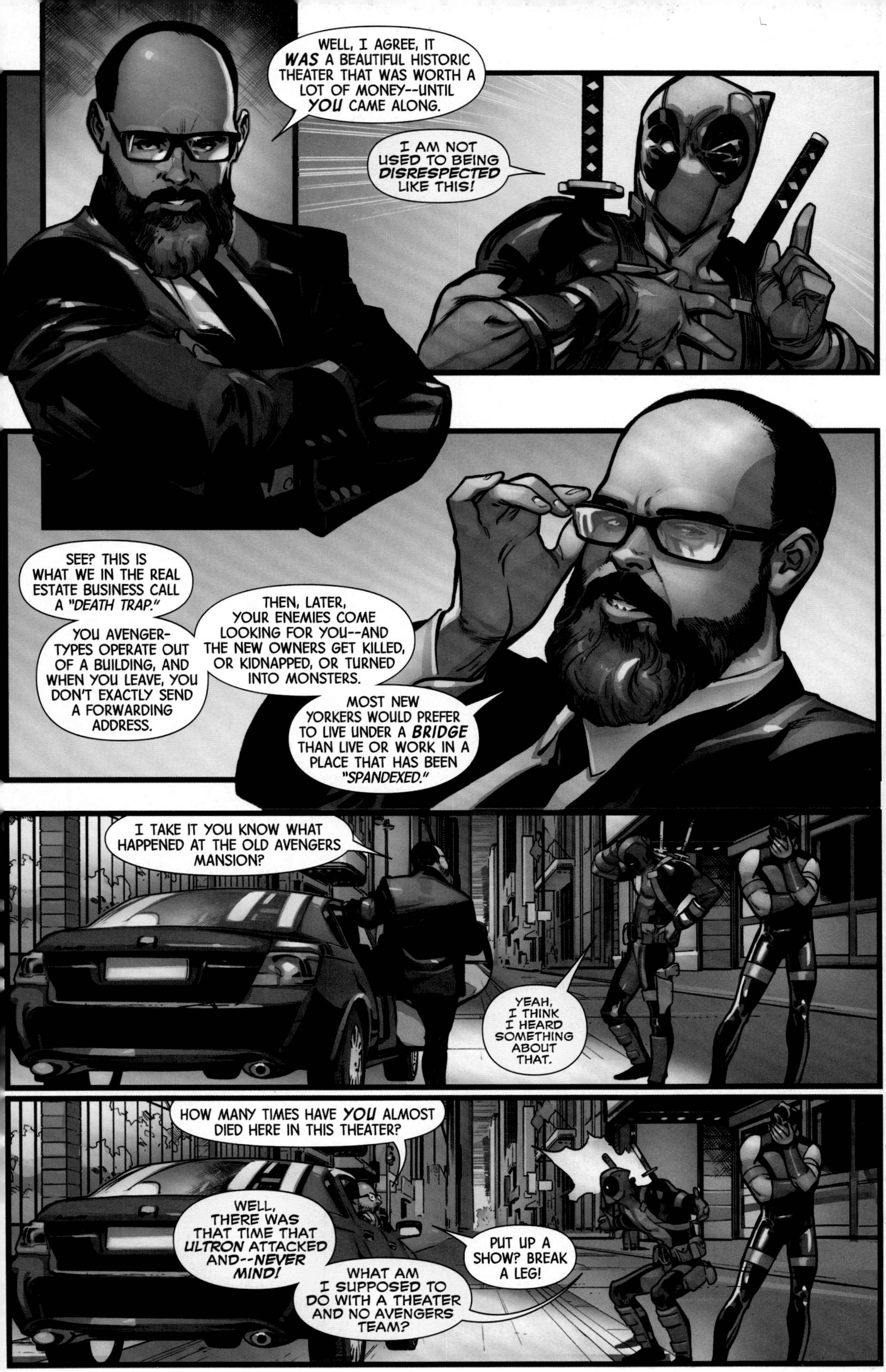
WELL, I AGREE, IT *WAS* A BEAUTIFUL HISTORIC THEATER THAT WAS WORTH A LOT OF MONEY--UNTIL *YOU* CAME ALONG.
I AM NOT USED TO BEING *DISRESPECTED* LIKE THIS!
SEE? THIS IS WHAT WE IN THE REAL ESTATE BUSINESS CALL A "*DEATH TRAP.*"
YOU AVENGER-TYPES OPERATE OUT OF A BUILDING, AND WHEN YOU LEAVE, YOU DON'T EXACTLY SEND A FORWARDING ADDRESS.
THEN, LATER, YOUR ENEMIES COME LOOKING FOR YOU--AND THE NEW OWNERS GET KILLED, OR KIDNAPPED, OR TURNED INTO MONSTERS.
MOST NEW YORKERS WOULD PREFER TO LIVE UNDER A *BRIDGE* THAN LIVE OR WORK IN A PLACE THAT HAS BEEN "*SPANDEXED.*"
I TAKE IT YOU KNOW WHAT HAPPENED AT THE OLD AVENGERS MANSION?
YEAH, I THINK I HEARD SOMETHING ABOUT THAT.
HOW MANY TIMES HAVE *YOU* ALMOST DIED HERE IN THIS THEATER?
WELL, THERE WAS THAT TIME THAT *ULTRON* ATTACKED AND--*NEVER MIND!*
WHAT AM I SUPPOSED TO DO WITH A THEATER AND NO AVENGERS TEAM?
PUT UP A SHOW? BREAK A LEG!

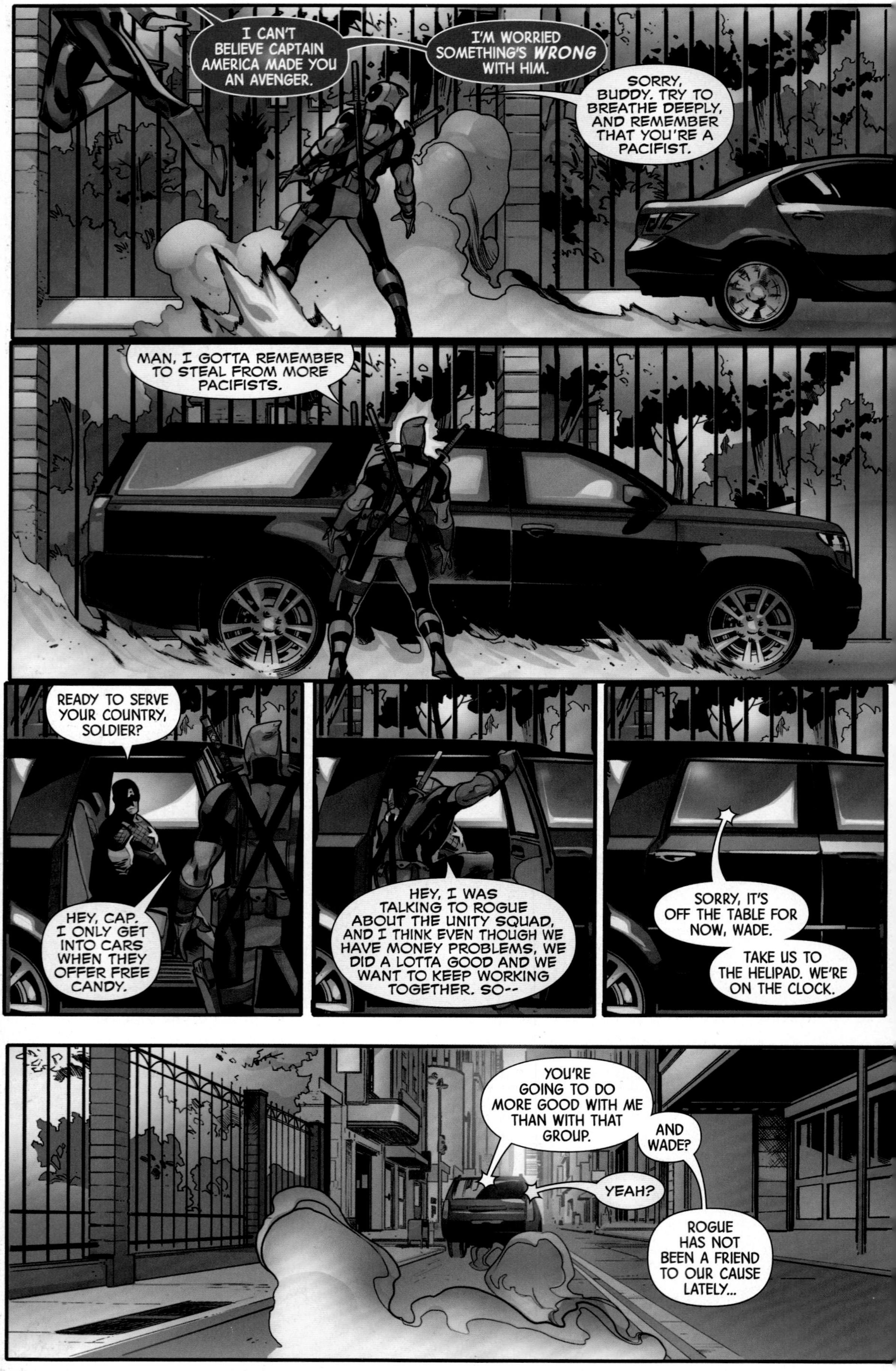
I CAN'T BELIEVE CAPTAIN AMERICA MADE YOU AN AVENGER.
I'M WORRIED SOMETHING'S WRONG WITH HIM.
SORRY, BUDDY. TRY TO BREATHE DEEPLY, AND REMEMBER THAT YOU'RE A PACIFIST.
MAN, I GOTTA REMEMBER TO STEAL FROM MORE PACIFISTS.
READY TO SERVE YOUR COUNTRY, SOLDIER?
HEY, CAP. I ONLY GET INTO CARS WHEN THEY OFFER FREE CANDY.
HEY, I WAS TALKING TO ROGUE ABOUT THE UNITY SQUAD, AND I THINK EVEN THOUGH WE HAVE MONEY PROBLEMS, WE DID A LOTTA GOOD AND WE WANT TO KEEP WORKING TOGETHER. SO--
SORRY, IT'S OFF THE TABLE FOR NOW, WADE.
TAKE US TO THE HELIPAD. WE'RE ON THE CLOCK.
YOU'RE GOING TO DO MORE GOOD WITH ME THAN WITH THAT GROUP.
AND WADE?
YEAH?
ROGUE HAS NOT BEEN A FRIEND TO OUR CAUSE LATELY...

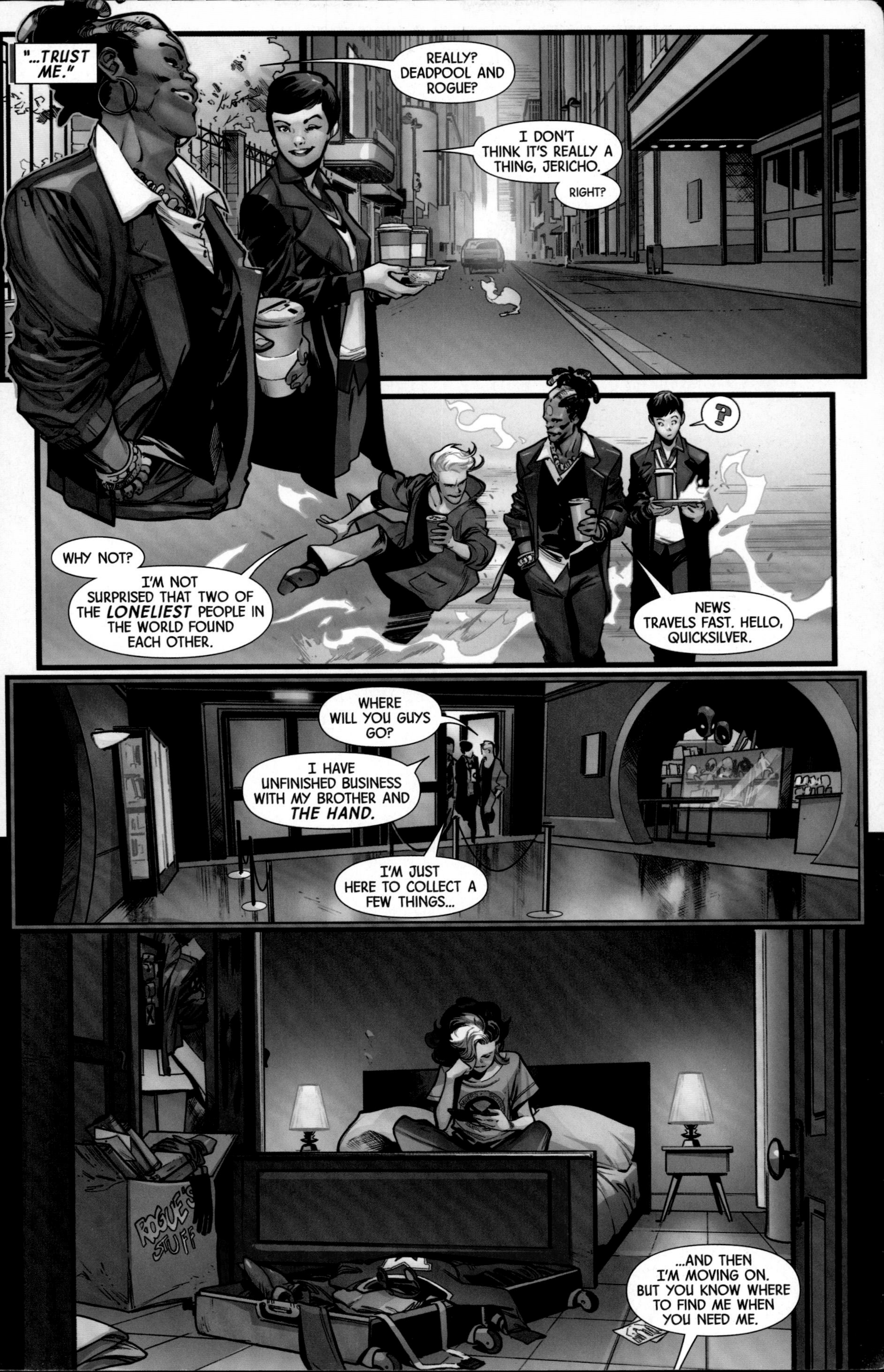
"...TRUST ME."
REALLY? DEADPOOL AND ROGUE?
I DON'T THINK IT'S REALLY A THING, JERICHO.
RIGHT?
?
WHY NOT?
I'M NOT SURPRISED THAT TWO OF THE LONELIEST PEOPLE IN THE WORLD FOUND EACH OTHER.
NEWS TRAVELS FAST. HELLO, QUICKSILVER.
WHERE WILL YOU GUYS GO?
I HAVE UNFINISHED BUSINESS WITH MY BROTHER AND THE HAND.
I'M JUST HERE TO COLLECT A FEW THINGS...
ROGUE'S STUFF
...AND THEN I'M MOVING ON. BUT YOU KNOW WHERE TO FIND ME WHEN YOU NEED ME.

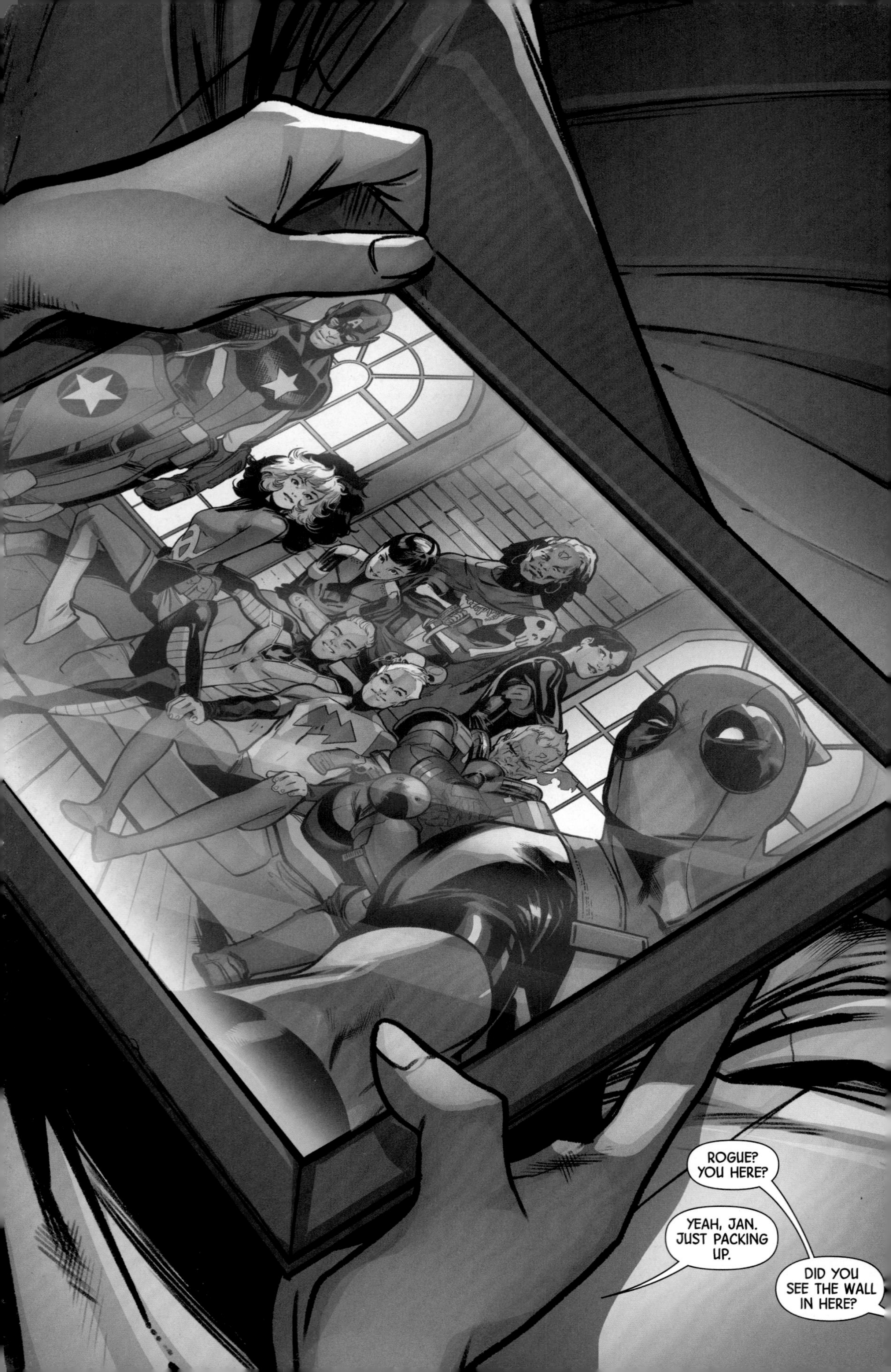
ROGUE? YOU HERE?
YEAH, JAN. JUST PACKING UP.
DID YOU SEE THE WALL IN HERE?

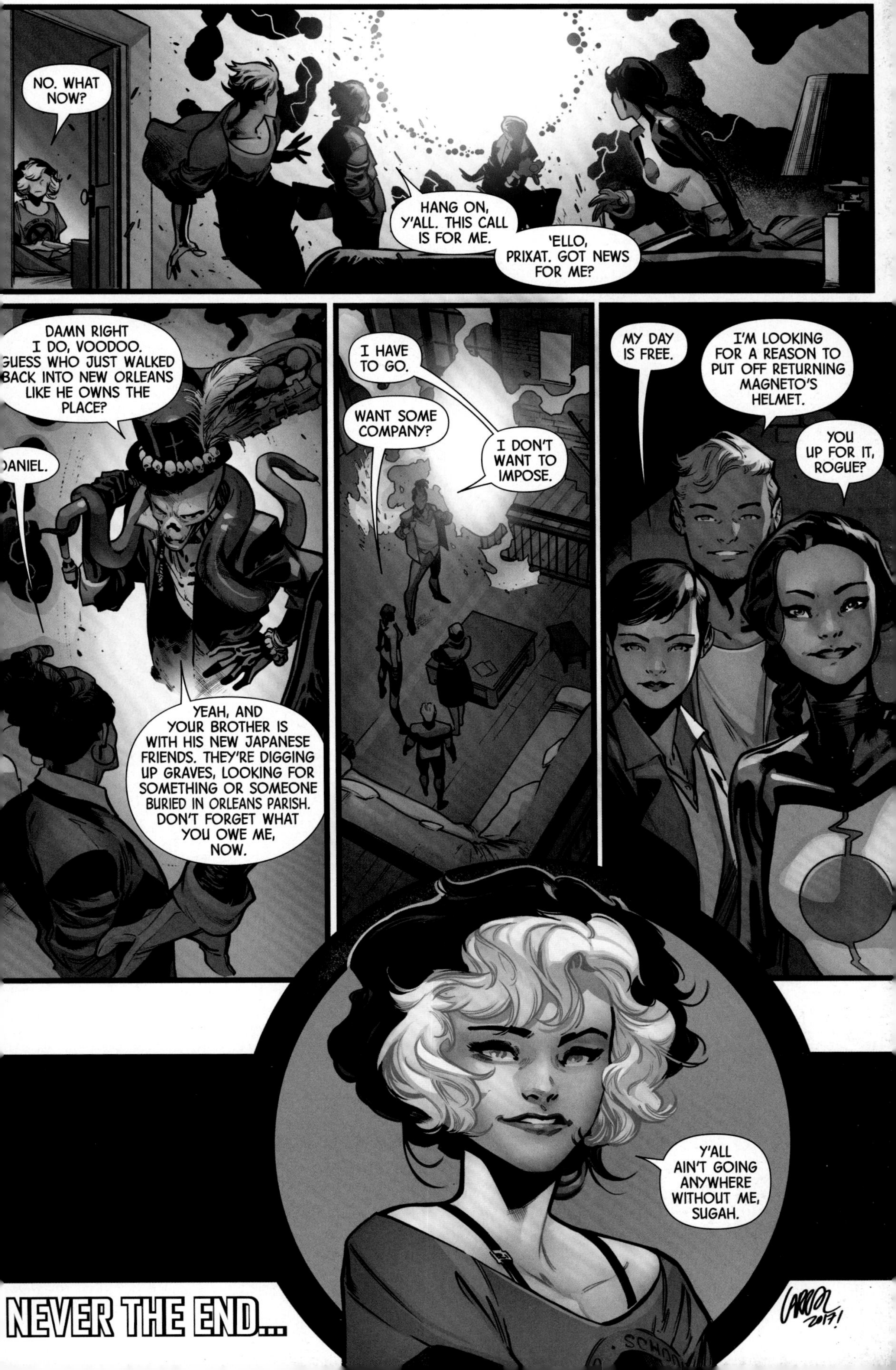
NO. WHAT NOW?
HANG ON, Y'ALL. THIS CALL IS FOR ME.
'ELLO, PRIXAT. GOT NEWS FOR ME?
DAMN RIGHT I DO, VOODOO. GUESS WHO JUST WALKED BACK INTO NEW ORLEANS LIKE HE OWNS THE PLACE?
DANIEL.
YEAH, AND YOUR BROTHER IS WITH HIS NEW JAPANESE FRIENDS. THEY'RE DIGGING UP GRAVES, LOOKING FOR SOMETHING OR SOMEONE BURIED IN ORLEANS PARISH. DON'T FORGET WHAT YOU OWE ME, NOW.
I HAVE TO GO.
WANT SOME COMPANY?
I DON'T WANT TO IMPOSE.
MY DAY IS FREE.
I'M LOOKING FOR A REASON TO PUT OFF RETURNING MAGNETO'S HELMET.
YOU UP FOR IT, ROGUE?
Y'ALL AIN'T GOING ANYWHERE WITHOUT ME, SUGAH.
NEVER THE END...

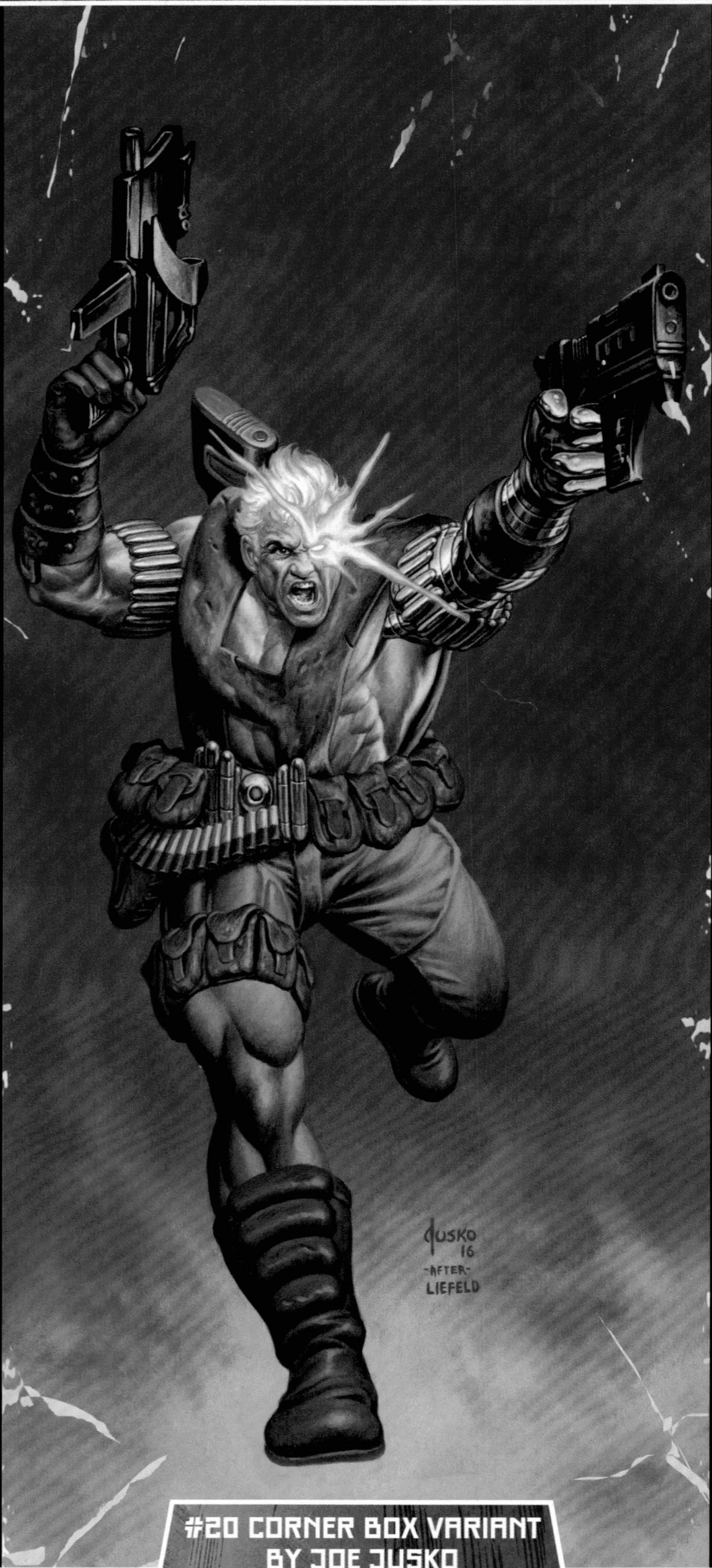
JUSKO 16 -AFTER- LIEFELD

#20 CORNER BOX VARIANT
BY JOE JUSKO

#19, PAGE 8
PENCILS AND INKS
BY PEPE LARAZ

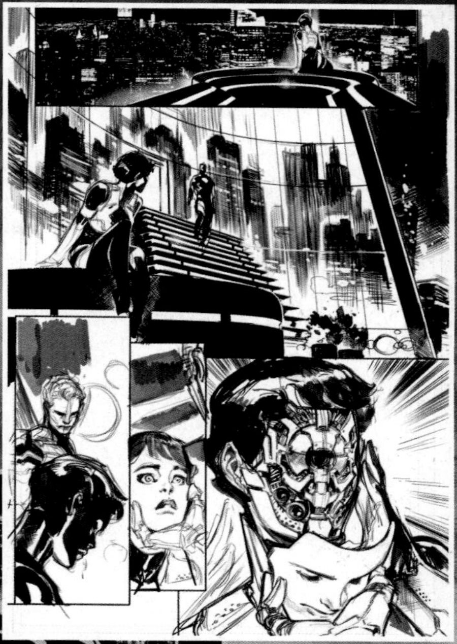

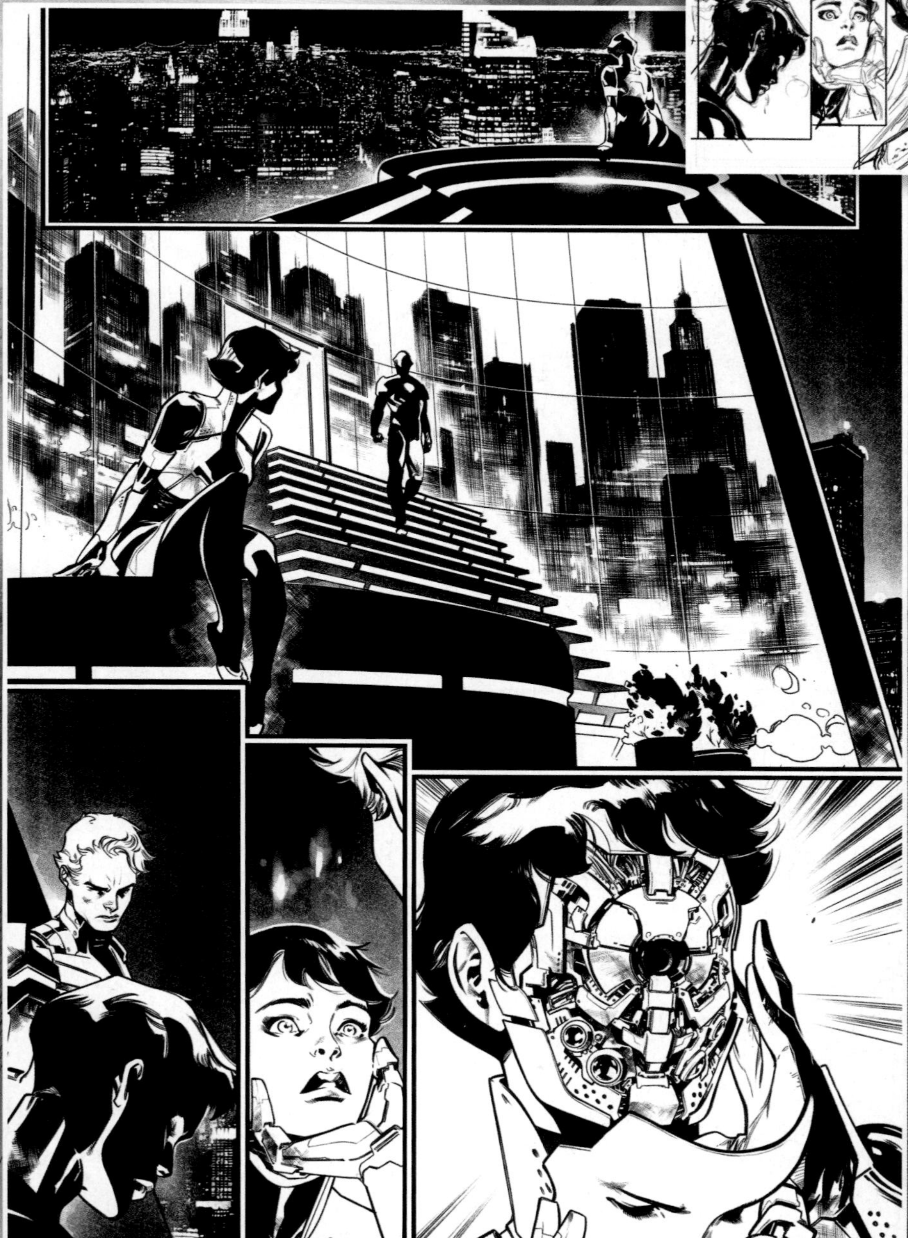

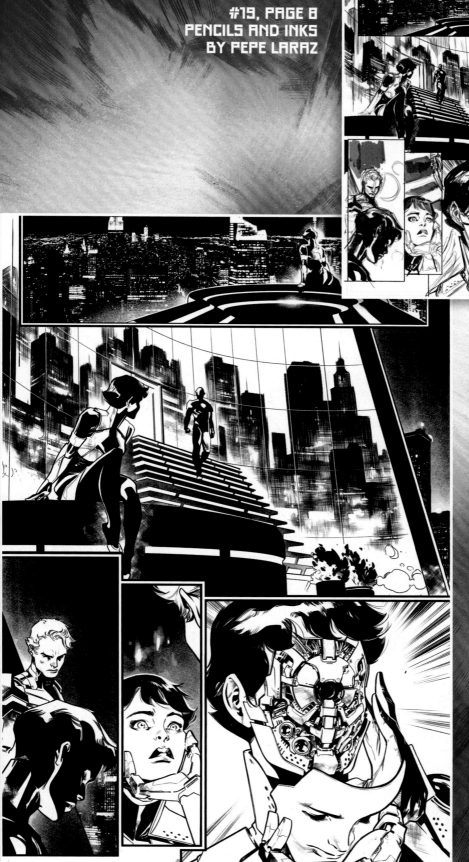

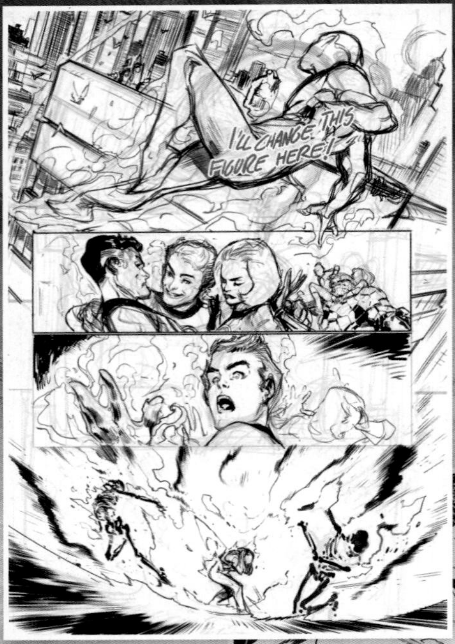
I'LL CHANGE THIS FIGURE HERE!

#19, PAGE 9
PENCILS AND INKS
BY PEPE LARAZ

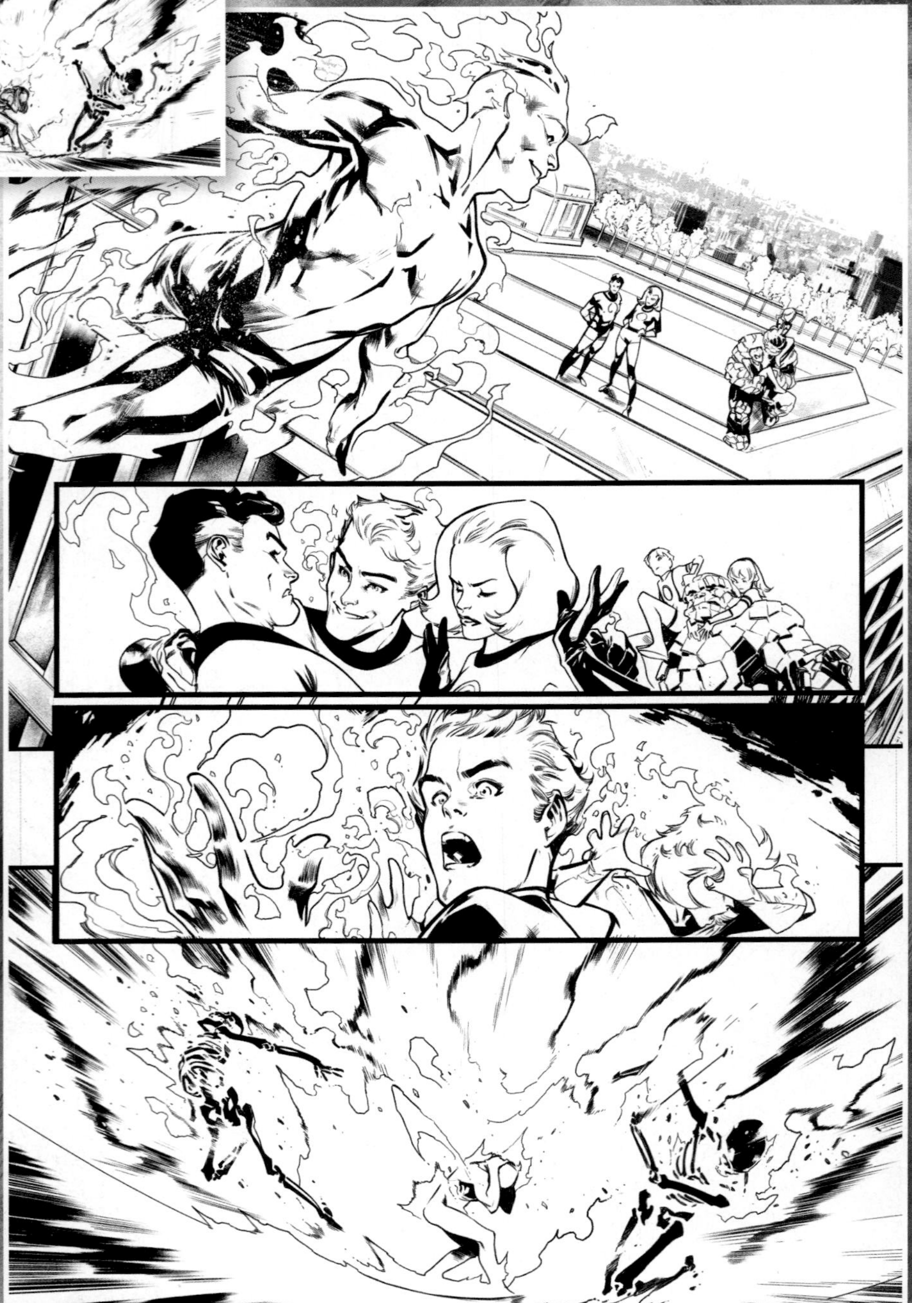

#19, PAGE 12
PENCILS AND INKS
BY PEPE LARAZ

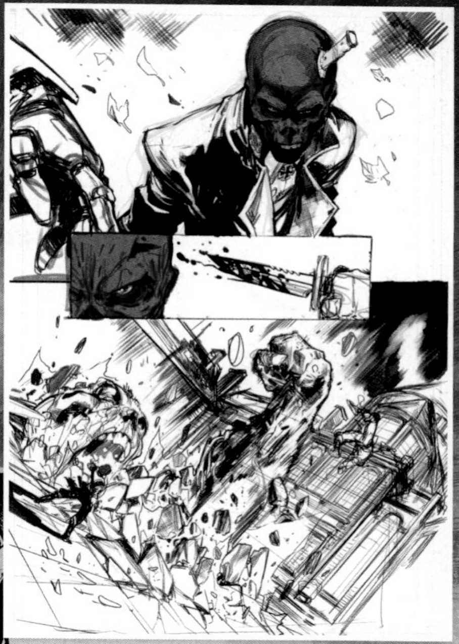

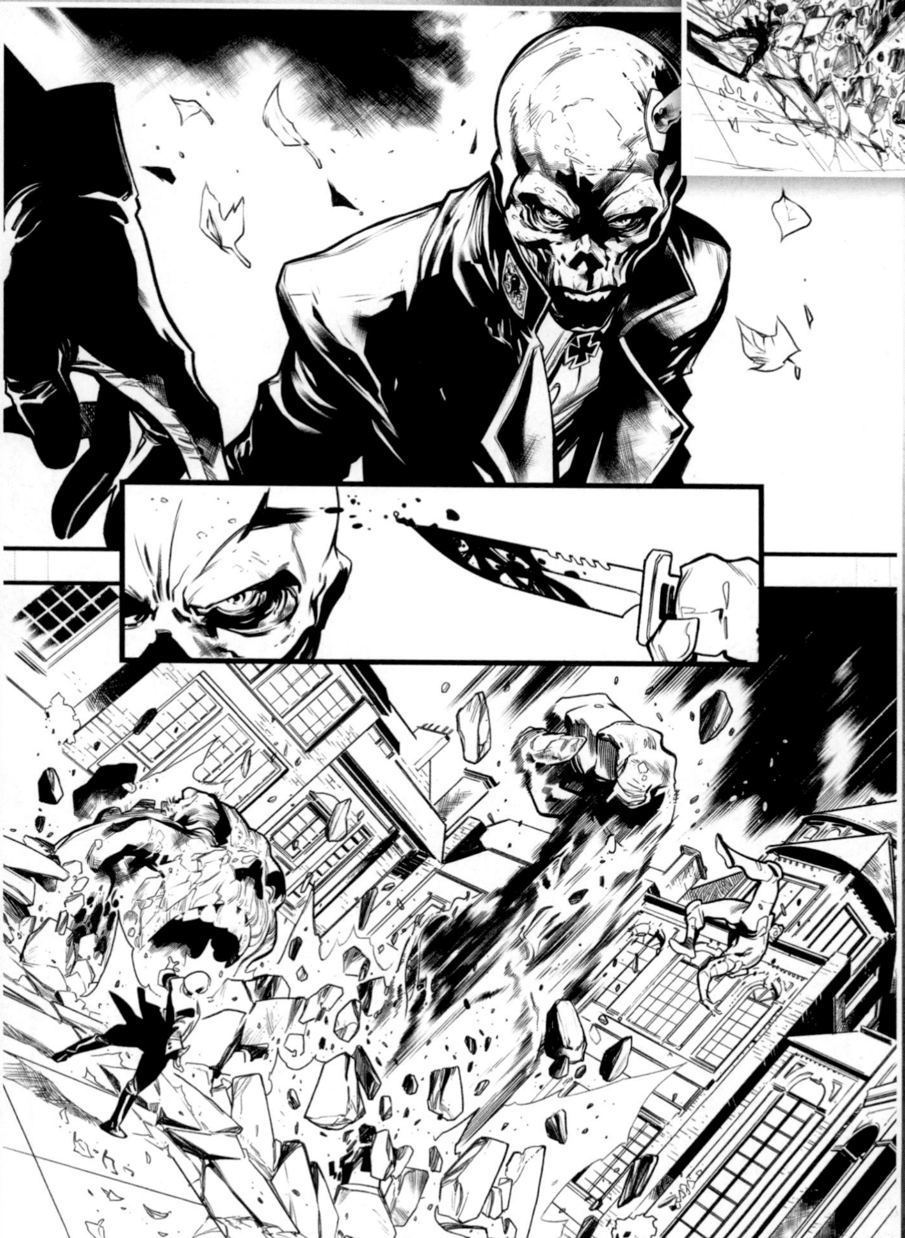

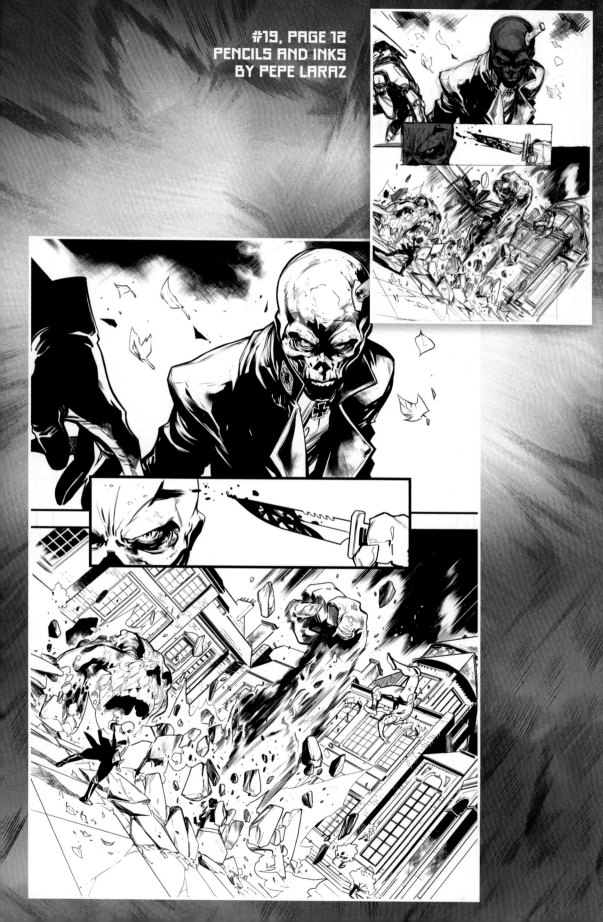

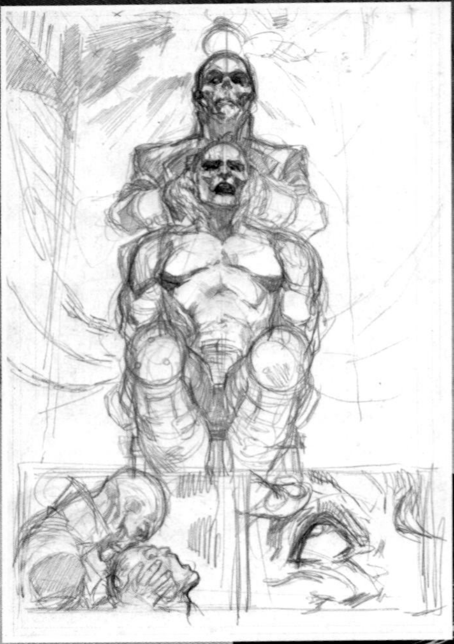

#19, PAGE 15
PENCILS AND INKS
BY PEPE LARAZ

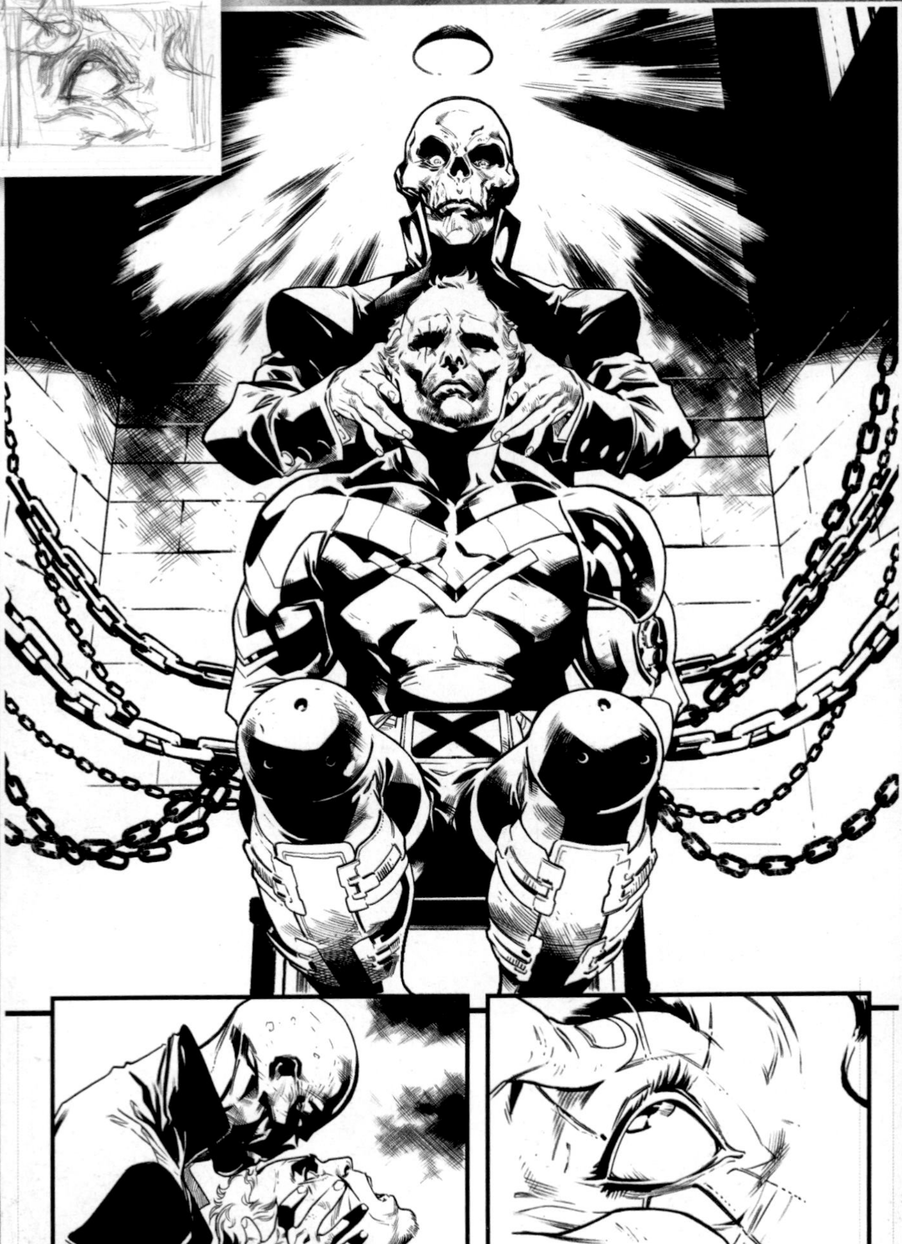

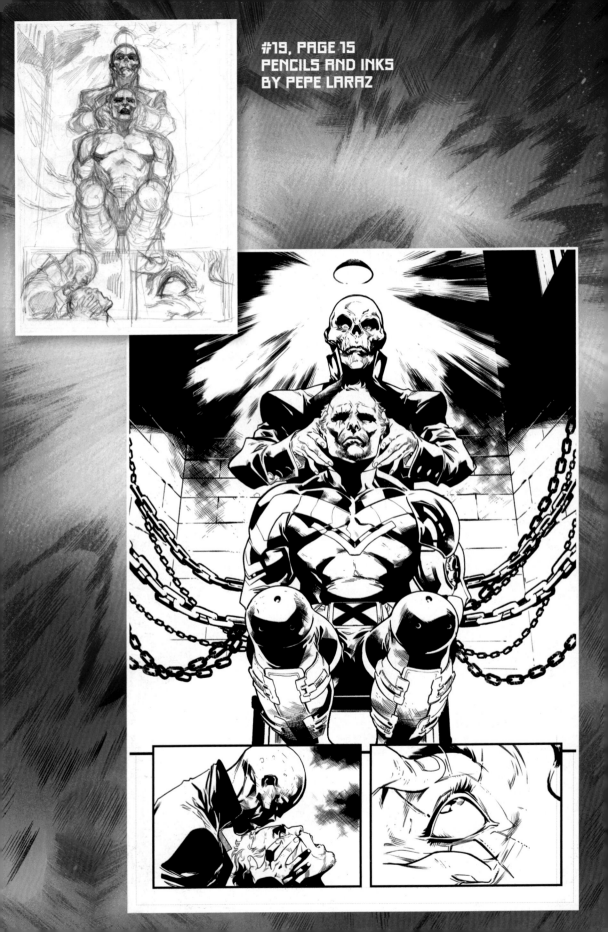

#19, PAGE 17
PENCILS AND INKS
BY PEPE LARAZ

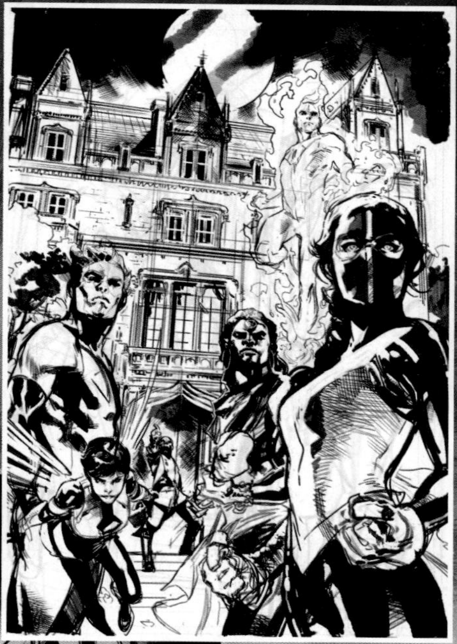

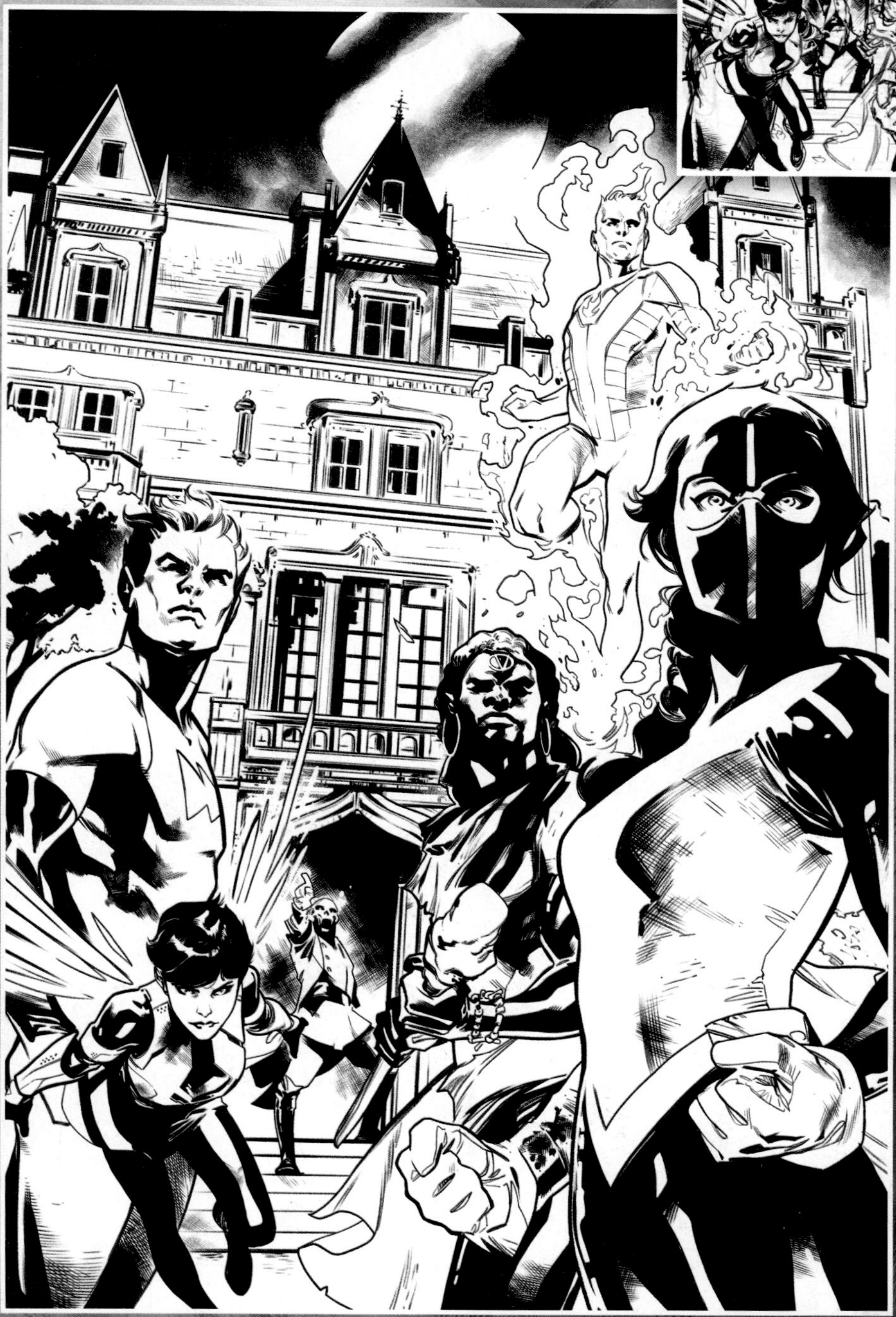

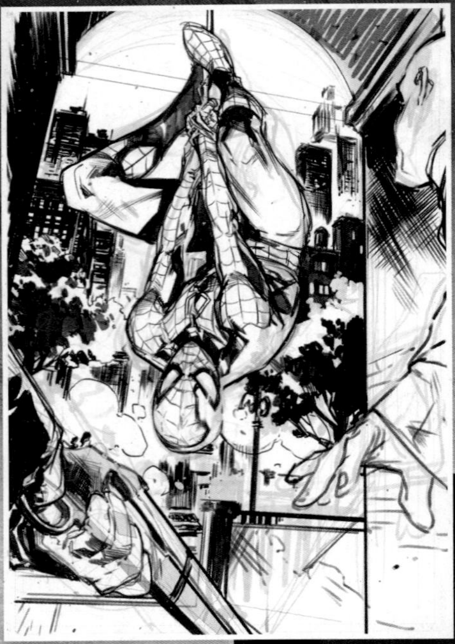

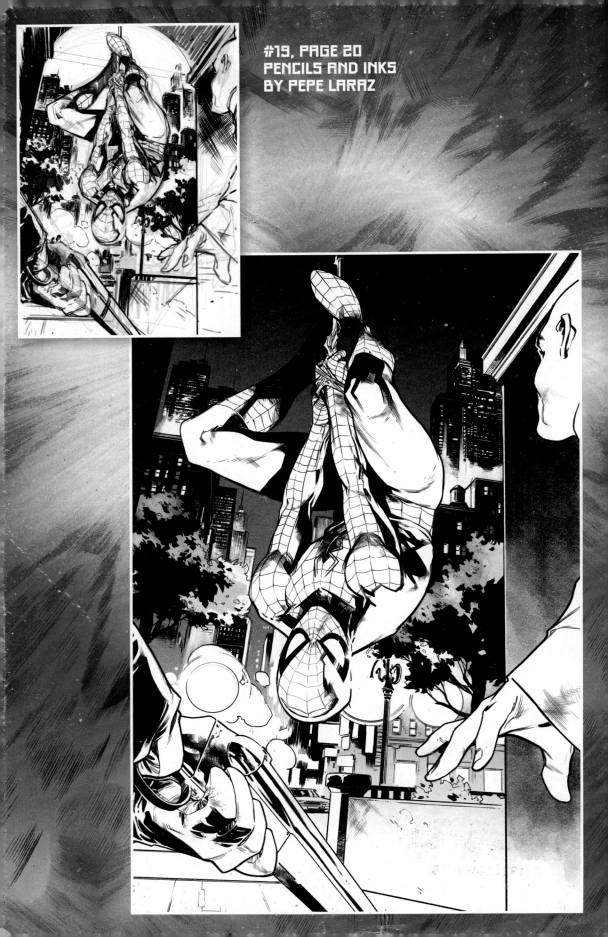

#19, PAGE 20
PENCILS AND INKS
BY PEPE LARAZ

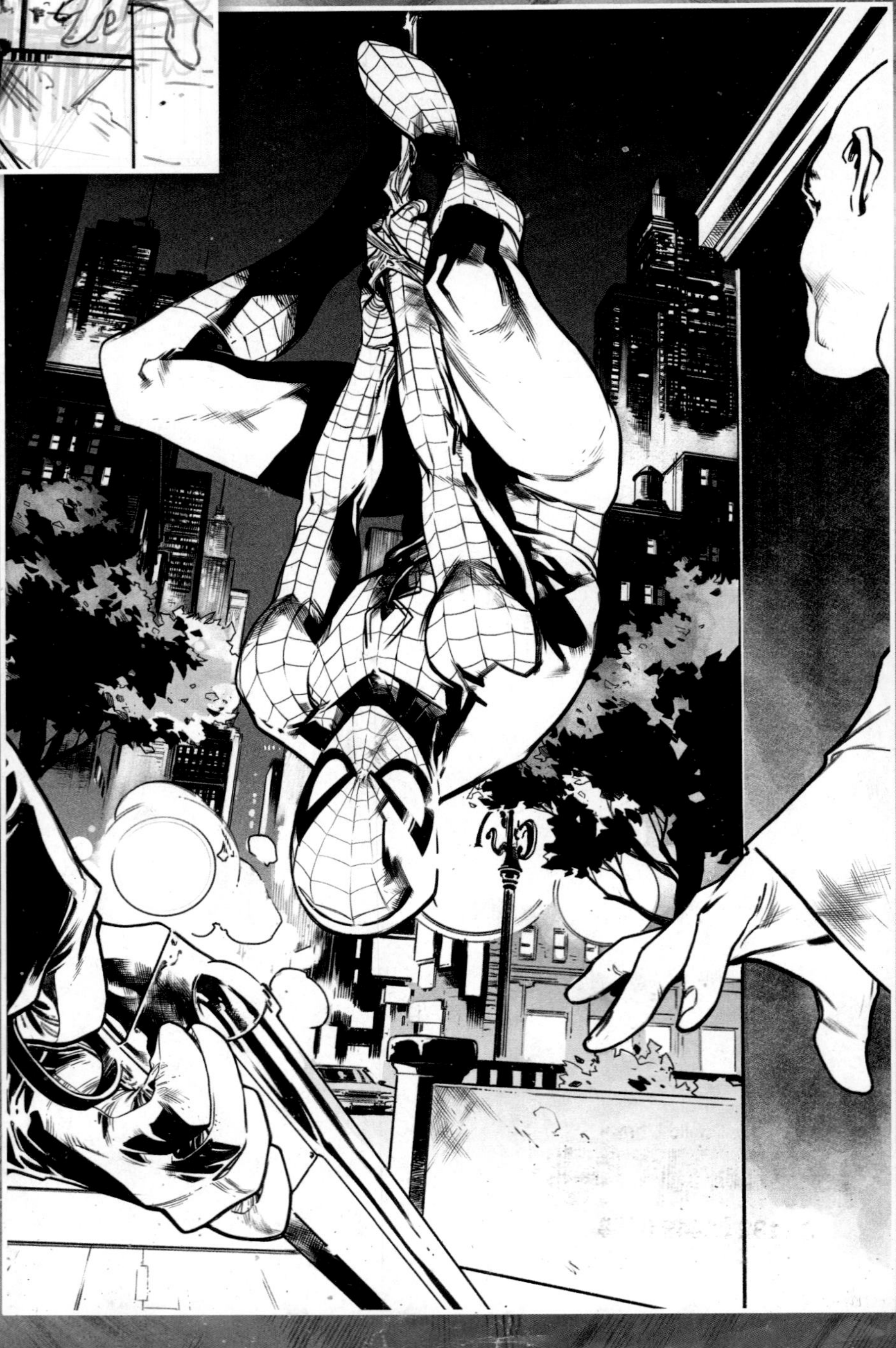